THE ART
OF LITERARY
PUBLISHING

THE ART
OF LITERARY
PUBLISHING

editors on their craft

with a new introduction
edited by Bill Henderson

PUSHCART

Fourth printing

Library of Congress Card Number: 78-69933
ISBN: 0-916366-05-7

Published in the United States by The Pushcart Press
Distributed by W. W. Norton Company

For information address:
The Pushcart Press
P. O.Box 380
Wainscott, New York 11975

Printed in the United States of America

ACKNOWLEDGMENTS

The dedication is excerpted from an August 15, 1979 article by John Leonard in the *New York Times* and is reprinted by permission of John Leonard.

"New Directions: An Interview with James Laughlin" is adapted from an interview originally broadcast by New York radio station WBAI and appears here with permission of Susan Howe, Charles Ruas, and James Laughlin.

"Letter to an Unpublished Writer" by John Farrar reprinted with permission of Farrar, Straus and Giroux, Inc., © 1948 *The Writer*.

"The Life and Death of an Academic Journal" by Cleanth Brooks is adapted from an article that appeared in *Editor's News*, a publication of the Conference of Editors of Learned Journals and is reprinted by permission of Cleanth Brooks.

"Small Publishing — Is It Beautiful" by Simon Michael Bessie was adapted from a speech delivered to the Association of American Publishers Conference for Smaller Publishers and is used with the permission of Mr. Bessie.

"A Quarter Century of the Jargon Society: An Interview wth Jonathan Williams" is adapted from an interview originally broadcast by New York radio station WBAI and appears here with permission of William Corbett and Jonathan Williams.

"The Fall of Liveright" by Saxe Commins reprinted from *What Is An Editor?* by Dorothy Commins with permission of The University of Chicago Press and Dorothy Commins, © 1978 The University of Chicago.

"The Struggle Against Censorship" is adapted from a discussion originally broadcast by New York radio station WBAI and appears here with permission of Charles Ruas, William Burroughs, and James Grauerholz.

"The Story of My Printing Press" by Anaïs Nin reprinted by permission of Guther Sthulman from *The Publish It Yourself Handbook*, © 1973 The Pushcart Press.

"Publishing Thomas Wolfe" by Maxwell Perkins reprinted with permission of *The Harvard Library Bulletin*, © 1947 The President and Fellows of Harvard College.

"The Curse of the Editorial Class" by Gerald Howard reprinted with permission of the author. First appeared in a slightly different version in *The Hungry Mind Review*, 1994

CONTENTS

DEDICATION:
for HENRY ROBBINS (1927-1979)

Henry Robbins was an editor of books. Among the books he edited were books written by the likes of John Irving, Joan Didion, Walker Percy, Wilfrid Sheed, Donald Barthelme, Doris Grumbach, Tom Wolfe, and John Gregory Dunne. The last time we had lunch, he handed me, in a brown paper wrapper, a fresh copy of "Metropolitan Lives" by Fran Lebowitz. "You'll like this," he said. I did. I am obedient.

*   *   *

Who knows what an editor does? There are the grabbers and the packagers and the promoters and the thieves. There are also those, like the late David Segal and the late Henry Robbins, who know how to enter a writer's silence and ask questions. They are perfect readers. In search of the perfect book, they nudge, blink, wheedle, sigh, expound, and publish you anyway. You know that they know that you could have done better, and so you try again.

Those of us in the agreeable racket of book-reviewing must sort out early on the packagers from the perfect readers. We all belong to the same service class of literature. We are middlemen, vendors of the ideas of other, more talented people. We agree to believe that publishing is the last honorable form of commerce. This leap of faith sprains the mind: If publishing were what we want to believe it is, literary agents would not be necessary.

But Henry, anonymous Henry, was unacquainted with the cheap. And what he did with his life was more important than any pennant, any movie, any noise. He civilized, by publishing books that will sneak into our unsuspecting heads and rearrange the neurons, the hierarchies, the values. When he died, The Times didn't write an editorial, The Post didn't run a series, The News didn't interview his colleagues, the wire services weren't around for the memorial service, 50,000 people didn't roar at his image on a scoreboard at a stadium, nobody named an airport after him. In France where they care about literature, they would have named a street. Part of the honor of my particular service class just plunged into the abyss. Why is it that the wrong heart is always attacked?

John Leonard

INTRODUCTION
TO THE 1995 EDITION

When I recently reread *The Art of Literary Publishing,* I was amazed at how little has changed in the fifteen years since its first publication. The problems are still the same: the bottom-line hucksters grab for more power and today's literary editors carry on in spite of eternal difficulties. I suggested then, and repeat now, that the value we place on our brief lives on this planet is reflected in the way we treat our literature and the authors and editors of that literature. In 1995, just as in 1980, literary editors and authors are endangered. Today's power grabbers tend to be other publishers and not Barbie Doll corporations. But the lust for power continues.

The first edition of this collection of distinguished editorial voices was hailed—"A unique over-the-editor's-shoulder perspective of the survival of quality in a world of slickness," *Publishers Weekly;* "A fascinating symposium," *Washington Post;* "Heartening," *Christian Science Monitor;* "Informative, provocative, and entertaining," *Library Journal.* Pushcart sold out the cloth edition and two paperback printings by the end of the 80s. But readers would not let the book go. Every month we received requests for another printing. The Radcliffe Publishing Course and other university programs informed me that *ALP* was a required text. Still, chronically short of funds, Pushcart delayed reprinting until this year. Finally *ALP*'s reputation demanded that we issue a slightly revised edition. In short, this book is "back by popular demand," a phrase I always distrusted as self-serving advertising until now.

I have resisted the urge to revise in any major way. Gerald Howard's essay is brand new and pays tribute to a few important editors left out of the 1980 edition—Pat Strachan and Cork Smith—to name but two. Otherwise there is simply no need to change or update.

What is clear is the continued necessity for this volume in an age that—because of the supposed "electronic revolution"—now fears for the very future of the printed word. In all ranks of the publishing community the panic rages. The cry ascends from publishing cocktail parties that soon we will all be pavement scrapings on the Info Superhighway. Commercial book corporations search for the exits; executives jump into the Internet. The fanatics from *Wired* are at the gates: "The computer age is the greatest revolution since the discovery of fire!" they holler. And the commercial print boys and girls bow down and plan to bail out.

When *ALP* was first published in 1980, computers were relatively new in town. "Word processors" they were dubbed—an obscene term that should have warned all of us about the mentality of their inventors. Now the processors of words process our very reality—"virtual reality" they term it as if it were so much sausage. In 1980 we called that "fake."

All of this would be mildly amusing if so many fine editors hadn't begun to tremble. I recently dined with the editor-in-chief of one of our better book publishing houses that dates back over 100 years. "I just hope books are around for another 20 years so I can retire," he moaned.

Balderdash!

And what a splendid reason to bring back the words of this volume to cheer him up. These editors may not be rediscovering fire, but they recognize what has endured and what will endure: words that care, and the editors and authors who nurture such words in books and journals that are not spat out for quick coin.

While the spirit of this book is crucial and unchanging, a few of its authors have moved here and there. Ted Solotaroff is now editor-at-large for HarperCollins; Hayden Carruth no longer edits nor teaches full-time, but Copper Canyon just issued his *Selected Essays* and a poetry collection, *Scrambled Eggs and Whiskey,* is set for 1996; Jon Galassi is now editor-in-chief of Farrar, Straus and Giroux; Cleanth Brooks died a few years ago; Ishmael Reed is devoting his time to writing—*Airing Dirty Laundry,* an essay collection from Addison-Wesley, is his latest; Simon Michael Bessie has formed a new firm, Counterpoint, with Jack Shoemaker, ex of North Point Press; Jim Landis left Morrow and now writes full time—*Lying in Bed,* a novel from Algonquin, is his latest; Ellen Ferber is teaching full time; Elliott Anderson took a spin in the film business; Gordon Lish runs *The Quarterly*; and Marjorie Fletcher now studies Chinese culture in Berkeley.

But no matter what their current jobs, these editors leave us with their courage, their sense of value and their determination to swim against the current. They, and all like them, will survive, somehow, some way. To paraphrase Faulkner, they will not only survive but what they do will prevail. These editors are dedicated to what endures while the commercial world surrounding them is enthralled only by what makes a cash splash and vanishes forever into the deep.

Bill Henderson

INTRODUCTION, 1980

It was an extraordinary front page.

On September 14, 1979, the *New York Times* featured three articles: "A RECORD $3.2 MILLION IS PLEDGED BY BANTAM FOR NEW KRANTZ NOVEL . . . for a record advance of $3,208,875 Bantam Books Wednesday night purchased the rights to publish in March 1981 a paperback edition of "Princess Daisy." The book is the recently completed second novel by Judith Krantz, author of the bestselling *Scruples* . . ."

Another article—"ABC OUTBIDS MATTEL FOR MACMIL-LAN INC. . . . The American Broadcasting Company made a surprise bid for Macmillan Inc. yesterday, upsetting a merger agreement Macmillan had reached just two weeks ago with Mattel, Inc., the toy company that built its fortune on Barbie Dolls."

The third front page account documented the fact that, across the country, students' reading ability was continuing a two decade decline.

Something disturbed me about that front page . . . Barbie Dolls, ABC, an increasing inability to find meaning in words (which implies that students don't care about meaning or words.)

I bought a copy of *Scruples* at the local drugstore. A review on the inside cover rejoiced that the novel was "as addictive as chocolate." I read a few hundred words that were calculated to titillate.

Perhaps, I mused, words aren't understood or valued today because some publishers are all too willing to be bought by Barbie Doll companies or by the purveyors of prime time (both mergers, by the way, failed as of this printing.) Perhaps the message from the publishing profession to the students and the rest of us is that books, TV, and Barbie Dolls are all the same and that words are valued and extravagantly paid for only when "as addictive as chocolate."

Why bother to read when you can just as easily gorge yourself on a box of Whitman Samplers?

A few editors still care about words and about the caring that words can convey. *The Art of Literary Publishing* is a celebration of these seldom-celebrated people, from both large and small firms, from past and present. To me these editors and others like them are heroes in a chocolate culture. Of course they would never give a thought to their heroism; most are doing what they have to do and want to do.

In assembling this collection over the past few years, I invited a variety of views—personal, practical, and philosophical. While this volume is in no way meant as a complete survey of all outstanding editors, it is intended to be a thorough sampling of prevailing—and usually very different—editorial opinion. Almost all of these chapters appear here for the first time in book form and most were written just for *The Art of Literary Publishing*.

Occasionally the editors speak from historical perspective— James Laughlin, head of New Directions (in an epic interview), or Cleanth Brooks, a founding editor of *The Southern Review,* for example; but more often they write resoundingly and directly of the present—Hayden Carruth, poetry editor of *Harper's* magazine, is mad about the state of things literary; Grace Schulman, poetry editor of *The Nation* is optimistic about the present and future of poetry; Ishmael Reed, director of Y'Bird publications, snaps that publishing has too often been a white male fortress; and Felix Stefanile, publisher of *Sparrow,* derides the current cultural ferment as "A Revolution of Twerps."

For every editor there is a different argument and here you will discover the opinions of today's most influential editorial minds: Simon Michael Bessie, a founder of Atheneum and now senior vice president of Harper and Row, Elliott Anderson, editor of *TriQuarterly*; Jonathan Galassi, an editor at Houghton Mifflin and poetry editor of *The Paris Review*; Len Fulton and Ellen Ferber, proprietors of Dustbooks; Maurice Girodias, publisher of the legendary Olympia Press (he is joined in a spirited round table discussion on censorship by Allen Ginsberg and William Burroughs); James Landis, editorial director of William Morrow Co.; Marjorie Fletcher, a founder of The Alice James Books Cooperative; David Ray, editor of *New Letters*; Gordon Lish, an editor at Knopf; Joyce Carol Oates and Raymond Smith of *The Ontario Review*; William Phillips, editor of *The Partisan Review;* Ted Solotaroff, former editor of *American Review*; and Jonathan Williams, head of The Jargon Society.

While we do look to the past—with chapters from Anaïs Nin, publisher and printer at Gemor Press; Maxwell Perkins, editor at Scribners; Saxe Commins, editor at Liveright and Random House; and John Farrar, a founder of Farrar, Straus and Giroux—this is not a book of yesterdays. Most of our editors thrive today in New York publishing corporations or in small presses across the country. These rare and special people carry on a tradition that words should mean and that meaning is important to all that we are and all that we seek to be.

Bill Henderson

THE ART
OF LITERARY
PUBLISHING

PUBLISHERS, BOOKSELLERS, READERS, AND WRITERS: SOME STRAWS IN A WHIRLWIND
by Ted Solotaroff

Ted Solotaroff was editor for many years of AMERICAN REVIEW *and is now an editor at Harper and Row, Inc.*

There appear to be two major developments in the publishing industry that work together like a pincers movement in the area of new writing. At both ends of the industry—editorial and sales—one sees the growing influence of the mentality and methods of big business. Until fairly recently, most of the publishing houses were managed by their owners, many of whom regarded their lists as in good part an expression of their own interests, tastes, and affections, which they could indulge since their profit expectations were relatively modest. A typical example is Alfred Knopf's support of Latin American and Japanese literature or James Laughlin's of experimental writing or Barney Rosset's of all manner of extreme and controversial work. In the past decade or so, the conglomerates have bought up many of the independent houses, and though the degree of control they exercise varies, their

3

general effect has been to create a considerably higher level of profit expectations. Moreover, the independent publisher and his backers accepted the variable nature of the business—that a major bestseller or two could make all the difference between a lean year and a fat one; the big corporation, with at least one eye always on the value of its shares, expects the profitability of its subsidiaries to grow with each year, not to mention each quarter.

This, of course, soon begins to affect the editorial decisions that are made: a good but unusual book begins to be "marginal"; a bad but faddish one becomes "highly commercial." The initiatives and risks of the editor give way to the prerogatives and assurances of the money managers—even to the money manager inside the editor. I know of one publishing house that reportedly measures its editors' performance by whether the net profit of the books they have sponsored is at least ten times greater than their salaries. But you don't need this kind of formula to get the same result. A friend who runs one of the more intellectual houses has been looking for an experienced junior editor for months. What he keeps running into are bright young people who come on very strong about plant costs and the like and who go blank when he asks them about their own ideas for books.

All of which is not to say that each of the conglomerate or otherwise publicly-owned houses are becoming intransigently venal or that the surviving independent ones are principally devoted to the original, the intellectual, and the otherwise problematic. Spiraling expenses, including those of acquisitions and royalties, and a spotty market drive everyone to consider the "bottom line." Also there are marked exceptions such as Knopf and Harper and Row or Avon and Bantam—all increasingly active in literary publishing, though all publicly owned. But, generally speaking, the thrust in publishing toward maximizing profits and minimizing losses and risks has sharply curtailed its overall receptivity to the kinds of writing I have been talking about.

A corollary development can be seen on the retail end of the industry that reinforces this trend. I am speaking of the advent of the bookstore chains which, likewise, look for higher profit than the privately owned store they are replacing

4

and which operate accordingly: so much a square foot in rent and overhead, so much in dollar volume: i.e., the efficiency of the supermarket. There is no question that these new operations are effective in attracting readers and moving books. Still, titles that aren't moving at a profitable rate don't linger in their stores, and those that don't have some sort of predictable following—first novels and the like—often don't enter them. In the past, publishers could count on those quirky, literate people who sold books because they liked to hang around them to get behind the worthy unfashionable title and steer readers to it. Again, not all of them were Frances Steloff of Gotham Book Mart, just as the buyers for a chain such as B. Dalton are not all computers with desks. On the contrary some of them like Dick Fontaine and Kay Sexton at B. Dalton and Mike Fox at Waldenbooks are genuine book people who favor quality and do what they can for it. But the fact remains that the chain stores themselves, which exert a powerful and growing influence on the publishing market, inevitably favor the fast-turnover title, more often than not the sort of book in which a gimmick meets a fad.

These, then, are two important structural changes in publishing that by and large foster a version of Gresham's Law. Fortunately there are still countervailing forces, for even commercial publishing doesn't lend itself all that readily to the kind of controls that big business likes to employ to standardize the product and the market. Even among the ''category books''—gothics, romances, westerns, mysteries, inspirational, etc.—those that most succeed are likely to have some distinctive edge to them of talent and conviction. Moreover, reading tastes and interests among the book-buying public tend to be as individual as their sexual ones. So once you get past the proven bestselling authors, you're in a gray area of crude comparisons (''it reminds me a little of *Portnoy's Complaint* . . .'') and hunches and surprises. Also we live in a very big and diverse country that has been educating a lot of people. This is why even the commercial publisher remains haunted by the tutelary spirit of art as well as of commerce. For the literary work that strikes it rich can strike it very rich indeed, and for years to come. First novels may generally lose money, but how would you like to

5

have passed up *The Naked and the Dead* or *Catcher in the Rye* or *The Invisible Man* or *Catch 22* or *V?* So all but the most shortsighted houses tend to maintain a margin of venture capital for at least a few of those strange, disturbing manuscripts that don't fit in anywhere but may turn out to have been written by the next Sylvia Plath or Kurt Vonnegut.

During the late '60s and for a few years thereafter, this margin widened significantly. Publishing itself was booming—the direct beneficiary of four developments that don't normally come at the same time: affluence; heavy federal spending for social welfare, including public schools, colleges, libraries, etc.; a series of political upheavals; a cultural revolution (or close to it). Money was pouring into publishing from all directions. Conglomerates were snapping up the houses, often at inflated prices, to strengthen their positions in the big new "learning industry." The interesting times we were living through stimulated book sales, both to those who wished to join or understand them and to those who wished to escape a bit from them. Moreover, the expanding educational market was turning more and more to the use of contemporary texts in response to the present-mindedness and demand for "relevance" that was sweeping the campuses and then even the high schools. This gave a terrific boost to the demand for contemporary literature. All of a sudden an obscure play by Samuel Beckett, whose work you hadn't been able to give away, was selling in the hundreds of thousands, or a novel by Nabokov that had been too gamy for American publishers only a few years before, was being distributed in the millions by several of them at the same time. Such diverse writers as Barth and Bellow, Borges and Burroughs, just to touch on the Bs, could now minister to the publisher's twin desires for profits and prestige.

Meanwhile, the powerful mood of unrest and change that swept over the culture favored the rebellious and innovative, or simply the personal and youthful, view of things. The "imagination of alternatives," as I wrote at the time, was awake in the land, and its principal bearers were the young and the young-hearted. A new audience came into being known as the "counterculture", which could turn an anthropology student at UCLA or a stoned son of Thoreau in San

6

Francisco into bestselling authors. For a time the young seemed to be the antennae of the race, and young writers were given unprecedented opportunities to publish—to the extent that literary agents and editors were scouting the creative writing centers and offering representation and contracts for manuscripts that might still have the instructor's grade or comments on them. Finally, an abundance of literary talents was springing up, for reasons that I've suggested elsewhere (*AR* 22) and to which I would add one other—that the proliferation of creative writing programs and courses was providing livelihoods for serious writers—a solution to their age-old problem of how to support themselves.

This, then, is the background—at least as much as I'm conscious of—for the bind we're in: a new and far more populous and diverse literary culture that we're trying to operate with the publishing institutions and mechanisms of the old culture. Without the unusually favorable circumstances of the '60s and with its own new problems and priorities, the performance of the industry is inadequate and increasingly unresponsive. I have not touched on commercial magazine publishing, where the negative tendencies I have been pointing to have been apparent for a long time and are now in an advanced state. What then are we to do?

I have little experience outside the circles of commercial publishing, and so what follows is mostly hearsay and speculation. But my sense of things is that the framework for an alternative system of publishing and distributing literary work is struggling to come together, and a different set of expectations among writers seems to be developing. This is particularly evident in poetry, the area of the literary culture that is most neglected by commercial publishing and its media and hence has had to fend most for itself. The poets have developed a national magazine, *American Poetry Review,* as a lively, nonsectarian, bluejeans alternative to *Poetry* magazine and the other more decorous and restricted poetry journals. *APR* is important, it seems to me, not only for the work it circulates to a relatively large audience but also for the sense of community it fosters and for the quarrels and other sources of energy it generates by its eclecticism and by its efforts to relate poetry to the culture around it. It expresses the demo-

7

cratic spirit of the poetry revival of the past decade in a particularly direct way.

The thrust of this revival comes from the development of small and local facilities, and the beginnings of a decentralized, grass-roots approach. The little magazines and small presses, beset by distribution problems outside their immediate areas, have been cultivating their own gardens. Poets involve themselves in arranging poetry readings by their colleagues, edit anthologies of local work, are active in the Poetry in the Schools program. Remarking on the indifference of the national print media to poetry, Donald Hall puts the matter as follows "Maybe poetry thrives because it lacks this sort of attention . . . the old metaphor of the poet's 'audience' has turned literal in the auditoriums and classrooms of the United States. Printed poetry thrives in personal magazines and in the efforts of one-man publishers. . . . We almost hand our poems around—the way they did in the 17th century."

My hunch is that writers of fiction and other forms of personal prose will follow in this direction as the centralization of commercial publishing in New York and the standardization of the market continue apace to frustrate their main aim and expectation, which is to be read. The Fiction Collective is a sign of writers banding together and taking an active role in getting their work published. But new modes of distribution will have to be found as well, on the order of Book People on the West Coast. Even in New York, there is the feeling that a significant audience for quality writing exists but that it is becoming too expensive and chancy to locate and develop, except in the college adoption area. The answer may well lie in the development of small-scale local and regional publishing, which is the way the industry, such as it was, worked in the 19th century and which is the way that theater and the other performing arts are working today.

The question that has been on my mind through the years of editing NAR/AR has been what this national literary audience is, and why it is so difficult to contact and marshall it. For example, in its early salad days, New American Review was selling close to one hundred thousand copies; its final issue, which virtually all the reviewers regarded as a banner one, will probably end up selling thirty thousand copies. What happened to those other seventy thousand readers, who soon got lost along the way? Or, to put it in another perspective: *Ragtime* has probably sold around three million copies in hardcover and paperback since it was published. Why did the issue of AR that featured a substantial part of its opening section only attract twenty-five thousand readers or less than 1%? Or again, with all the fanfare that attended the appearance of Robert Coover's *The Public Burning*, why did the issue of *AR* that published its opening section fail to do significantly better than the other less publicized issues of that year? The same is relatively true of A. Alvarez's famous essay on Sylvia Plath in *AR* 12, or Harold Brodkey's much-touted story of a girl's first orgasm in *AR* 16, or John Schaar's very influential essay, "The Case for Patriotism," in *AR* 17, or Peter Handke's extraordinary memoir of his mother, "A Sorrow Beyond Dreams," in AR 20.

The point I'm driving toward is that the potential literary audience, as witnessed by the sale of a book like *Ragtime,* numbers in the millions. And once or twice a year a significant literary work by a Joseph Heller or John Cheever or John Fowles or Thomas Pynchon will enlist a sizable portion of it. But, as with those North Vietnamese divisions that attacked in force and then disappeared into the countryside, it's very hard to know most of the time where this audience is and how to engage its interest and purchasing power.

Thus the problem of distribution is only partly solved by improving the mechanisms. After all, *American Review* had a distribution that was the envy of the little magazines, and yet no matter how many or few copies we published and placed in the bookstores, airline terminals, and various other outlets in likely places such as college campuses and the more cosmopolitan urban centers, its three publishers normally ended up taking back nearly half of what they put out. And bear in mind too that most issues of *NAR/AR* were well publicized in the review media and even had a small advertising budget. Why, too, were we unable to convert an initial readership of nearly one hundred thousand to no more than four thousand subscribers, most of them libraries?

So, to my mind and experience, these are the large and

enigmatic questions about the market for literary writing. Some say the audience is waning, that film is where it's at. But why, then, does the audience now and then turn out in droves? And what of the unprecedented wave of interest in creative writing and the steadily increasing numbers of capable poets and writers turning up everywhere? After ten years or more of trying to figure out this situation, I don't have any answers, only hunches. One is that it no longer makes sense most of the time to speak of the literary audience or market as a coherent entity. Instead of the former small elite of higher literary education and taste who supported the literary culture and defended it against the mass culture, there is now a much larger and much more amorphous and volatile entity that I think of as the literate class. Every now and then it will be brought together by a particular writer or book, but mostly it remains fragmented, diffuse, and dispersed, composed as it is of diverse and contending interests, values, and tastes. In one area of this audience, for example, are those who set their minds by Tom Robbins and Richard Brautigan, in another it's Saul Bellow and Philip Roth, in another Nabokov and Borges, in another Ishmael Reed, Thomas Pynchon, or Robert Coover. Or again, I suspect, the readers of Charles Bukowsky don't have much in common with the readers of Richard Wilbur, and neither with those of Louise Gluck, or of Patti Smith. In other words, defensible literary interests and tastes and judgments are no longer as they were twenty years ago the province of the high brow quarterlies, a kind of Supreme Court, as it were, but rather are found in the upper levels of literacy throughout the society. Rather like the House of Representatives they form various constituencies, lobbies, priorities. Occasionally a book like *Catch-22* or *Portnoy's Complaint* or *A Separate Reality* or *Sexual Politics* will force almost everyone who reads seriously to pay attention; or again, a writer like Vonnegut will join the contemporary campus market to the post-60's market to the SF market and his sales will soar. Or a novel will come out of the blue, like *Rubyfruit Jungle,* catch on with the young, with feminists, with gays, and be very successful. The net effect of this situation is that now and then a book or a writer draws together a large audience and makes a lot of money, or else circulates among its own constituency, or more likely a small segment of it, and otherwise sinks without a trace. Theodore Roszak has described how "The Movement" of the sixties has not disappeared, but has rather reorganized into a loose network of "small bands of kindred spirits . . . blacks, Chicanos, native Americans, men, women, kids, students, old folks, dope addicts, convicts, homosexuals, transsexuals, mental patients, the terminally ill . . .," who are drawn together by their specific personal situations. Even as broadly based and seemingly coherent a movement as feminism tends to break down, in Roszak's view, into a "congeries of local, finely discriminated groupings: third-world women, divorced and widowed women, rape victims, Gray Panther women, inorgasmic women, country women (living in rural communes), hookers, faculty women, bisexual women, lesbians, radical lesbians, lesbian mothers, unwed mothers, women in the arts, women in-and-just-out-of prison."

To a lesser but still important extent this is also true of the literary audiences. The paradox of it all is that as commercial publishing becomes more and more standardized and routinized, as though one's fall list were so many models of shoes, the upper levels of literacy, at least, become more and more diversified, specialized, and personalized. Hence, there are the moments in almost every editorial meeting, hardcover and paperback, when the book comes up that doesn't fall into one of the standard slots, and the hard-headed among us ask who's going to buy this book, and one or two editors grow passionate about its quality and about the larger issues involved, the others look blank, and the publisher looks grim. On the other hand, this development provides a very strong rationale for the small press movement, and the outcropping of small specialized bookstores, which are likely to become more and more plugged into this disparate constituency of American letters. On the third hand, there is the steamroller of the mass economy, that works directly against the small, the local, the marginal, and the personal in publishing and bookselling. So I just don't know. Like everyone else who is in this perplexing business of publishing more for love than money or status, one can only play his hunches, pursue his desires, do what he can, and hope for the best.

11

As for the writers themselves, I hardly know what to say. In some ways the situation is one of rising expectations, which, as James Baldwin has observed in connection with the Third World, is likely to be the most anguished time of all. The struggling author of the three thousand copy novel sees this or that serious writer, or even a difficult one like Samuel Beckett or Thomas Pynchon, making hatfuls of money, and justifiably wonders why the pea never turns up under the shell that he has placed his stake on. Or why it hasn't for his last three works, when it paid off so lavishly for his first or second. Twenty-five years ago, when members of my generation contemplated the literary vocation, it was with the expectation of joining a more or less permanently depressed class: the models being Joyce or Henry Miller or George Orwell or e.e. cummings or Doris Lessing or Louise Bogan—an unremitting struggle, not without its heroism, to get by, until eventually, around the age of forty or fifty it might all pay off. I don't think younger writers today are much inspired by these models: for one thing, there is the chance to teach and live comfortably; for another, the pot of gold may seem to be just around the corner. Hence, they tend to pay a lot of attention to *Literary Marketplace* and *Publisher's Weekly* and to the right agents, houses, editors, etc. Not that, in the end this heightened sense of opportunity makes much difference as to whether the young writer will succeed or not, but it can make a difference in disorienting him about the facts of publishing life, particularly in these days of dwindling lists of commercially published first novels, books of poems, and other one-of-a-kind works. Whenever I visit a writing program and listen to the questions that are asked, and the ingenuous savvy they float on, I think that perhaps the most appropriate workshop that could be given is one in how to deal with rejection for years to come, and how to support yourself if a teaching job doesn't materialize.

Well, that's about what's on my mind these days, as I, like everyone else in publishing, press on into the mists and turbulences.

NEW DIRECTIONS:
AN INTERVIEW WITH
JAMES LAUGHLIN

James Laughlin is a poet and is also founder, President and Publisher of New Directions Publishing Corporation. This interview was conducted by Susan Howe and Charles Ruas and edited by Mr. Ruas and Mr. Laughlin.

Why did you leave Harvard as a student in 1935 to go to Europe? What long term effect, if any, do you think that Harvard had on your taste, your thinking, and what you did subsequently?

I left Harvard because I found it extremely stuffy. There were in those days some really great men and I was fortunate to be able to work with some of them, such as Ted Spencer and F.O. Matthiessen. But in general I would say that the academic ambience was not hospitable to the modern literature in which I was already getting interested at that age. In my secondary school at Choate, I had had one of the masters of all time, a great English teacher, Dudley Fitts, the poet and translator of Greek Drama, who worked with Robert Fitzgerald on the early versions of the Greek plays. When I

13

came to Harvard I'd already been indoctrinated with a considerable passion for people such as Eliot, Pound, Yeats and Joyce. At Harvard in '33, believe it or not, there still were no courses being given in these writers. They were not yet accepted, although they were men of stature already on the international scene. There was one course which was given by the Professor of Rhetoric, the holder of the Boylston Chair, that as you know is the great honorary chair to have at Harvard. Robert Fitzgerald has it now, Archie MacLeish has had it, and others before them. It has, by the way, the prerogative that the holder of the Boylston Chair may pasture a cow in the Harvard Yard. I've always been trying to put Bob Fitzgerald up to the idea of renting a cow for the day and bringing it into Harvard to see whether this tradition would stand up. But the students walk on the grass so much I think that the cow would have a very hungry day. Anyway, in those days, the Professor of Rhetoric, whose name has now passed into oblivion, would get so angry if the name of Eliot or Pound were mentioned in his course that he would ask the student to leave the room. That was a little bit the tenor of official, established, Harvard at that time, and I found it oppressive. When the opportunity came for me to get a leave of absence to go abroad and to meet some literary people, I rapidly jumped at it, and took off for Europe. There my first opportunity was working with Gertrude Stein for several months.

That was plunging right into the midst of the expatriate's Paris. How did it come about?

It came about completely through happenstance. I had read her work at Choate, and was very fascinated by the experiments she was doing with association and language, and her attempts to purify language by getting away from conventional connotations and styles. I knew her work, but I'd never had any contact with her. I happened to be in Salzburg during the summer after attending the music festival and quite by serendipity, or whatever you want to call it, I met in the Schwimmbad, the town swimming pool, Professor Bernard Fay, the great French scholar of American Literature who was a dear friend of Gertrude Stein's. Swimming there and

14

sunning ourselves, we got to talking about modern American Literature. Fay had spotted me as a young American student, so he wanted to pump me about what was going on with the young in America, and we got to talking about Gertrude. I expressed admiration and he said, "Why she's one of my best friends, would you like to meet her?" So, he wrote to her and arranged for me to go to stay with her at her farm. It was down near the Lac d'Annecy in the foothills of the French Alps. Her house was in a little village and was called Bilignin. She invited me to come to visit but there was a little catch in it I found when I arrived. It was one of the most delightful months I ever spent, because Gertrude was one of the most extraordinarily charismatic women that I have known, though she did have a few, shall we say, eccentricities. Alice B. Toklas was equally fascinating in her totally different way. They complimented each other perfectly because Gertrude was the dominating, strong, powerful intellectual force, while Alice was the tidier-up-afterer, the housekeeper, the marvelous cook, and the one who kept things rolling. She was what you call in old vaudeville, the end man. She saw that the guests kept arriving, that the proper questions were asked at the proper time. Well, the catch to this visit with Gertrude was that she had some work she wanted done. She was just about to set out for this country after many years of hoping for it. She'd been invited to give lectures at various universities. She had written six lectures, which, under the title of *Narration,* were published by the University of Chicago Press. She needed press releases, or she thought she needed press releases. Somebody in the Paris press corps told her. "Nobody will understand what you're talking about, when you give these lectures. You've got to have press digests of them. You must have them reduced to one page for each of the lectures, which you will give out to reporters when you meet them." So she put me to writing these boiled-down versions of the lectures. It was one of the most difficult things I've ever attempted in my life. The lectures were highly epistemological, and highly metaphysical, and written entirely in that extraordinary Steinese dialect of the disembodied word and the floating phrase. To attempt to boil down the essential ideas out of a half-hour lecture to one page was a task in which I repeatedly failed. I would bring Gertrude these pages and she would read them and shake her head and say, "No, no, this is wrong. You've missed this, you've missed that. Go back and do it again." But I spent a really wonderful month there in that beautiful countryside with Alice and Gertrude in their stone house which was bigger than a normal farmhouse but smaller than a chateau, and called a chateau-ferme. It had a marvelous terrace out in front, with a lovely view looking out over hills and valleys and poplar trees and fields. I remember that Gertrude used always to sit on the terrace wall with her back to the view because she said that the only way that you could properly take in a view, was by sitting with your back to it. That was the way she was. She had these really quite extraordinary points of view about things.

After spending a month with her, what was your feeling about her work and Gertrude Stein as a person?

Well, she simply riveted your attention, whenever she was talking. The work itself, I think, divides into so many different categories that you have to pick and choose what is best. A lot of it was in my opinion definitely what we would call automatic writing. I say that because I used to watch her do it. She would sit out on the terrace in a deck chair with a pad, and her hand would simply move ceaselessly, without pause. The words, the ideas, were coming from somewhere deep down inside, and she never rewrote. As far as I know, she never rewrote anything. Alice would type out the pieces that were going to be sent to magazines. She would type them out from Gertrude's hand notations but when you looked at the original pages they were almost indecipherable, showing, I think, to what extent they were coming from the unconscious mind. Alice had developed a great proficiency in reading this scrawl. You can see the notebooks in the Beinecke Library at Yale. It was automatic writing, which is really nothing against it. After all, lots of people have done automatic writing, Kerouac for example.

Also at that time the whole Surrealist school in France was experimenting with it.

The French were very deep into that kind of thing. But Gertrude was very independent. She was not at all tied up with the Dadaists, or with the Surrealists. She felt very much on her own, and while she was willing to be published in magazines which printed surrealists, she always felt completely apart from them and rather resentful if anyone attempted to identify her with them. I think for that reason she was a little bit annoyed with Edmund Wilson. In *Axel's Castle*, he put her in the same book with other figures in modern French Literature, and she really didn't like that.

That brings up the question I wanted to ask you next. How did it feel to grow up in a country where the best literature was in Europe, the best American writers or the most exciting artists were abroad.

It seemed a very good reason to go to Europe.

You spoke of the sterility of Harvard, for you, so there must have been a strange cultural gap for you. . . .

At that point there was almost nothing. It's hard to imagine, for a young kid now who is growing up in a country which has hundreds of little magazines, and which has so many schools for writers and writers seminars and writers groups and poetry readings. It's a totally different climate. When I was eighteen and in Harvard there was none of this. Poetry readings were practically unheard of. There was one poetry reading a year given at Harvard under the Morris Grey Fund. Usually it was some venerable fellow who had thoroughly proven himself respectable who was chosen by the older members of the faculty. You've got to remember that this was just after the depression and there was no money around. The publishers, such as Liveright a bit earlier, and the Boni brothers, who had been engaged in bringing out avant-garde literature, had mostly gone broke and dropped out of business so there was nothing left. The *Dial* had stopped publication, Margaret Anderson's *Little Review* had stopped publication, Bill Williams *Contact* and Richard John's *Pagany* had stopped publication. The only important little magazine that was going at that time was Lincoln Kirstein's *Hound & Horn*, which was not a hunting magazine, as you know, but was one of the great literary and artistic magazines of that time. Lincoln had founded it shortly after he finished Harvard.

Nowadays, in the '70's, the major publishing companies are not publishing poetry. There are many, many small presses, and small magazines now. From poets I get the idea that over the past few years it's almost impossible to get a book of poems published by a large publishing house.

I wouldn't say that that is quite fair. If you look over the lists of the large publishers you will find that there are at least half a dozen of the very best ones who make a regular practice of bringing out three or four volumes of good quality poetry each year. Then you have some presses, I think particularily of The Wesleyan University Press, The Princeton University Press, or The University of Pittsburgh Press, which do even more than that. It is true that there are now in this country hundreds of small presses, thanks largely to two machines: the IBM composer is a wonderful machine on which a poet can turn out himself a page of poetry which looks like printed type; the other, of course, is the offset press, where you don't have to go through Linotype procedures, or through plate making procedures. You simply lay out your pages, and almost anybody can run a small offset press. Then all you need is a cutter and a staple binder and you have a little magazine. These books and magazines keep cropping up. Every week, I get an announcement of a new little magazine from some group of poets, the young and they get stuff around. While their circulations are extremely small they are influential.

How did you decide that you would start a publishing firm?

That was entirely due to the influence, in fact, the order, the directive, of Ezra Pound. After I had spent the summer with Gertrude, and finally after great, great labor had turned out a few scraps of paper which she thought possibly might be acceptable as press releases, she left the farm and went back up to Paris and I went up to Paris too. I had a room which I rented, I think for seven francs a month, which was near the Eiffel Tower. I was rather poverty stricken in those days because my parents didn't approve of my not coming back to Harvard and so they stopped sending me any money. The only reason that I was able to stay in Europe was that I had a cousin of my mother's who was very sympathetic to my rebellion from my native city of Pittsburgh. She would surreptitiously send me a check for a hundred dollars about every second month and that's what I lived off. Anyway, it was fine in Paris, and I could go anytime I wanted, to see Gertrude and get a free meal, or Bernard Fay, or various of her friends or other writers that I met. But when the weather got cold, there was no heat in my little room, which was, actually, not in a boarding house. It was a little closet room in an insurance office, a fly-by-night insurance company, on the second floor of a building near the Champs de Mars. When there was no longer any heat and I didn't have any heavy sweaters, all I had was a loden mantel that I'd brought from Austria, life in Paris became a little bit difficult. Dudley Fitts, my master at Choate, had corresponded with Pound considerably and taking advantage of the Fitts connection, I wrote to Pound and asked if I could come to Rapallo to see him. I received, to my amazement, a telegram in reply. The telegram said "Visibility high", so I took off by the next third-class night train and went down to Rapallo and found that here was this marvelous, dynamic eccentric, a most hospitable man, a born teacher, a person who loved to talk to young people, carrying on fantastic pedagogical monologues. Pound was a teacher manqué if ever there was one. I found that it was possible to enroll without any tuition fees whatever, in what was known as the Ezuversity. This meant that you could have lunch with Ezra—you paid for your own lunch, but things were very inexpensive then in Italy. You could spend the afternoon with Ezra, either taking walks, or playing tennis with him, or going rowing with him when it came to be summer. Then you could have tea with Ezra and Mrs. Pound, and you could even have dinner. If you could stand it, after dinner you could go to the ghastly Italian movies. These were the days before art had arrived in the Italian film industry. All the while that this was going on there was this continuous monologue of information on every conceivable subject coming out of Ezra, and this is what constituted the Ezuversity.

What was he working on at that time?

By 1935, Pound was chiefly immersed in history, that is, his reevaluations of history, and particularily his studies of the early American founding fathers, the *Adams Cantos,* the Jefferson material. He was working also on his economic theories, the ideas of Social Credit which he had picked up chiefly from A.R. Orage and C.H. Douglass in England. And he was doing research on the connections between banks and armament manufacturers, and things of that kind.

Was he also at that time, developing his theory of history?

Yes, this was the period when his rather unusual interpretation of history was being hammered out from his reading. People from all over the world with whom he was corresponding—and he had an enormous correspondence—would send him books, which he would read and put the pieces together. He had a network all over the world of young people to whom he would write who would find books for him and who were supposed to start inserting pieces of propaganda derived from his theories in magazines. The Ezuversity gave a marvelous course, because people kept dropping through Rapallo—it's on the main train line between Genoa and Rome—all kinds of writers would stop off for a few days and would join in on the discussions. While I was there I was the principal permanent student in Ezuversity, but other people were always dropping in—Basil Bunting and Louis Zukofsky and any number of different writers, who'd be passing through, so that you kept meeting interesting people, and learning all sorts of interesting things. Ezra would give us books to read, too, from his large library.

What were his working habits, from what you said it sounded like he was talking and mixing all day.

He got up fairly early and he worked all morning either on writing or correspondence. Then of course he read late at night. His office was a marvelous place. The Pounds had the penthouse floor in an apartment on the sea front in Rapallo. It was a very narrow structure, a series of little rooms in line, and one of these rooms was his office. He had many of his things hanging by strings from the ceiling. Thus, his pencil and his pen and his scissors and his eraser and his extra spectacles, and other things were hanging by strings from the ceiling above his typewriter. His files were hung up either by strings or on hooks on the wall so that he could reach back from his chair and get at them. He used to say that his biggest living expense was postage, because he carried on an enormous correspondence with people all over the world, answering letters and exhorting the writers to get to the roots of the money evil, and how the banking systems were abusing credit, how history was being distorted for the benefit of the bankers and the armament makers.

Was his daughter Mary born at that time?

Mary was born in 1925. When I first met her she was living up in northeastern Italy, in the mountains with the Marcher family, the peasants who were her adoptive family. Ezra never wanted children around; he didn't want the noise and fuss of children. I worked on my writing in Rapallo with Ezra. I would write little things and show them to him, and he would break the points off his pencils stabbing out the extra words. He'd say, "You don't need that word, take that out." Cross, crash, bang. Half of what I'd written would come out, so that these manuscripts that I'd present to him would look like battlefields. Finally in the end he said to me "Jas, it's no use." I said, "What do you mean, Boss?" He said, "It's no use. You are not going to make a writer, you're too verbose. You've had too much Harvard. You're not going to make a writer. So, why don't you do something useful?" I said, "What do you mean by useful?" He said, "Go back to America and start printin' things. None of my friends have any publishers. All their publishers have gone broke with the depression. There needs to be a publisher to print them." Following his directive, I returned to America. I reenlisted at Harvard which took me back, without any hard feeling, and I started to bring out books. The first ones were actually printed by the same fellow up in Vermont who printed the *Harvard Advocate*. Later, I found three or four printers right in Harvard Square. I did the distribution by climbing into my car during reading periods and vacations and driving around the country trying to peddle them to stores and libraries, where I was regarded as a very curious beast. This tall young man would come in in his strange outfit, (I was still wearing my Austrian cape), to try to sell them such odd authors as Kay Boyle and William Carlos Williams and Robert McAlmon and Ezra Pound. Most of the storekeepers didn't know what in God's name this stuff was. Usually, out of pity for this eccentric young man, they would buy two or three copies, and that's how the business got started.

Did Ezra Pound turn you towards the work of William Carlos Williams?

Yes, that's how I got to know Williams. You see Williams' early publishing history had been very difficult. He had had to pay for the printing of one of his early books which Ezra had arranged to be done by Elkin Mathews. His other early experimental books, the prose books such as *The Great American Novel* and *Spring and All,* were done in Paris, published by Ezra's friends such as Bob McAlmon, who was running the Contact Press, or by Bill Bird, who worked as a night editor at the *Paris Tribune* and had the Three Mountains Press on the side. Almost all of Bill's early books were published in France and were hardly distributed in this country at all. They were known only to a small and select group of his friends, who passed them around from hand to hand. *A Novelette and other Prose* was published by George Oppen, the poet, who was then living in the South of France. He had something called the To Press which led to George's Objectivist Press and that's how the Objectivist School got started with people such as Zukofsky, Reznikoff, Rakosi, Oppen himself and several others. Ezra published *The Objectivist Anthology* with them. Almost all of Bill's early books were published you might say semi-privately. There had been two books published by established publishers in this country: there was *In The American Grain,* published by Albert and Charles Boni, and then there was the early novel *A Voyage to Pagany*, which was published by a firm named Macaulay, which fairly soon went broke. By the time that I came along, Bill had accumulated a lot of poems and he also had the first parts of the novel *White Mule* ready, and he had no publishers. Ezra immediately sent me to Bill, "Here's this young guy who's willing to print your books for you." Bill said, "Well what do you know about publishing?" and I said, "Nothing," and he said, "That all right, I don't know anything about it either." He let me have his next books and they of course helped greatly to strengthen the list and get it going because they did begin to have some limited acceptance, though it wasn't really until the Sixties that William Carlos Williams became properly famous.

In the beginning was your venture into publishing influenced by private presses such as Sylvia Beach's Shakespeare and Co. in Paris and Hogarth in London?

I didn't know much about the Hogarth Press. I didn't get to London often in those days. I was particularly influenced by McAlmon's Contact Press books and I did also know the books that Sylvia Beach had done. Actually Sylvia didn't do a great many books, you know. She did *Ulysses*, but what else did she bring out? Sylvia's was more an institution, it was a place. She was the Frances Steloff of Paris and Shakespeare & Co. in the rue de L'Odeon was the Gotham Book Mart of Paris. It was the place where Hemingway could get his mail and everybody else could drop in to see Hemingway.

What about Harry Crosby, the Black Sun Press, did you know them at all in Paris?

I didn't get to meet Caresse Crosby until considerably later. I never knew Harry. I think he had done himself in before I came to Paris. But Caresse was a remarkably attractive and dynamic woman.

They put out beautiful books.

Oh, they were lovely books. Of course, there was plenty of money, they both came from well-off families, so they were able to print their books extremely handsomely. They did books of Pound and they did some D. H. Lawrence and any number of interesting people.

I'd be very curious to know what happened for example to your list which included Pound, during the Second World War and afterwards the position it must have forced you into, especially when Pound was committed to St. Elizabeth's.

You've got several questions there. First of all, the list began to grow in various sideways ways, because I didn't limit myself to publishing Ezra's friends and those he recommended. I also came strongly under the influence of various other people, and some of quite different schools of thought than Ezra. For example, I was very much influenced by Yvor Winters, the critic and poet and professor at Stanford. I did a number of books which he suggested including a couple of his own books of criticism and an anthology that he put together. Very soon thereafter I met Kenneth Rexroth who became a strong influence in directing me toward various authors whom I should publish. Rexroth was already established in San Francisco by then. I began a series of modern classics, translations particularly, texts, which were not available, that is, Rimbaud and Baudelaire and Lorca and other classics which were the forerunners of the modern movement. We did a little Surrealist anthology in one of our annuals.

I can also remember that you were one of the few presses that had some Henry James on its list.

Yes, thanks chiefly to F. O. Matthiessen, with whom I became friends after I returned to Harvard, we were very much involved in the James revival. We did Matthiessen's collection of James' *Stories of Artists and Writers,* and a new edition of *The Spoils of Poynton,* which was out of print then. We also helped to revive a number of other people. For example, believe it or not, in the Forties, F. Scott Fitzgerald was totally out of print.

That's pretty startling.

24

It's hard to believe but after Fitzgerald's initial success there'd been a kind of eclipse. After he'd had his troubles and gone to Hollywood and was having such a hard time, he was totally out of print. The way Fitzgerald came to me was that Edmund Wilson was his literary executor and Wilson had been showing around *The Crack-Up,* which was a collection he had assembled of Fitzgerald's miscellaneous papers that he wrote during the later part of his life and illness. Every big publisher in New York had turned it down, so he brought it to me and I jumped at it, of course. Later I talked to Scribner's and found that they had no Fitzgerald in print. *The Crack-Up* went through five printings, I think, and that was the start of the Fitzgerald revival. For a while we leased *The Great Gatsby* from Scribner's and we had Lionel Trilling do an introduction for it. But of course we lost the lease on *Gatsby* later when the boom really got going and Scribner's saw that it was profitable to put all of Fitzgerald back into print. Then there was a similar situation with E. M. Forster, owing to a tiff over an invitation to lunch in London, which Forster had had with my dear friend Alfred Knopf, a man whom I love and enormously respect but who can be a little, shall we say, acerb. Knopf had allowed the Forster books to go out of print, so that we were able to lease two of those from him. We had *The Longest Journey* and *Where Angels Fear to Tread* for many years. I say that we were instrumental in the Forster revival, because I persuaded Lionel Trilling to write a book about him, which was so brilliant it put him back into popularity.

It's hard for me, at this point, to understand how certain writers could have been eclipsed so totally, and yet revived by an introduction by an academic critic.

Oh, I think I can explain that. The general reading public, you see, had forgotten about these writers because they weren't bringing out new books. The tendency to teach modern literature in the colleges had not yet gotten started, so there was a kind of a hiatus. You had people such as Matthiessen and Spencer at Harvard, and others such as Robert Penn Warren, Cleanth Brooks, John Crowe Ransom, and others who wanted to teach modern writing, but it took them a long time to get it into the curriculum because it was so very bitterly resisted by the old guard of the English Departments. Actually you had the same situation in England, until recently, I'm told, where it was considered that the teaching of contemporary literature was ridiculous, that contemporary literature was something students read for diversion and what they should be studying was the classics. Nowadays it's completely reversed. If you go into almost any English Department in this country, you will find that the popular courses are the courses in the modern novel or in modern poetry and the professors really have to struggle to get students to read Milton and Pope.

Then you spoke about the war. The war was very hard on us because of the paper rationing. Just at the start of the Second World War we were really beginning to make headway. The books were becoming better known and I'd set up better distribution arrangements. I had a marvelous man named George Stuart who was the salesman and went around the country visiting the bookstores. We were getting more reviews. Then, suddenly, the government imposed paper rationing. You could only have as much paper as you had used in the year 1937, a year when we'd done almost nothing. There we were sitting, unable to buy paper legally—and I didn't want to do it illegally—and we had more and more good manuscripts coming in and no way to get them printed. That was very very difficult. It meant that we had to hold back on a lot of things, even reprints. We had to delay a long time on certain of William Carlos Williams' books which had to be done by other presses simply because we couldn't stir up the paper.

Can we go back to Ezra Pound? First, how did WWII effect you?

We were totally cut off, we didn't know what had happened to Ezra, because there was no mail coming through from Italy. Ezra had come to the States just before the war, he had made his last trip to this country in what was a futile effort to try to persuade the American Government that a war was coming

26

and they should stay out of it if they could. He had absolutely no success. He had relied on his friendship with Congressman Tinkham of Boston, the man who was famous for having ridden his horse into saloons in Roxbury to get votes. Tinkham was a wealthy eccentric of the Boston aristocracy whom Ezra had met on the beach at the Lido in Venice. Ezra had hoped that through Tinkham all doors would be open to him in Washington and that he would be able to meet Roosevelt and other politicians. He hoped to explain to them that the wicked international bankers were stirring up another war and that America must, at all cost, stay out. People in Washington just wouldn't pay any attention to him, so the trip was a terrible letdown for Ezra. After the war started, Mr. and Mrs. Pound stayed in Italy. Ezra wanted to come back, but couldn't get a passport for his daughter because of technical irregularities and a nasty American consul who didn't want to cooperate. There they were stuck in Italy, and almost starving. We couldn't get any word from them, they couldn't get any word out. We were much concerned but could do nothing. The first thing I finally heard was when I read in the papers that Ezra was being brought to Washington for a trial for having made broadcasts from Rome during the war. In all good faith I must say he was still trying to get America *out* of the war. It didn't fit in with his concepts of history that we should be fighting that war.

I'm interested in the political aspect of your career at this point. You'd always known Ezra Pound as an avant-garde poet who to some extent stayed, let's say, on the outside, and suddenly you saw him tried politically as a traitor, or accused of being a traitor. I'm wondering what shift in attitude you may have had at that point, and how you understood the situation.

Except for the anti-Semitism which I never could tolerate— that was one thing that Ezra and I used to fight about, because I just couldn't stomach that—I think his Fascist learnings were definitely a part of his mental condition. The psychiatrists who treated him after he was brought to Washington told me that the anti-Semitism was a recognized symptom of the kind of paranoid mental state which he had developed as a result of not being listened to by anybody in power who could put his ideas into practice. Apart from the anti-Semitic stuff, which I find repulsive and which I'm happy to say he repudiated in his old age, I always agreed with most of his economic theories. I'm a Social Creditor to this day. I still think that the economic system which we have, which is a pyramid of debt financing, is absolutely ridiculous and is going to bring us to a complete crash and dissolution of our system if it is not corrected within a reasonable time. We see that in the condition of the City of New York, with its vast debt on which it cannot pay the interest without getting further into debt. Ezra was saying for years that money was credit, that money was social credit, that it must be used as a ticket, and that it must not be something on which somebody charged rent. A banker or a government charged rent in order that creative production might take place. I was a Social Creditor and I was totally sympathetic to his economic ideas all along.

But did you think that he should have been hospitalized for those views, if you were in such sympathy with him?

You've got to look back to the hysterical climate of those days. Pound, technically, had made those broadcasts, even though he prefaced each one by saying he was doing his duty as an American citizen by making them, that he was upholding the Constitution and warning people of Roosevelt's mistakes and against the tie-ups between the American government and the international bankers. You've got to realize that there was a very good chance that he would have either been hung, because there was no legal precedent for what you did with people who made broadcasts which could be considered treasonable, or that he would have received a long term. Another fellow, Douglas Chandler, who broadcast from Germany, got something like thirty years, part of which he worked off by good behavior. He was in Danbury and then he was in Lewisburg, Pennsylvania, for about twenty years. This could very well have happened to Ezra. I think that the feeling of all of us, Ezra's friends, was that although we believed in his good intentions and were convinced of his honesty and

28

integrity, it might have been very difficult to convince a jury of these facts, and that it was preferable to go along with the ruling of the sanity hearing jury and the government psychiatrists that he was too confused in mind to stand trial.

But it was a shattering experience for him.

Yes, it was traumatic for him. When the Army had him in the DTC, the camp for criminal soldiers in Italy, for a while there they had him locked up in a cage made out of airplane landing strip mats. It gave him a nervous breakdown. But he gradually made some recovery. When he arrived in this country he was not able to understand why they were trying him. When I heard that he was coming, I asked my lawyer, Julien Cornell, who's a wonderful chap, to go down to meet him in Washington, to see what could be done to look after him and to defend him. Julien talked to him at great length and reported to me: "I cannot make Ezra understand what his situation is. He cannot grasp that he has done anything that was treasonable, he considers himself an American. He considers himself a better American than most of the people who are running the country. He cannot see why he should be tried for anything. In fact, he thought that when they brought him back what they were doing really was bringing him to this country because of his great knowledge of Confucius, to brief men at the State Department and then send him over to Japan to be a special aide to General MacArthur, to help with the rebuilding of Japan, along Confucian lines." This gives you an indication of how, shall we say, removed from common reality Ezra had become.

The last ten years of his life he was supposed to have been silent, did you see him during that time?

Yes and it was true he spoke hardly at all.

What do you think it was, do you think it was remorse, old age, rage, or what? Why do you think?

I think it was a withdrawal brought about by acute disappointment that the world didn't listen to his ideas about economics and history. Also in a philosophical sense, although Ezra was never a mystic, he pooh-poohed mysticism—it was a withdrawal into his own spiritual domain and a rejection of the world which had rejected him.

Was he aware of the growing influence of his work at that time, during the last ten years of his life?

He must have been aware of it, because so many books and so many articles were being written about him, and we'd always send them to him. Admirers and students were constantly trying to stop by to talk with him in Venice or Rapallo. He certainly was aware that he had become famous. At the same time, it was really tragic that he couldn't accept the admiration for his poetry with very much happiness, because what was more basic to him, what seemed to him more important were his economic, political and historical ideas. He couldn't separate the two, and he couldn't find happiness in the fact that people thought that the Chinese translations or the *Mauberley* or bits and pieces of the beauty spots of the *Cantos* were great. He couldn't take much pleasure in that when they wouldn't pay attention to his economic ideas. He felt, almost, that he'd failed in what was to him his main mission.

They made records of his reading of the Cantos *at that period, and I was wondering, did he continue writing?*

Oh yes, he was writing all the time that he was in St. Elizabeth's Hospital in Washington. He was translating Chinese, he was doing the translation from the Greek of the *Women of Trachis* and he also did a translation of Sopocles's *Electra,* which we are trying to find. The typescript is lost somewhere, but we hope to find it in a collection of papers that was rescued from his wife's Washington apartment. He was working on *Thrones,* which is the last section of the *Cantos.* He was enormously industrious while he was in St. Elizabeth's Hospital. It was simply incredible, the way he kept on working. He didn't let his spirits flag at all. He thought of himself as a political prisoner and he remembered other great political prisoners throughout history. You know, Nehru wrote a history of the world in prison. He kept right on with his work the whole time and turned out some marvelous things.

I'm wondering if your relationship with Pound affected New Directions during the McCarthy era. Were any writers you published brought up before the McCarthy committee?

I don't think any of our immediate group were particularily bothered by McCarthy. The only one who had trouble was William Carlos Williams, and that came later, when he had the appointment for the Chair of Poetry at the Library of Congress. That was taken away from him on some very flimsy and undefinable grounds of some political connection. I think my reaction to the McCarthy era was one that everybody else had, that this was a perfectly dreadful man and couldn't somebody please get rid of him somehow. But I had no intimate contact with him through writers.

I'm amazed by your list, especially now that most of the writers are so recognized and taught in school. How did you, for example, decide to bring out Nightwood?

I think *Nightwood* was recommended to me by T.S. Eliot. Eliot had been a devoted friend of Djuna Barnes, oh, for many many years. You know she lived in Paris when she was younger. She was one of the great beauties of the expatriate set, and she was very well known in Paris literary circles. Eliot used to get over to Paris occasionally, and I think he met her there and became friends with her and recognized her genius and they were very close. He was extremely helpful to her in doing the polishing, the final putting together of *Nightwood*. He had first arranged for the book to be published here by Harcourt Brace. Harcourt Brace brought it out, and nobody paid much attention, and it just fell flat. Harcourt Brace let it go out of print. Then Eliot called it to my attention. New Directions brought it out again and we've had it on our list ever since. It is taught in many colleges, recognized not only as one of the most important works of imaginative prose of the century, but also you could say that Djuna Barnes, in her way, was a pioneer of the Woman's Liberation Movement.

Would you know why she never received the recognition of her contemporaries in this country? I met with her recently. She is still hard at work, and a recluse. Her vision of mankind is rather Swiftian.

I think because she's lived such a quiet and withdrawn life, which is of her own choosing, and has never played any kind of literary politics. In fact, she resents any kind of promotional activity. For example, you can't get her to do interviews. People want to see her to write articles about her and she says, "I'm busy, I don't want to be bothered." She feels apart from such activities. She's confident that *Nightwood* is a masterpiece which will endure, as I myself think, and she leaves it at that.

When did you come into contact with Hilda Dolittle, was that through Pound?

I had always known about H.D., because she was part of the whole Pound scene and was married to Aldington and friends with Bryher and so many other people, that I had always known her work. We didn't actually begin publishing her until the late Prof. Norman Pearson of Yale suggested, "Wouldn't you like to start republishing some of the works of H.D. which have gone out of print, and which are so good?" And I agreed. I think she's a very important writer who gradually will come to be known as one of the ranking poets and writers of her period.

At what point do you decide to let a book go out of print? For instance Reznikoff's By The Waters of Manhattan *has gone out of print.*

I think that's only temporary. At the moment, because of the combination of inflation and recession, the lowered purchasing power of students, it's a very difficult period for our kind of book. This has meant that we have temporarily been

32

obliged to let a number of books, which I'm sure we will later reprint, go temporarily out of, let's call them out of stock, rather than out of print.

How did you come to publish Delmore Schwartz?

I knew about him first when he sent me his work, and I read him in *Partisan Review*. Then he was teaching at Harvard, and we became very close friends. He and his wife ran the New Directions business during the later years of my period at Harvard. They had the business in the basement of their flat on the Charles River, near where Dunster House now stands. It was a little block of flats near Ted Spencer's house, and Harry Levin was in the flat next to Delmore Schwartz. Delmore was an enormous influence on me. He was continually recommending things to me which we published; he had marvelous taste and was a fascinating figure.

Who would he have recommended, what example would you say?

I think he brought in John Berryman and quite a number of other people we published. We had Randall Jarrell in one of the early anthologies, we had almost all of Delmore's friends, or people whom he admired, if not in books in numbers of our annual anthology, *New Directions In Prose and Poetry*. Delmore later moved to New York after he stopped teaching at Harvard. At about that period, the work of New Directions got to a size where we had to have a real office. We took it to George Stuart who had an office in New York, who sheltered it for a time. One person we haven't mentioned is I think, one of the most important writers we have ever published—John Hawkes. Hawkes in my opinion is of Nobel stature. I think he is really one of the great prose writers and innovators of our time. That again was a Harvard connection, since I learned about Hawkes through Al Guerard who was teaching composition at Harvard and Radcliffe. He asked, "Have you heard about this young guy in one of my courses who's really terrific." That's really the way that New Directions has grown. Most of our writers have come to us through the recommendations of another writer friend. For example, it was Kenneth Rexroth who recommended both Denise Levertov, whom I think is one of our very finest poets, and Gary Synder, who is remarkable as a poet and as a theoretician of the ecology and of social conditions. Jerome Rothenberg was also sent by Rexroth.

Did the Patchens take over as your assistants, after Delmore Schwartz?

Yes, Kenneth and Miriam Patchen took over. I'm always bad on chronology, but before New York and George Stuart we moved the business to my Aunt's place in Connecticut where she gave me an old horse stable which was converted into an office. Kenneth and Miriam Patchen lived in a little cottage nearby and did all the routine work of shipping the books out and keeping the records. I still looked after the selection of books and getting them produced. Well can I remember the hours of toil that Kenneth put in there in that old stable in Norfolk.

Your first editors, so to speak, were people you published. Then eventually as the business grew you took on professional editors rather than writers.

Yes, many of the early editors were writers, Bob Lowry, the novelist, was an editor for a while. Hubert Creekmore, the poet, novelist and translator, was an editor. Another one was Jimmy Higgins, who later became famous as editor of a labor newspaper down in York, Pennsylvania. Tony Bower, who's dead now, was more of a translator than a writer. We did use a lot of writers in the early days. Another person who did wonderful service for New Directions was the sister, Sue, of Alvin Lustig, the great designer. It was Alvin who was responsible for so many miraculous book jackets.

They were, they are miraculous.

They were incredible. There's never been anybody quite like

Alvin and his premature death was a very great tragedy. He had diabetes and went blind, and it finally killed him. He was an extraordinary designer, right up with the very best. He set a whole style of covers for New Directions which we used on our New Classics Series, particularly during the period when we were reviving older writers. Those covers are works of art in themselves.

Of course another writer we haven't mentioned, whom I think is terribly important although we've only published his short stories is James Purdy, one of the most remarkable and powerful and individual and off-beat writers whom we have in this culture today. I think it's one of the great tragedies and defects of our cultural situation that Purdy, who is very accessible, doesn't get the amount of attention that he really deserves.

Do you have editors that you closely rely on?

I listen to advice, wherever I can hear good advice. Our great loss was the death of Bob MacGregor, who was with me for twenty years and who was an extraordinarily gifted publisher and editor who helped with so many of the writers we published. He was deeply involved with the editing of Tennessee Williams and the editing of Dylan Thomas, of Enid Starkie who wrote books about Rimbaud and Baudelaire, and Montale and quite a few others. His recent death was a very hard blow for the firm. But we do have new young people who are with us now, who are very gifted, Fred Martin, Peter Glassgold, Griselda Ohannessian, Peggy Fox and others who are carrying on in the tradition of the firm. I lean on them very heavily, particularly for the actual mechanics of getting the books out. I still do try to read everything that is recommended to me, either by a friend whom I trust or who is recommended by one of the editors.

What do you feel about the work that is being done right now?

I think the process of the disintegration of the novel, form and structure, is producing a lot of bad work. So many pieces come in which show that the author is sensitive and talented but is striving so hard to break away from the traditional narrative form, that his book is almost unintelligible. I hope that this is something that will be corrected.

Do you feel that the '70's continue the sort of reaction and rebellion of the '60's, in literature?

That's the kind of question I find awfully difficult to answer. I don't see movements clearly, I don't see literary history as being divided into neat little blocks and bands and tendencies that you could mark with colored pencils. It seems to me the good people are all such individualists, you just have to look at their work as individual entities. You could say, for example, that somebody like Walter Abish, the author of *Alphabetical Africa* and of *Minds Meet,* who is certainly one of the most gifted experimental writers writing today, you could say that he comes out of the tradition of Kafka perhaps. There might even be a little link with Gertrude Stein there, in the way he treats words. But I think you have to look at these people as individuals and not attempt to construct movements and groups. This has never been a movement country. Paris and even London have been movement countries. Writers would sit around in cafés, and they would take a name, put out a manifesto and they would have a movement. I don't think we've ever had that pattern in this country.

Well, the Beats, for example, did Ginsberg ever submit his poetry to you?

We've had him a number of times in the annual. Right from the first he was great friends with one of our most admired authors, one of the ones who we've done the best with and who is one of my closest friends. That's Lawrence Ferlinghetti, the poet who has the City Lights publishing firm and bookshop in San Francisco and whose book, *Coney Island of The Mind,* has had one of the most phenomenal sales of any modern book of what I would call serious poetry. Right from the first, Ginsberg was out in San Francisco at the height of the Beat period. *Howl* was published by Ferlinghetti, and Ferlinghetti has continued to publish almost all of Ginsberg's

36

important books since then. Ferlinghetti is another writer of whom we are particularly proud. His work is changing in character, it's becoming much more mystical, much more metaphysical, much more serious, if you will, and less the light hearted satire of *Coney Island of The Mind*. I think that it is getting stronger and stronger, and the new book of his that is coming out soon that's called *Who Are We Now?*, is extremely powerful. It deals not only with social and ecological, but also metaphysical issues in a new and very powerful way.

How did you find out about Stevie Smith? How did you come to publish her?

Stevie came through Jonathan Williams, and I'd like to take this opportunity to tip my hat to Jonathan, who is one of the great culture heros of our country, and who, in spite of the most incredible difficulties over the years has continued to produce books that are remarkable both for design and for content. He just keeps blithely going on, even though the stores don't give him the support which he ought to have. I would say that he, along with men such as Ferlinghetti and a number of others are the really important publishers of our time. I mean the important publishers are not the big firms here in New York, who have been bought up by the conglomerates. They do some good books, sure, but the ones who are finding the essential writers, the ones who are finding the writers who will last and who will survive are these individualists, people like Ferlinghetti and Jonathan Williams. And I could name half a dozen others, small presses. For example, a man who is doing a marvelous job is John Martin at The Black Sparrow Press in California. I sometimes think that John is carrying half the load of poetry on his back, he and his wife. They do all the work themselves, you know. They've got no big financial backing behind them; it's all just sheer leg work and labor. There are so many other good presses of this kind in California. There's Robert Hawley and his Oyez Press and the Capra Press in Santa Barbara; both do fine books. All over the country you find these small presses springing up. Warren Hecht's Street Fiction Press in Ann Arbor is another good example. They're all over the place.

It's a new spirit, it's so totally different from the way things were when I began, when there were only two or three small presses.

Well you're the father of them all, really, of those presses.

Well, don't condemn them to that terrible fate.

Looking back are there books that you wished you had published that for some reason you didn't?

Oh I suppose that every publisher has missed the boat. If I'd listened to my friend John Slocum, I would have published Samuel Beckett. Long before Grove Press was in existence, John sent me an early book of Beckett's, I think it was *Watt*. I started to read it and then put it aside. I was intrigued by it but I was busy doing other things and running my ski resort out in Utah. The next thing I knew, he'd been taken on by Grove Press, so we lost out on Beckett, who has become such an extraordinarily important figure. I think there are many cases of that kind. In certain instances, things have been offered to me which have become very successful. I'm very proud to say, and I don't mind being quoted, that I turned down the work of Rod McKuen, who has sold I don't know how many million copies, but he just wasn't my dish of tea. I mean, it's poetry, sure, I admit it's poetry, but its not a kind of poetry that I like. I hope I am modest about my critical judgement. I have done over the years, what I liked, what personally rang true—as Gertrude used to say, "the thing that rings the bell." I have tried to publish the things that for me rang the bell. Take for example, this fascinating novelist we're doing now, Coleman Dowell, who is still far too little known. The minute that I read Coleman Dowell's first manuscript, a marvelous, crazy, wild, delirious satire, called *Mrs. October,* the bell rang and I knew, and I said this is a writer, this is somebody who is different. This has been borne out by the work that he has done since. His current novel *Island People* is an extraordinary work, which in its subtleness (although there is no derivation whatever and no relationship,) recalls Proust, although it is a work on a much more modest scale. The new

38

book which he has just completed, *Too Much Flesh and Jabez*, is a fable of erotic homosexual life in the South.

This has always been the way I operated, and that I was able to operate, because of good luck in my situation in life, that I could do the things that I wanted to do, without having to waste a lot of time publishing junk to support them.

You say that you began New Directions at the behest of Ezra Pound. At some point, did you arrive at some definition of the role you wanted to play, as a publisher?

Just what I told you, that I wanted to keep on doing the books that I liked. The books that if I were a reader I would want to read. An absolutely selfish, self-centered, egotistical undertaking it has always been. I did what pleased me or what pleased my friends and what my friends could convince me was worth doing.

When you read just for yourself, not considering what you're going to publish, who would be the writer that you would pick up over and over again of all writers?

Oh I suppose, if you want to look at the novelists, Tolstoy and Stendhal. And then recently I've been reading Trollope, Dickens, Conrad, Hardy and Proust. My personal tastes are remarkably conventional and traditional, compared with the modern books I do. Among the poets, it sticks pretty much to the Pound canon. I mean going back to the Greeks and coming up through Catullus and Propertius and then the Provençal poets to Villon and then moving into the French Symbolists and the moderns.

Could you tell us how you came to publish Tennessee Williams, you seem to have published so much of his work?

Yes, I think we published almost all of Tennesee Williams' plays and his poetry and most of his stories. One day, many years ago, I was at Lincoln Kirstein's house, and there was this very shy young man, who was wandering about and who didn't seem to know anybody. I've always been very shy at literary cocktail parties, so I singled him out and we started to talk and I found out that he was a young poet. We first started talking about Hart Crane, whom he greatly admired as did I. That made us friends, and he modestly said that he'd written his play *Battle Of Angels*, which had been a terrible flop up in Boston. Miriam Hopkins was in it, it wasn't her fault, there was one part where it had to have a smoke bomb and all the smoke went out into the audience. All the people fled out of the theater and it got terrible reviews, and the play closed. He said, "Would you like to read it?" I said, "Sure I'd love to read it." So, he sent it to me. It's a marvelous play, *Battle Of Angels*, which he later rewrote as *Orpheus Descending*, and I was enthusiastic about it. I had a funny time with that book. It was when I was living out in Utah, working on my ski resort there. I had wanted to start a paperback series, and I needed a printer. So I took the script down to the printers in Salt Lake City who put out the Mormon newspaper, *The Deseret News*. They said yes, they'd be glad to print it for me. They started the composition and then I began getting telephone calls from them. They were very nice about it, but, they'd say, are you aware that such and such words appear on page so and so of this text, and aren't you, and don't you think, that people are going to be upset by them? I said, I don't really think they're going to be upset by them back East and that's where were're going to market the book. Let's compromise: don't put your name as printer in the book and nobody will know it was done at the *Deseret News Press*. I'll be responsible, I'll hold you harmless, and you don't need to worry—and that's how *Battle Of Angels* got printed. Since then Tennessee and I have been friends and we've published all his plays. I particularily like Tennessee's poetry and his stories. I think that if he had not been such a famous playwright, he would be much better known as a poet and as a story writer than he is. The best of his stories, are incomparable. He has a lovely narrative gift. And his poems, to me have a wonderful wild romanticism, that nobody else has. There's a deep passionate romantic feeling in his poems, and a lyricism in them that is very beautiful. Both of these qualities of his have been obscured by his great fame as a playwright.

40

What about Dylan Thomas, you seem to have published a lot of his books.

Yes, I think we published all of Dylan, except one or two little things that we weren't interested in. I first heard about Dylan Thomas after the war. The first time I went back to England I was privileged to visit with Edith Sitwell at her wonderful family home, Renishaw, up in the Midlands—beautiful gardens, marvelous old place. I'll never forget, when the butler brought in my bath in the morning in a large tin tub and a series of pitchers of hot water—I didn't really believe that such things still existed. She was wonderfully gracious, Dame Edith, and she told me about Dylan Thomas. She said, "There's a young Welshman who is, I think, a genius, and you ought to look at him," and so I said, where do you get his books. She said, "You go to Red Lion Square in London, to the Parton Press and you ask for his book, I think its called *Eighteen Poems*." So I went to Red Lion Square, got the book, took it around to a nearby pub, sat down, read it, and after I'd read it, the bell rang. I knew immediately that this poet had it, that he was something out of this world. I got in touch with Thomas, and we first published him in the annuals. Then we brought out a combination book of his stories and poems called *The World I Breathe*. After that, we got Jack Sweeney, who used to run the Poetry Room at Harvard, to edit *The Selected Writings of Dylan Thomas*, and that made quite an impression. After that Dylan began coming to this country for his beautiful and dramatic poetry readings. There has never been such a poetry reader.

Henry Miller and Anais Nin, and that whole group, Bowles and so on, they've all become recognized.

I've never published Anais Nin. I've never felt much affinity with her work, though I admired her as a person very much, and I respect her work. It's rather interesting how I got started with Henry Miller. That began way back when I was studying with Pound at the Ezuversity, in Rapallo. Henry had sent *Tropic Of Cancer* to Ezra, and Ezra had read it. I remember one day we were having tea, and Ezra picked up a paperback book and tossed it to me. He said "Here Jas, here's a dirty book that's really good, and you oughta read it." So I read it and I was very impressed. I wrote at once to Henry Miller, in Paris, and asked him about his work and if he had any short pieces that we could publish. I realized of course, that at that time, in the climate of those days, it would have been impossible to print *Tropic Of Cancer* in this country. That was only possible later when another one of our culture heros, Barney Rosset at Grove Press, had the guts to bring *Tropic Of Cancer* out here. I think at one time Barney told me that he had nearly seventy court cases going, defending various booksellers in different parts of the country. Fortunately, Henry had a number of shorter works, other books, philosophical works, and books of reminiscences and I think over the years we've published perhaps twenty of Henry's books, which we keep in print.

Since you mentioned Barney Rosset, you bring up the interesting point that Grove Press literally had a campaign to sort of eliminate self-censorship among publishers in this country.

I think that's true, yes. Barney had a very heroic attitude and my hat is off to him for what he accomplished.

How did the problem of censorship affect you, and the people you wanted to publish?

I don't think it affected us a great deal really. I think the only censorship case we were involved with was Maude Hutchins' *Diary Of Love,* which was attacked by the newspapers in Chicago. She was at that time married to Bob Hutchins, who was president of the University of Chicago so that she was a very nice target for some district attorney who was running for office and made an issue out of the book. It was really a very funny and innocuous book, but it had a little bit of mild sex in it. The Civil Liberties Union took up the case and it never went to court.

We have had a certain amount of attempted censorship on

Ferlinghetti's poem "Christ Climbed Down". (It's one of the poems in *Coney Island*.) To me it's a very reverential poem, but because of the beat way in which it is expressed it has upset some local censorship groups at various times. There have been attempts to throw it out of the school library here and there, but nothing very much has come of it, because anybody who reads it with an open mind sees that it is a religious poem.

In your consideration of a manuscript, has the subject matter and the content ever come as a consideration?

My test is always whether if there is, let's call it frankness or outspokenness, is that an essential part of the structure and the art form. If it is, fine, don't worry about it. But if it's gratuitous, if it's obviously there for the sake of sex, for the sake of sensation, then I just send the book back.

How would you evaluate Tropic, *for example? Did you think it was not as serious as let's say* Colossus of Maroussi?

I thought it was entirely serious, and that the sex is an integral part of the work. But I realized, from the practical point of view, that at the moment when that book first came to my attention, given the moral climate or mores, the way people felt about what they read in this country, it would be impossible to bring it out, unless one were prepared to spend a fortune, which I didn't have, in legal fees, to defend it. It was a case where I knew that I couldn't bite off something that big.

Was that before Olympia Press was established in Paris?

No. The edition that Henry had sent to Ezra, was the Olympia Press edition. It was not called Olympia then, though, it was the Obelisk Press, which had been started by Maurice Girodias' father, a man named Jack Kahane, an Irishman, who flourished in Paris. He wrote a book called *Memories Of A Booklegger*. His business was the publication of erotic books in English in Paris, for sale to tourists. He was a wonderful jolly fellow. It was he, the father, Jack Kahane,

43

who had first brought out *Tropic Of Cancer,* in the Obelisk Press edition, and who also first published Lawrence Durrell's *The Black Book,* and a number of other very good works. Kahane was not adverse to doing literature, as long as it would move.

What has been the best selling book, that you've published?

Strangely enough, the best selling book that we've ever published is Hermann Hesse's *Siddhartha* and the story of how that came to us was interesting too. It was all due to Henry Miller. The lady in England, Hilda Rosner who had first translated the book, sent it to Henry in California, and Henry was wild about it. He sent the script to me, saying "Here's a book you ought to publish." When I first read it, I felt it was Buddhism once over lightly, a sugaring of the pill of the Buddha's life and I wasn't too excited about it. I put it aside and told Henry, well yes it's got something, we'll get to it. But Henry kept after me, writing every few months "You've got to do this book, this is a very important book." So finally I heeded "Uncle Henry," as I should have in the first place and we brought it out. I think the first year it sold only four hundred copies. But we stuck with it. Then when the Hesse boom reached its peak with the young people in this country we were selling a quarter of a million copies a year. That's all thanks to Henry Miller; that good fortune and the persistence on his part enabled us to publish I don't know how many young unknown poets whom we might not have otherwise been able to tackle.

To go to the other end of the literary spectrum, how did you first get involved with Merton, how did you come to publish him first?

That came about through Mark Van Doren. Van Doren lived near me in Connecticut and we'd been friends for a long time. He was a great teacher, as you know, at Columbia. Merton had been one of his students when he was there. He had been writing poetry for Van Doren at Colombia and later, after

Merton had converted to Catholicism and had entered the Monastery down in Kentucky, Mark sent me a little sheaf of Merton's poems. I could see right away from the imagery in these devotional poems that Merton was an important poet. So I snapped up his *Thirty Poems* for our Poets of the Year Series. After that we published all of Merton's poetry and recently brought out his *Collected Poems*. Merton's work in poetry changed completely during his lifetime. He began writing devotional poems, and then he became increasingly concerned with social issues. Thus, when you get to the period of a book such as *Embers Of A Season Of Fury,* most of the poems are social poems. There are poems about segregation, about peace, about the nuclear danger, there are poems about things that are wrong in the social system. Gradually, while he still continued to write some religious poems, he moved more and more toward secular themes. His next move was influenced by the Chilean poet Nicanor Parra, whom we published, the author of *Poems and Anti-Poems.* Thus Merton's final move was toward anti-poetry, where he attempted to write a poetry totally different from what he had done before which would fully exploit the resources of the sub-conscious. This tendency begins to become manifest, in the book called *Cables To The Ace,* and it reaches its peak, in what I consider to be his masterpiece, the poem, which was going to be, had he lived, his *Cantos,* his *Paterson,* his *Bridge,* his long personal epic *The Geography Of Lograire.* That was the last book of poems that we published for him during his lifetime. Although it is hardly known now, I have every confidence that, twenty years from now, after the time lag, *Lograire* will be recognized as one of the significant long poems of this period, particularly because of its use of parody and myth and what Merton does in it with the melding of personal intuition with historical material. It's a very important book, but still hardly known. When it came out, it had only two serious reviews and yet I am as certain as I am of anything, that this is a seminal book, a book which more and more young poets will be reading and will be taking off from, because of the remarkable way that he uses passages from his historical reading or passages from mythology, be it the myths of the Cargo Cults of Melanasia or the myths of the American Indians. He uses them as a springboard for parody on contemporary affairs and thought.

Do you feel that Olson was a pivotal figure like that?

Olson has had a very great influence. He takes off from Pound and there is a certain derivation from Pound. In his own theoretical work, particularly in the theories of "projective verse" and in the "field theory," he has been a strong influence on the whole Black Mountain group, that is Creeley, Levertov, Robert Duncan, and others. Now there is a person that I haven't said nearly enough about. I think Robert Duncan is one of the great poets today. There is a man who, just as much as Pound ever did, but in an entirely different way, has totally created his own poetic world. It's a world which is constructed out of literature and out of himself, in which all the points of reference are central to him, and are quite different from anything else that anyone else is doing. Unfortunately, about ten years ago, Duncan took, in a very different way than Pound, a vow not of silence, but he said that he wasn't going to have any more commercial books published for ten years, that he was just going to write and work and think. Fortunately that period is over soon, and we will be able to have a new and important Robert Duncan book on the market.

The curious thing is I think, that between Olson, Duncan, William Carlos Williams, you do seem to be following or publishing the poets who are in the Ezra Pound tradition, of trying to write an epic poem. You say that also about Merton's Geography Of Lograire.

I think that's accidental. The fact that different poets try to write big works is just their natures. When Williams began writing he had no idea that there would be a *Paterson*. Although he worked on it for twenty years, *Paterson* was something that came along later. His objective in starting to write was anything at all but to write an imposing poem of length. Look at the little snippets that were the most famous work of his early poetry. I think it's a mistake to link Williams and Pound too closely as poets, because, although they were friends, they were fighting friends, always yakking at each other all their lives. Ezra was very patronizing to Bill, and Bill resented it and tried to get back by sticking a few pins in Ezra when he could. Although they grew up together as young men and knew the same people, in their objectives they were so very different. Bill Williams' big thing was the American idiom. It became an obsession with him, the idea that there would come, deriving from Whitman, a kind of writing, a rhythm of writing, a form of writing, a method of speech, which would be absolutely American—completely divorced from the tradition of English poetry. You know, of course—it's been spelled out in many places—of his antagonism to Eliot. He felt that Eliot sold out when he went to England and aligned himself with the traditions of British poetry. Pound was trying to do something entirely different in the *Cantos*. In many of his poems you will find bits and pieces of parody of different American dialects and speech, but what he was really striving for was an international language for poetry. You know all the different languages that he uses in the *Cantos*, there must be ten of them, including Chinese. Ezra was always working toward an intercultural form of expression.

Both Eliot and Pound were really descendents of James, in terms of American Literature, whereas William Carlos Williams strongly took the Whitman side.

Yes, I think that is true. Ezra was devoted to James and so was Eliot. Ezra always said that in fiction the line went, Stendhal, Flaubert, James and Joyce.

What about Balzac?

Ezra never liked Balzac.

He eliminated Proust?

Ezra, strangely enough, was never interested in Proust. I

don't recall talking to him much about Proust. I think I once said, "Oh what about Proust"? and he answered something like, "Oh you don't need to bother with him." Ezra had many blind spots. After all, it's no wonder, someone trying to cover all world literature is bound to have a lot of blind spots, or figures he doesn't like.

Ezra often talked about the "time lag," in publishing. When a writer comes along who really does something new, who does something different, who is a true original and who produces a new concept, there's often a time lag which can last anywhere from ten to twenty years before the general public catches on to what is going on. That has been true in so many cases of writers whom we have published. It's very trying, it's very hard, it's very nerveracking for the authors, because they know that what they're doing is good. We just patiently try to comfort them and say, "Well you wait and your ship will come in, your time will come. Just be patient and don't sell out. Don't give up and keep on going and in time it will pay off." Usually it has.

SOME PERSONAL NOTATIONS
by Hayden Carruth

Hayden Carruth is poetry editor of HARPER'S, *publisher of The Crow's Mark Press, writing teacher at Syracuse University, and advisory editor of* THE HUDSON REVIEW.

One wonders what is the use of an essay about my experience in literary publishing. Doesn't everyone in publishing know what the problems are, know and know and know? Exactly, and everyone outside publishing doesn't care. Those millions and millions: believe me, they don't care at all. So what's to be gained by it?

Something, one hopes. At the least, ventilation; at the most, real solutions and reforms. Still I cannot suppress my feeling that this exercise is just that, i.e. on a par with those essays we had in school forty-odd years ago, "My Summer Vacation," "What I Did During the Blizzard of 1931," etc.; and I feel now, sitting here at my typewriter, just as I felt then in those dreary classrooms. What could I say that had any conceivable value? This in spite of the fact that the summer vacation and the blizzard were as clear in my mind then as my experience in publishing is now. But a commonness is a commonness.

My experience in publishing began when I was four, I suppose, seated on a stool in the corner of my father's office. Not his actually; he was only the paid editor, but I didn't know that then. My father was transformed from the person I knew at home; now he wore a green eyeshade and sleeve garters, his collar was unbuttoned, he spoke on an upright telephone that came out of the wall on an extending arm, he clipped and pasted with huge shears and a professional-looking pastebrush, he pounded with three fingers on an old Underwood. He was putting together tomorrow morning's editorial page. Afterward I was taken downstairs to the oddly green-lighted pressroom where I sat on a steel step and watched the enormous rotary press, as big as three or four houses, and held my ears against the roar. Or possibly my experience in publishing began when I was only one and fell asleep at night in my crib with the sound of my father's typewriter rumbling in my ears. After the long day at the office he wrote poetry and fiction standing up, with his typewriter on top of the wooden icebox in the corner of the kitchen. My birth was paid for, I was always told, with a check from the *Saturday Evening Post.*

And so on and so on: a commonness. When I was ten I had my own paper, set by hand and printed on an old Meriden eight-by-ten. When I was twelve my first "article" was published. In high school I reported sports for the local weekly. In college I wrote for various student publications, was night editor of the school daily, and freelanced for papers throughout the state to pay part of my expenses. During the war I wrote mission reports, press releases, and radio scripts for the Army Air Corps in Italy. After that I went to graduate school, discovered "modern literature," became serious about my own writing, and in a couple of years was editor of *Poetry,* then associate editor of the University of Chicago Press, then for a while an allround editor in a posh office in New York (one of the Ford Foundation subsidiaries). And for the past thirty years I have been free-lancing: copy editing, blurb-writing, manuscript-reading, ghostwriting, book reviewing. Once in a hard time I typed manuscripts at home for a vanity

50

publisher in New York, ten dollars for each fifty pages. Now I am a 'poetry editor of *Harper's,* advisory editor of the *Hudson Review,* book reviewer for various publications, and I even have my own small press, though so small it hardly counts.

A rich and varied publishing experience? I can almost hear some young voice saying it. But the upshot for me is that I am broke, jaded, half a lifetime behind schedule in my own writing, and utterly dismayed with the whole publishing scene.

When I was a young poet in the 1940s I and my friends complained bitterly about the state of American publishing. The established firms in New York seemed stuffy and conservative. We knew what a hard time Cummings had had with them, for example; we knew that we had only James Laughlin and his New Directions to thank for bringing Pound and Williams into print and keeping them there. We had a few small presses, of course, and good ones too, Cummington, the Prairie Press, Alan Swallow, the Golden Goose, a number of others; but they were few and their programs were limited. No university press would look at a manuscript of poetry. In 1951 when I tried to persuade the governing faculty committee of the University of Chicago Press to consider a couple of books of poetry a year, I was told flatly no. An academic press was for the publication of academic materials, and that was that. So it wasn't easy to get out a book in those days. In fact it was extremely difficult, all the more if one hadn't received the approbation of the reigning New Criticism and hadn't been published regularly in *Kenyon, Sewanee, Partisan,* etc. Many resorted to self-publication, including my friend Paul Goodman.

Yet in looking back I wonder if we weren't better off than we thought. When my first book was accepted by Macmillan —by then I was 39 and my manuscript had been the rounds of many publishers, most of whom simply refused to read it— I was delighted. I found editors who knew what I was doing in my work, could discuss it intelligently, were seriously interested in literature as a living, if not wildly experimental, art. They had an active, distinguished backlist and were proud of it. So was I. Who wouldn't be pleased to be on the same list with Yeats, Robinson, and so many others? But we all know what has happened to Macmillan since then. Staff turnovers half a dozen times; the company bought and sold and bought again, put at the mercy of stockholders in some gigantic conglomerate or other; the backlist neglected while the editors hustle for best-selling cookbooks, juveniles, sensational political reports, and novels that can be sold to the movies.

The same with many other firms too, almost all of them. I don't say a few literate, conscientious editors aren't left in New York, nor that some publishers, two or three, aren't still doing a creditable job with poetry. But in general and proportionately the big houses are publishing less poetry, or serious writing of any kind, than ever.

Meanwhile the subsidized presses have taken over, and I don't know what to say about that. Hundreds of them, both academic and small independents. They go hand in hand with the enormous expansion of "creative writing programs" in our universities. It is true that some of the books I treasure most have come from subsidized presses, including a few I have received in the past year or two; I wouldn't want to be without them. But it is also true, as everyone knows, that the deluge of books and booklets from subsidized presses now is 95% competent dullness. And "deluge" is the right word. I receive more books than I have time to unwrap, much less to read.

That percentage of dullness is too high, and it is something for us to worry about, but suppose it were lower, we would still know in our hearts the danger of subsidization. It means the indirect support of a more and more marginal artistic endeavor by a society that doesn't want it and doesn't even know it exists. It means greater and greater inbreeding among artists, remoteness, imitativeness, and specialization, i.e. dullness. It means cultural exhaustion, artificially prolonged. We used to think—a sort of melting-pot theory—that if we had enough artistic ferment, artists of genuine importance would emerge from it. Maybe this is true. But what I see emerging is a huge bureaucracy which supports a huge publishing mechanism, operating without standards, promoting nepotism, favoritism, and failure. It is vanity publishing. It is just what we have always scorned and deplored, and the fact that the National Endowment for the Arts foots the bill doesn't change it in the least.

Recently I took down from my shelf George Gissing's *New Grub Street,* which I had first read, according to a notation inside the cover, in 1938 and had not looked at since. I had forgotten what a fine novel it is. I recommend it to everyone, but especially to readers of this essay, because in addition to its literary excellence it gives us a remarkably acute psychological and moral analysis of what happens to literary culture in conditions of social change. Gissing was writing about the time in England a hundred years or more ago when the spread of popular education had induced a change in publishing. The rise of the cheap press was a disaster for serious writers. Every serious writer in the novel, poet, novelist, or critic, comes to ruination, while the villain, Jasper Milvain, rises to fame and fortune through political conniving, social manipulation, and particularly through his cleverness in manufacturing tasteless, ephemeral reading matter for the popular magazines. It is a gloomy novel. Yet with only superficial changes it can be applied to our situation in America today. What popular education was to Gissing's England, television is to our America. The time for joking about television is past. I don't know what else we can do about it, but joking is definitely not in order.

Of course it is perfectly possible to say that in 1891 when Gissing's novel was published, Hardy, James, and Conrad were in mid-career, Yeats was just beginning, and the whole flowering of 20th-century literature lay ahead. Literature survived the crisis in publishing which Gissing wrote about, and perhaps this gives us hope that it will survive our own crisis. We know we have splendid poets and novelists living and working among us today. But one can also say, I think with equal reason, that what Gissing saw in its inception has continued ever since, perhaps less precipitately than he expected. Can anyone argue that the popular press today, including book publishing, is not worse than it was a hundred years ago, worse and bigger? And if you add in television the effect is obvious. Hardy and Conrad did succeed, after all, and they did make money for themselves and their publishers, a lot of money. Name one American writer today of comparable literary status whose publications are not subsidized one way or another.

Well, I will name Paul Goodman, who did, late in life and after very protracted, very difficult struggle, achieve a little success. No doubt there are others, and my statement above is an exaggeration. But I still say a general comparison of our time with Gissing's can show only that we are going downhill.

I have already mentioned my own little press, the Crow's Mark Press, which is very small indeed, having brought out only two printed and two xeroxed booklets in ten years. Until recently it was never a thing I took very seriously; I had neither the time, money, nor energy to do so. But then I became angry because no one would pay attention to David Budbill's poems about life in northern Appalachia, meaning Vermont, and so I published them myself. *The Chain Saw Dance* came out in March, 1977. (This is a condensed account of what happened, but sufficient for our purpose here.) It has been a success, a quite remarkable success, considering what one might normally have anticipated from a book by a little-known poet and a publisher the smallest of the small. It isn't my privilege to say anything about the quality of the book here, and I won't except that David's poems are anything but dull. But quality isn't relevant anyway. I have seen too many good books fail and far too many bad ones succeed. *The Chain Saw Dance* is a success for many reasons, but the two principal ones are the hundreds of hours of volunteer labor by several people who have worked on promotion and distribution, and then a controversy which arose locally after the book appeared and which resulted in publicity far more extensive than we could have dreamed of otherwise. There was even a featured national wire story, with consequent telephone interviews broadcast in Miami, California, and elsewhere. What has this meant? Nine months after the publication (and before the appearance of any significant reviews) the book has gone through two printings and we are contemplating a third.* Yet the total sale is still less than two thousand copies, and the total profit is zilch.

I don't mean that David and I aren't pleased. We have reached more people than we expected to, we are confident we will reach still more, and my original purpose, to bring the poems to the attention of at least some of those who might be expected to take an interest, has been fulfilled. We *are* pleased. Yet our success is almost a travesty of our function. To *publish,* meaning to make public. Are less than two thousand in a total populace of more than two hundred million a public? It seems indubitable that no more than a tiny fraction of those who have heard of the book, owing to its unexpected publicity, have tried to read it. Why? Because it is poetry. Because it is art. Because, in spite of its freshness and originality and truth, it is anathema. It could and ought to be read with pleasure by many, many more people, but it won't be. David and I are pleased; but beyond that we know something else, namely, that the very fact of our need to be pleased with such a small success is a cause of further, greater displeasure.

We who are in publishing know the problems: the financial squeeze, the labor squeeze, the distribution squeeze, the technological squeeze, and all the rest. They affect publishing from top to bottom, from big to small. It would be wonderful if solutions could be found, just as it would be wonderful if reforms could be made in the system of subsidization before it is too late. (Perhaps a committee of writers and publishers should be established, much as I dislike committees, to look into the possibilities.) But in fact solutions have been found. In Russia, where all publishing is subsidized, serious writing is distributed in editions of hundreds of thousands, with a minimum of technical difficulties (though plenty of political ones). Or take England a little more than a century ago. Robert Browning was a best-seller, and there were Browning Societies in half the cities and towns of the English-speaking world. Perhaps that was a zenith in the evolution of the printed word, the published word, as a medium for imaginative endeavor. Now already the published word in that sense has gone far toward obsolescence.

Gissing was a pessimist, and I have become one. I wasn't always. In 1970 when I wrote the introduction to my anthology, *The Voice That Is Great Within Us,* I thought American poetry was going full steam and would continue. I thought the age of affluence was upon us, leisure for the life of imagination. I thought the great expansion of our universities, creative writing programs, poetry appreciation courses, would give new impetus to serious writing. I thought the increasing number of small presses would create active regional vortices of interest and sensibility. In short, I thought the burgeoning cultural mechanism would produce not only poets but an audience for poetry, readers with passionate understanding. Instead it was produced poetasters and publicasters; ignorance, sloth, shoddiness, imitativeness, and vanity. The audience is smaller than ever.

This doesn't mean I know the answers. I don't. Nor does it mean I will quit trying, either in my own writing or in my work as publisher, editor, and reviewer; trying to maintain standards, at least as I perceive them, and at the same time to bring more people to poetry, as I have for thirty years. What it does mean is that I am discouraged. In fact, I am very discouraged.

*Addendum: The third has sold out and we have now printed a fourth. But the general statement still holds true.

LITERATURE, THE NATION, AND THE WORLD
by Grace Schulman

Grace Schulman is a poet, critic, translator, Director of New York's YM-YWHA Poetry Center, and Poetry Editor of THE NATION. *She is author of* BURN DOWN THE ICONS *(Princeton).*

The past is prologue, especially for the poetry editor of a weekly newsmagazine that is one hundred fourteen years old. Considering that past, I can conclude only that the future is bright. I cannot agree with the cheerless views of the literary arts present and future found in several other essays here.

From bound volumes of *The Nation* in the library that serves as the poetry editor's office come the massed voices of the century's poets, essayists and critics. For more than a century the work of established writers, as well as promising new ones, has appeared in *The Nation's* so-called "back of the book"—that section dealing with the arts in contrast with public affairs. In *The Nation's* first issue, dated July 6, 1865, and subtitled "A Weekly Journal Devoted to Politics, Literature, Science, and Art," the publisher, Joseph H. Richards, spoke of the arts in his credo: "The criticism of books and works of art will form one of its most prominent features; and pains will be taken to have this task performed in every case by writers possessing special qualifications for it." The first editor, Edwin Lawrence Godkin, wrote of world events but also considered philosophical trends generated by writers such as Thomas Carlyle and John Stuart Mill. And literary figures were among the original contributors: Henry Wadsworth Longfellow, James Russell Lowell, John Greenleaf Whittier and Henry James.

Although the first issue included a poem that was more topical than literary, dealing with war and reconstruction ("The American Struggle," by Aubrey de Vere), *The Nation's* poems and criticism have been more consistently literary, whatever their subject matter. In one sense, then, the "front" and "back" of the book are disparate entities. In a more subtle way, though, they are related. To know literature is to apprehend works of art as they exist in time, and *The Nation's* concern with precisely what is happening at a given moment has afforded a sophisticated perspective on a century of good writing.

The earliest event to break the closed circles of politics and poetry was, of course, the American Civil War, whose shadow fell across the front and back of the book, simultaneously. An unsigned review of Walt Whitman's *Drum-Taps* appeared in *The Nation* on Thursday, November 16, 1865. The reviewer (Henry James at 22) said that the poem "exhibits the effort of an essentially prosaic mind to lift itself, by a muscular strain, into poetry." He asserted:

> Like hundreds of other good patriots, during the last four years, Mr. Walt Whitman has imagined that a certain amount of violent sympathy with the great deeds and sufferings of our soldiers, and of admiration for our national energy, together with a ready command of a picturesque language, are sufficient inspiration for a poet. If this were the case, we had been a nation of poets. The constant developments of the war moved us continually to strong feeling and to strong expression of it.

The reviewer objected to Whitman's abandonment of structural devices ("Frequent capitals are the only marks of

58

verse in Mr. Whitman's writing . . . *Drum-Taps* begins for all the world like verse and turns out to be arrant prose.") He wrote that "no triumph, however small, is won but through the exercise of art and . . . this volume is an offense against art."

The writer called for poetry that embodied America's crisis and, at the same time, transfigured it. He argued:

> This democratic, liberty-loving, American populace, this stern and war-tried people, is a great civilizer. It is devoted to refinement. If it has sustained a monstrous war, and practised human nature's best in so many ways for the last five years, it is not to put up with spurious poetry afterwards. To sing aright our battles and our glories it is not enough to have served in a hospital (however praiseworthy the task in itself), to be aggressively careless, inelegant, and ignorant, and to be constantly preoccupied with yourself.

A year later, an article called "More Poetry of the War" appeared, addressed to *Battle Pieces and Aspects of the War* by Herman Melville, who perceived war's tragic significance. The reviewer wrote:

> . . . Accustomed as we have been of late, in certain works professing to be poetry, to astonishing crudity and formlessness, we yet cannot refrain from expressing surprise that a man of Mr. Melville's literary experience and cultivation should have mistaken some of these compositions for poetry, or even for verse. There are some of them in which it is difficult to discover rhythm, measure or consonance and rhyme.

On the other hand, the reviewer praised "Commemoration Ode," by James Russell Lowell ("not only among the finest works of our generation, but among the noblest poems of all time"), and "The Old Sergeant," by Forceythe Wilson.

My reason for recalling those views is not to underline their dimness, but, on the contrary, to show their struggle to perceive new directions in modern poetry and in poetic form during times of political upheaval and death. In 1968, Robert Bly was to observe, writing in "On Political Poetry," in *The*

Nation, that the true political poem moves inward, deepening awareness of the self. Other poets, such as Michael Hamburger, have noted that artists who are keenly conscious of human suffering tend to write poems that assimilate prose rhythms. What Henry James considered formless and self-indulgent was actually profound self-knowledge and the crowded, hurried effect of urgent speech. In Whitman's *Drum-Taps,* "Reconciliation," for example, ends with the lines: "I draw near, / Bend down and touch lightly with my lips the white face in the coffin." And ironically, the emphasis on self, a device that foreshadowed the modern poet's use of the self to permit discoveries on a deep, psychic level, was an essential characteristic of Henry James's later work.

As *The Nation* continued to study the direction of American letters, critics came to regard Walt Whitman's poetry with greater esteem, considering it distinctively national. On January 2, 1868, three years after Henry James's attack on Whitman, J. R. Dennett wrote that he was a "truly American poet" who "may well be honored as a preacher of democracy—democracy in its wider, humanitarian sense." And by 1905, fourteen years after Whitman's death, *The Nation's* poetry reviewer praised him above all American poets.

In the 1860's when volumes by English writers such as Tennyson, Carlyle and Burke still dominated many American bookshelves, *The Nation* reported in its first issue "an increasing interest in things American." Ticknor & Fields, a leading publisher, advertised books by Longfellow, Whittier and Holmes.

The Nation's literary comment included books that dealt with the woods and cities of a growing America. In its second year, on August 2, a reviewer said, in connection with Hawthorne's *Note-Book,* "the Concord River in rain and shine, a wet day in the fall, an exasperating walk in the underbrush, are perfectly depicted . . . ." And on July 19, 1866, a critic compared social issues and literary matters in a striking way. Longfellow's *On Translating the Divina Commedia* and Bryant's "The Death of Slavery" have in them, he wrote, the same image, embodied in similar language. In one case the image refers to Dante's Hell; in the other, to the American institution of slavery. While Longfellow addresses the shade of the "poet Saturnine" ("I enter and see thee in thy gloom . . . make room / for thee to pass"), Bryant addresses the shade of the "Great Wrong" ("Lo the foul phantoms, silent in the gloom / of the flown ages, part to yield thee room").

In those early issues, the "back of the book" contained a surprising number of essays about literary women, such as Catherine Fanshawe and Margaret Fuller. As for the "body section" of the journal, writers commented frequently on woman-suffrage. Moreover, women wrote for *The Nation:* one of the finest journalists of the time was Jesse White Mario, who covered Italy for the magazine from 1866 through 1906.

Essays about women writers in the 1860s have a curious resemblance to those of our time. In an unsigned review called "A Woman in the Pulpit," the writer argued that Gail Hamilton, author of *A New Atmosphere*, was a maiden lady who advocated women's right to remain single and to be treated with respect. Though shrill, she must be heeded:

> As critics, we must regret her style; it is muscular, ungraceful, and wants taste, and does not attain the artistic. We deprecate her tone . . . . But because she pleads for a higher life—because she assails courseness and brutality in men—because she proclaims to twenty-nine thousand sisters in her native State that they may be happy and useful women, even though destined never to know the happiness of wife and mother—and because she increases strength, we forgive her for being noisy and devoid of art.

The reviewer wrote that New England cannot shelve her book as a tract: "It is the cry of its women. In many respects it is the résumé of the wants and thoughts of all women who are other than passive beings."

The subject of women novelists was dear to Henry James, who praised George Sand as novelist, romancer, poet, philosopher and moralist. On July 16, 1868, he wrote: "To read George Sand in America was to be a socialist, a transcendentalist, and an abolitionist." Actually, he claimed, she was superior to Thackeray and Dickens in many ways.

61

"Whereas those writers expressed in a satisfactory manner certain facts, certain ideas of a peculiar and limited order, Mme. Sand expresses with equal facility and equal ideas and facts the most various and the most general." He asserted that "the movement of Mme. Sand's thoughts seems to us as free as the air of heaven," and said that she "contemplates all things with a superior and impartial mind."

A colorful, controversial critic of poetry was Colonel Thomas Wentworth Higginson, who wrote regularly on contemporary verse for *The Nation* from 1877 through 1904. Colonel Higginson, who had been a pastor of Unitarian Churches in Massachusetts, was an abolitionist and a friend of John Brown. In the Civil War he became colonel of the first Negro regiment, the First South Carolina Volunteers. Wounded in the war, he retired in 1864 to a life of writing and of furthering liberal reforms, including the woman-suffrage movement.

In American literary history, he is known, unfortunately, for his obtuseness regarding the genius of Emily Dickinson. In 1861, sixteen years before he came to *The Nation*, he had, in a "Letter to a Young Contributor" in *The Atlantic Monthly*, advised beginners to avoid prolixity and high-flown language. "Change your style with life," he said, and Emily Dickinson asked, in a letter that contained poems, "Are you too deeply occupied to say if my Verse is alive?" Although he judged her work unfit to publish, he answered her letter, asking for more poems and inquiring about her age, her reading and her companionships. He encouraged her, and invited her correspondence.

After her death in 1886, Higginson, with Mabel Loomis Todd, prepared the volume of *Poems* that appeared in 1890 and 1891, but with punctuation and even words changed to suit conventional practices. He felt the poems were formless and imperfectly rhymed. He believed they were metrically erratic, unaware that her rhythm, foreshadowing the practice of modern poetry, depended on inner mood and was organic to the subject.

Judging from his work in *The Nation*, however, Colonel Higginson was haunted by the knowledge that he had not published Emily Dickinson's poetry. Her genius hovered over many of his reviews of other writers. In 1891, he said of Stephen Crane: "He grasps his thought as nakedly and simply as Emily Dickinson." In 1900, he remarked of Louise Chandler Moulton's poems: "Many a single verse by Emily Dickinson has more power of imagination than is to be found in this whole volume." And in 1902, in one of the first notices of Edwin Arlington Robinson's Captain Craig," he wrote that Robinson was "like Dickinson when she piques your curiosity through half a dozen readings and suddenly makes all clear."

Forty years after her death, *The Nation*, under Freda Kirchwey, carried a full page of work that was forthcoming in *Further Poems of Emily Dickinson, Witheld from Publication by her Sister Lavinia*. The book was edited by the poet's niece, Martha Dickinson Bianchi and, when published, was reviewed by Mark Van Doren.

Although *The Nation* was not, like *Poetry*, primarily an outlet for twentieth-century verse, it did provide a forum for literary opinion. The major writers of the century were represented over a period of many years. Ezra Pound's *The Spirit of Romance* was reviewed in 1911, and T. S. Eliot's *The Waste Land* was evaluated in 1922. Although the poetry of William Carlos Williams was not seriously evaluated until 1950, Wallace Stevens was noticed as early as 1925, when *Harmonium* appeared. The work of the major figures was published sporadically, including Marianne Moore's "The Mind is an Enchanting Thing," in 1943.

Many progenitors of the new American poetry were women, and *The Nation* recorded their activities. Although Harriet Monroe became more widely known as founder and editor of *Poetry*, *The Nation* honored her as a poet by praising her "Commemoration Ode" as early as 1892. H. D., upon whose manuscript Ezra Pound had scrawled "Imagiste" in 1912, was the subject of an essay in 1924. Matthew Josephson celebrated those "inspired women" in 1930, writing an essay on *My Thirty Years War*, by Margaret Anderson, who had been editor of *The Little Review*.

As for the poetry that emerged as a consequence of the Imagist movement, the dividing year is 1919 for *The Nation's* literary section. Concrete imagery and conversational directness characterize poems of that year by Margaret Widdemer,

Padraic Colum and Rolfe Humphries. *The Nation* encouraged many unknown writers, such as John Erskin, whose "Kings and Stars," published on November 15, 1919, ends with a king's words:

> *One said:*
> *The world widens*
> *By starlight*
> *And the mind reaches;*
> *Stars beget journeys.*

The 1920s generated a storm that rattled the book section. Robert Frost's *North of Boston* (1919), T. S. Eliot's *The Waste Land* (1922) and John Crowe Ransom's *City of God* surged like breakers on the literary scene. Mark Van Doren, who was literary editor from September 3, 1924, through September 26, 1928, wrote in a manner that expressed excitement, wit and profound irreverence. Among his many amusing comments was his remark about the six-volume *Autobiographies* of William Butler Yeats: "Mr. Yeats, like Mark Twain, and surely the two are alike in no other respect, has the power of remembering anything whether it happened or not."

In general, the decade was one of controversy and dissenting views. The masthead of July 18, 1923, lists artists, critics and political figures. Freda Kirchwey was managing editor (and became literary editor in 1929, after Mark Van Doren's tenure); Ludwig Lewisohn, who wrote of himself, "I knew from the beginning that I would please no one," was associate editor; John Macy was literary editor. In "Truth and Realism in Literature" (October 8, 1924), Maxwell Bodenheim, a frequent contributor to *The Nation*, said that the experimental novels of Virginia Woolf and Dorothy Richardson were more exciting than the conventional novels of D. H. Lawrence.

D. H. Lawrence's extraordinary poems, though, covered a full page of the "Fall Book Section" on October 10, 1923. The poems, "Bare Almond Trees," "Tropic," "Peace" and "Humming-Bird," are powerful songs of death and resurrection. In "Peace," the image of a volcanic eruption bodies forth the violent end of a dying civilization. Lawrence's poetic force is his passionate rhythm and strange, vivid images which, as they depict the death of the old world, also suggest the risen self and the discovery of a new harmony. The poem begins:

> *Peace is written on the doorstep*
> *In lava.*
>
> *Peace, black peace congealed.*
> *My heart will know no peace*
> *Till the hill bursts.*
>
> *Brilliant, intolerable lava*
> *Brilliant as a powerful burning-glass*
> *Walking like a royal snake down the mountain*
>   *towards the sea.*

The striking quality of the poems that appeared in the 1920s is their diversity. There were poems in set forms and poems in freer rhythms. There appeared on December 25, 1925, "Sonnet: The Hold Bonds," by Carl Rakosi, whose style changed sharply in subsequent years; on January 22, 1930, there was a Petrarchan sonnet, "Parting," by Stanley Kunitz, whose versatility permits him to use conventional forms. On the other hand, there were songs in freer cadences by Babette Deutsch, Margaret Widdemer and Witter Bynner.

The best had passion and intensity, such as Louise Bogan's "Dark Summer," that appeared on October 13, 1926. The poet captures the danger of waiting:

> *Under the thunder-dark, the cicadas resound.*
> *The storm in the sky mounts, but is not yet heard.*
> *The shaft and the flash wait, but are not yet found.*
> *The apples that hang and swell for the late comer,*
> *The simple spell, the rite not for our word,*
> *The kisses not for our mouths, light the dark summer.*

In the 1930s, the decade of the Spanish Civil War, a prevailing theme in the arts and in political thought was the

65

revolutionary search for a new civilization. In the minds of artists and social philosophers, there was a growing awareness that men and women were death-driven. In that sad time, there appeared two important obituaries, one of D. H. Lawrence, by Joseph Wood Krutch, in 1930; the other of Antonio Machado, by Waldo Frank, 1939. Joseph Wood Krutch connected Lawrence's nomadic life and his hatred of civilization:

> . . . Lawrence's abandonment of England and his wanderings in Australia, Mexico, and the American Southwest were outward signs of the fact that he had given up that white man's civilization which he so bitterly reviled. He had no political interests and no social program. It was only incidentally that he condescended to touch a detail of the system, as he did, for example, when he attacked the censorship, for he had repudiated it in toto and he saw no reason for meddling with the details.

And in a moving portrait of Machado, the author of *La Guerra,* who died just after the fall of Barcelona, Waldo Frank said that the poet made art of Spain's great tragedy and that he sang of his country's rebirth:

> Within wars Machado sings of the spring "stronger than war," the spring that has flowered in this war, in the lives of the soldiers, and in that other avatar of Spain's arduous, ever ardent body, her friends and *huertas*.

In 1939, three months after the sudden death of William Butler Yeats, two of his last great poems appeared in *The Nation.* They were "The Statues" and "Long-Legged Fly," subsequently in *Last Poems, 1936-1939.* Yeats wrote of the chaos of modern times and, on the other hand, of the heroic possibilities in Western society. In "The Statues," Yeats wrote:

> *We Irish, born into that ancient sect*
> *But thrown upon this filthy modern tide*
> *And by its formless spawning fury wrecked,*
> *Climb to its proper dark, that we may trace*
> *The lineaments of a plummet-measured face.*

Although *The Nation* had followed the work of the Irish poet since December 15, 1892, when Thomas Wentworth Higginson had called *The Countess Kathleen* "one of the most original and powerful of recent poetic volumes," Yeats's transformation of current issues was not always apparent to his critics. On June 7, 1919, the reviewer of *The Wild Swans at Coole* asserted that despite Yeats's sure ear, he "ignores the late war," quoting his lines:

> *I think it better that in times like these*
> *A poet keep his mouth shut, for in truth*
> *We have no gift to set a statesman right.*

Actually Yeats built his art on patterns of interdependent opposites—innocence and heroic action, for example—as a way of exploring the human dilemma. In the title poem of this volume, he was concerned with the death that modern civilization appeared to be seeking, and, on the other hand, with the nobility of art and great deeds.

Beginning in April 1956, *The Nation* appointed a special editor for poetry, and the number of poems appearing in the magazine increased sharply. The first editor was M. L. Rosenthal, and his successors were W. S. Merwin, Paul Blackburn, David Ignatow, A. R. Ammons, Alexander Laing, John Logan, Denise Levertov, Michael Goldman, Allen Planz and Robert Hazel. The "back of the book" carried poems by new writers and by established ones, in English and in translation. And many of the translations were from the less common languages, such as Vietnamese, Turkish and Slovene.

If the major American poets have been represented in *The Nation's* literary comment since 1865, more of their poems have appeared in the past two decades than ever before. During that period there have been poems by John Berryman, James Wright, Muriel Rukeyser, Denise Levertov, David Ignatow, Richard Howard, Adrienne Rich, James Merrill and William Stafford, as well as many of the younger figures, such as Louise Glück and Charles Simic.

In recent years, I have been astonished by the poems of W. S. Merwin, and by the poet's deceptively calm, chilling manner of presenting terror. Lately, his poems, such as "The Gift," convey truth of the psyche:

> *I must be led by what was given to me*
> *as streams are led by it*
> *and braiding flights of birds*
> *the gropings of veins the learning of plants*
> *the thankful days*
> *breath by breath*

I have been struck by the poems of James Wright, and especially "To a Blossoming Pear Tree," with its vision of beauty and compassion:

> *Young tree, unburdened*
> *By anything but your beautiful natural blossoms*
> *And dew, the dark*
> *Blood in my body drags me*
> *Down with my brother*
> *In pain.*

Outstanding in my mind are "Oak Leaves," by William Stafford; "Lenses," by James Merrill; "Lightning," by Marvin Bell; "The Village," by Alfred Corn; "After Grief," by Stanley Plumly; "The Point" by Hayden Carruth; "Charles Baudelaire," by Richard Howard; "Like Laocoön, by Arthur Gregor; and "Marsh, Hawk" by Margaret Atwood. I recall poems by Octavio Paz in translations by Mark Strand and by Eliot Weinberger, both precise and musical; poems by Natalya Gorbanyevskaya in versions by Ronald Walter and by Daniel Weissbort. I remember Merwin's translations of poems by Roberts Juarroz; Talat Halman's versions of Turkish poems; and the poems of Janos Pilinsky, translated by William Jay Smith and Gyula Kodolanyi.

I dwell on the consequence of *The Nation's* Poetry Prize of 1923, which went to Edwin Arlington Robinson. The prize, last awarded in 1927, was revived in 1974, and has survived in "Discovery-*The Nation*," representing a union of *The Nation*'s contest with that of the 92nd Street YM-YWHA. Recent winners of startling promise and accomplishment are Ellen Bryant Voigt, Philip Schultz, Gary Soto, David St. John, Katha Pollitt, Debra Greger and Jean Feraca.

I think of poems of the past, such as "Woodsman," by Genevieve Taggard (1923); "A Pagan Reinvokes the Twenty-Third Psalm" by Robert L. Wolf (1923); and "The River," by James Rorty (1926). Although those poets do not rank with their major contemporaries, they, too, had moments of blazing intensity that is recorded forever in the "back of the book." And in our own time, I recall striking poems by lesser-known writers whose work is instinct with promise: some of them are "Myth," by Ricardo Sternberg; "Padre Island: A Sanctuary," by Cleopatra Mathis; "Flowers of Winter: Four Songs," by Duane BigEagle; "Harvesting," by Charles Elster; and "Four Things Choctaw," by Jim Barnes.

I remember a poem by Lallo called "The Harvester" (April, 1977), dealing with women who worked a farm machine. Tough-minded and precise, the poem ended:

> *They walked home*
> *through dark fields,*
> *mashing tomatoes*
> *on their soles*
>
> *Their shoes*
> *by the side of their cots*
> *are carrying seeds . . .*

I think, too, of the many good poems that come in envelopes marked "Whiskey Creek Road, Tillamook, Oregon" and "Ferndale, Washington." The best of them are in a new American tradition that was predicted by Ezra Pound early in the century, based on the precepts of Whitman but overlayered with international influences. If American writers have felt the impact of Stevens and Eliot, they have absorbed the lessons of foreign masters as well, such as Vallejo, Cavafy, Ruben Darío, Appolinaire and Khlebnikov.

There is, then, a subtle connection between the poetry of *The Nation* and the news in the "front of the book." Of course, both sections have been set apart from the beginning, and poems that are overtly political are no more common than those that respond to any other subject. (In recent years, I recall "April 30, 1975," by John Balaban, and "The Arrival," by Ernesto Cardenal, translated by Donald Walsh, as examples of poems that transcend ideologies.) In a larger sense, though, literature and politics are joined, for modern poetry is international in character. American writers are using the same techniques and subjects as writers in disparate parts of the world, and they speak in a dialogue with the voices of many nations. And because poetry refuses any political identification it is, paradoxically, the medium of all people. It speaks of commonplace things and of remote beauty, of human joy and suffering, of truths that concern everyone. It sings of the future.

LETTER TO
AN UNPUBLISHED WRITER
by John Farrar

John Farrar was a partner in the publishing house of Farrar, Straus and Cudahy when he wrote the following letter in 1948. The firm today is Farrar, Straus & Giroux, Inc.

Dear Madame:

That I was unable to return your manuscript to you sooner was due to the weakness of the editorial spirit. You will remember that I promised to write you honestly about it. After you submitted it, one of my staff read it immediately, and I also read it at that time. However, hanging over me was that promise I had made to write you *honestly*. The more I pondered the question of what honesty would be in your case, the more confused I became. The problem became not yours and mine, but a general one, and in many respects, a typical one, although the urgency and insistence of your appeal placed it somewhat apart from the ordinary. At long last, then, I have found a quiet Sunday, deliberately planned it so, in order to attempt to explain your problem as writer and mine as

71

publisher to you as honestly as the limitation of my mind and character permit.

The would-be writer is, of course, of first importance to the publisher. The writer can exist without the publisher; but this truth does not reverse itself. The writer can go on writing, even though unpublished. He can publish his own works if he can afford to do so. The publisher vanishes completely without writers, unless he were to reduce it to the absurd and write all the books he publishes, but then he would simply become the writer publishing his own books.

It follows, then, that the publisher's conduct toward writers must be both wise and generous, and he must be as interested in the beginner as in the accomplished professional. It is his business, whether his heart is in it or not; and in pursuing it, lie not only his self-respect but his profits. However, to achieve in author relations a balance between paternalism and objectivity is a tricky task, in a business which demands the creative spirit as well as the common sense scanning of the budget and the balance sheet. Modern publishing presents many harassing problems; but the one I am discussing with you is the first one we must solve for ourselves. To achieve a perfection in the handling of manuscripts and their writers is enormously costly in emotion, integrity, eye-strain and the expenditure of cash. Time is the first necessity. Someone must have *time to read* and *time to interview*, and *time to think* in between the reading and the interview, and an interview preceding the reading of a manuscript means more time on someone's part.

You must accept from me the fact that publishing is a business of great and varied detail, so varied and changing, in fact, that it is peculiarly difficult to organize, and were its details either too often delegated by management, or stylized, or frozen in a pattern, the success of a publishing house might vanish. If I point out that each book, in practically every one of its details from writing through design and production to merchandising, is an individual and has a personality, you may perhaps see what I mean, and also appreciate the demands on the time and energy of those engaged in the creation of a book and the operation of a publishing house.

I tell you this because you will remember, when you

72

talked with me on the telephone, you told me that you had come on to New York and were planning to stay here until you were able to achieve your purpose, that you intended to be a writer and were willing to spend time and effort in becoming one, that in approaching any other business you would be able to talk with the management about your problems. You could not understand why you encountered special difficulties in publishing, difficulties in seeing publishers, and, I presume, in gaining a reaction to your work or advice about it. You were most gracious in thanking me for talking with you on the telephone.

Before our telephone conversation, you had come in and had told my secretary that you wanted to see me on a personal matter. I was trying to cope with my correspondence. I have only one secretary who is also my personal assistant. When she was seeing you, I waited. Since I did not know you, "a personal matter" did not make sense. I, myself, never hesitate to make my business known when I ask for an interview. I ask for the same courtesy from others. Had you told her that you wanted to submit a manuscript, you would have been interviewed, or an appointment would have been made for you with an intelligent and sympathetic editor, although actually, my advice to any beginning writer, unless there is a real problem to explain about a manuscript, is to send it in by messenger or mail to a publisher, or to leave it without conversation. You then sent a message to me that you wanted my personal advice about a publishing problem and would I telephone you and make an appointment. My secretary was so distressed, I presume because you are a charming and persuasive person, and she is young and has a warm heart, that I told her to tell you I would telephone you. You then left.

There followed our telephone conversation, in which it appeared that you had written a novel, that you wanted a publisher to read it, and to tell you what he thought of it. I suggested that you send it to us, rather than talk with me before I read it, and that, although it would probably take time, I would read it myself and write to you *honestly*.

Now, whether you would have had more success in reaching the principals in other business with a different kind of product, I don't know. I do know that to make absolutely certain that you and other nice folk, of varying talents, should be satisfied with the speed and tact used in the reception or rejection of their manuscripts, would be absolutely prohibitive for a publisher, from a cold financial standpoint alone. Moreover, were it possible to achieve such perfection, it would probably only be a surface perfection and the basic results would not be altered. Suppose we could afford to hire enough secretaries, assistant secretaries, editors, assistant editors, to give the appearance of this perfection? For one thing, certain rare characteristics are needed in such personnel. One of them is patience, which often comes only with maturity and experience. To discover and train such assistants is costly. Moreover, salaries in publishing are not high and the men and woman who work in it, often because they love it, partly because of their special abilities, find the establishing and carrying out of this kind of "front" distressing and practically impossible. In many commercial establishments, such public relations are essential and the margin of profit great enough so that they can be maintained.

Speaking only for our own house, which is new and small, the number of manuscripts submitted to us averages about two hundred a month. Of those that are sent in without introduction either from literary agent or other friendly sources, the number accepted for publication is pitifully small, at best one or two a year. This meager result is not because the manuscripts are not read. It is rare that a manuscript of distinction is not carefully considered, and also rare that it does not ultimately find a publisher. That so many successful books are first rejected by several publishing houses is for quite other reasons with which I won't bother you in this letter. The actual cost of maintaining such a manuscript operation would be widely varying; but depending on the size of the house, etc., it probably runs from $3,500 to $15,000 a year and upward.

I'd like to explain to you my own theories about interviews and rejection letters. They undoubtedly differ from those of many publishers although my co-editor and partner, Roger W. Straus, Jr., agrees with me. They are the result of some twenty-five years of magazine and book-publishing experience—the exceptions to them, for me, are when one is driven by some overpowering feeling, call it hunch if you like, to do just the opposite. I prefer not to see an author until I have read *something* he has written. It may be only a lively letter; but preferably a long enough piece of writing to prove that he has at least the ability to catch my own interest, which is, after all, what *I* go by. If a manuscript catches my interest and I believe it can be made into a publishable book for us, naturally I want to see the author. If, on the other hand, we are rejecting a book, it becomes both a human and a business question, largely again of time.

In principle, I believe a letter of rejection should not give editorial advice. I believe this is dangerous both for author and publisher. An author may be told one thing by one publisher, a different thing by another. He may rewrite his book on the advice of one editor, only to find a completely different reaction from another editor. A nice woman told me recently that she had been struggling for several years with a manuscript, that she had worked on it for months with one editor who finally did not publish it. She was told by another house that the book was unpublishable, by another that with re-work it could be made as successful as *Gone With the Wind*. This, I consider cruel and unnecessary. When I say to an author, "We'd be interested in seeing your next," I mean it. When I say, "I think you may find a publisher for your book," I mean it. Otherwise, the simple statement that it is not a book for our list is kinder, truer and safer.

That last statement is the one I would have made to you, if I had not made you a promise. So far as I am able to judge from reading your book, you do not have the equipment to write the kind of fiction we would be likely to publish. I did not read every word of your novel. You are an educated woman, therefore it was literate; but I was not caught by your characters, your dialogue, your plot or your prose style. You have practically everything to learn about the craft of fiction. It is possible that, with your determination, you might with your present equipment write stories for the pulp paper magazines, which is a perfectly good way to start. But since I promised to be honest, I do not honestly think you will be able to do that.

It is my belief that you do not have the temperament of a writer. With your force and charm, you would probably be successful at many other things.

You may ask, if you are not too pained or angered by this letter, if you may see me to talk this out. I feel the same way, only more strongly, about such post-mortem interviews, as I do about rejection letters. An interview cannot change my reaction to your novel, nor have I any advice to give you. Such interviews are often upsetting; because it is difficult to be honest, in person, to charming individuals, especially ladies, and I might give you some crumb of comfort which would send you off on a wrong track. Also, humanly, you would quiz me on details of your book and want detailed criticism and I would be embarrassed because I don't remember such details, and my criticisms were and are sweepingly general. So let's not foregather.

The above is even often true of interviews on promising manuscripts, although I should make it clear that many of the most exciting moments in publishing are in the editorial conference room. However, if something is wrong with a promising manuscript, there are usually a dozen ways to fix it; but the best way is always one which the author discovers himself, and the responsibility must be his. When one hears an editor say, "Why, I practically rewrote that book!" one feels, first, that it may not be true, and second, that the editor is not quite what was once called a gentleman. It is a little like a doctor talking about his patient's symptoms.

You must realize how painful this letter is for me to write. I am sure you will also realize that, in any particular case, my reaction may be wrong. You have the whole world of publishing to test it in, one way or another. I remember that, years ago, I told a young woman much the same sort of thing. She burst into hysterical tears, slammed the door in my face as she went out—determined to become a successful writer. She became one.

Beside me on the table are two manuscripts. One is a novel by a young woman who has been writing and learning to write ever since she was a child. She has studied the great masters and she is becoming a fine writer. The first book she showed us, we did not publish. This one will be on our spring list. She asked me if I would read it again and look for the kind of thing in it that worried her and that she thought I might discover where she has become blinded. The other is a mass of wild poetry from a young man, not ready for publication; but he's coming to town tomorrow and if he can achieve a certain kind of discipline, he may write a great poem one day. Those will be the rest of my Sunday.

I hope you will not mind my publishing this letter somewhere, if I can find a home for it. It is general enough so that I like to think it may prove helpful to others. Unless you tell someone that it was written to you, they won't know.

Now, I hope you'll prove me wrong. And that's honest too!

Sincerely Yours,
John Farrar

P.S.—After I finished this letter, I read the young man's poems, then picked up the novel. I found that I was too tired to do the detailed editorial reading and checking so I picked up a manuscript from the pile waiting to be read. On it was a memo from an assistant editor saying simply that this was a manuscript that I ought to read. It had been preceded by a good straightforward two-page letter from a young Negro, the writer, and we had asked him to send in the manuscript rather than bring it in himself. I read, fascinated, until two o'clock this morning. Whether we publish this book or not, the man has great gifts. Sometime when one is so moved as I was by his book, one does not quite know for twenty-four hours what it is all about. But, it was an experience and in a sense I have you to thank for it, for otherwise, my Sunday might not have been free to reading.

THE DOUBLE AGENT: THE ROLE OF THE LITERARY EDITOR IN THE COMMERCIAL PUBLISHING HOUSE
by Jonathan Galassi

Jonathan Galassi, senior editor in the Trade Division of Houghton Mifflin Company, was the founder of Houghton Mifflin's New Poetry Series. He is also a poet, critic and translator—currently editing and translating a selection of essays by Eugenio Montale for the Ecco Press—and he serves as Poetry Editor for THE PARIS REVIEW.

To some observers today the phrase "literary publishing" is a contradiction in terms. Literature, after all, is essentially an expression of the spirit, a human activity without quantitative dimensions. Publishing first of all is business (publishers make up an important arm of the modern "communications industry") and the publisher's primary concern, of necessity, is survival in the marketplace. And since most major publishers today are either part of the diversified portfolios of large corporations or are themselves big companies, survival for a publisher means having rates of profit and growth which are commensurate with those of the other businesses that are its counterparts and competitors on the stock exchange. As a result, the trade publisher today tends to behave very much like other big businesses and treats its product, the book, as a commodity to be exploited like a new brand of toothpaste or cereal or whiskey.

This approach works well enough for certain kinds of books, particularly those which have readily identifiable large markets due to the timeliness of their subjects or the visibility or popularity of their authors (in the publisher's eye, the writer is an "author", a subcontractor who manufactures the publisher's product). What I am concerned with here, however, is the publishing of serious books, books which can be said to make some sort of real contribution to the furthering of human knowledge or understanding; I am especially interested in new work which, by virtue of its originality or difficulty or very newness, is not assured of an immediate, predictable audience. The first novel, the essay in cultural criticism by an unknown or foreign writer, the book of poems or stories, are high-risk ventures for modern publishers who have inherited the overhead of big business along with its management techniques and managers, and who have become increasingly reluctant to invest even very modest sums in projects which promise little in the way of immediate return.

Because of this reluctance, more and more "marginal" or financially unpromising "quality" publishing is being undertaken by small and university presses, and at times it seems probable that eventually most serious writers may first be published in this manner. If that day comes, trade publishing will have become nothing more than the calculated marketing of slickly-packaged materials, another "leisure-time" industry as it is already seen in some quarters, unconnected to its own past or to the intellectual and cultural roots of the society it purports to serve. For the time being, however, a significant number of trade publishers continue to devote part of their resources to the presentation of new talents whom they believe to be important or promising, and I am convinced that despite the pressures of the contemporary marketplace they will continue to do so. I believe "literary" publishing must remain an essential activity for any trade publisher who can see beyond the short-term balance sheet and who understands that remaining in touch with and encouraging what is original and new is vital for his own future.

But how does the meritorious but problematic literary work

find its way into the highly competitive world of commercial publishing, where it is if not always precisely unwelcome, usually only tolerated? The responsibility for the presence of this kind of book on commercial lists usually rests with the surprisingly large group of editors in trade publishing who are interested in writing for its own sake, who do not agree with one of their glamorous colleagues that "there is no such thing as a good book that doesn't sell," who persist in the conviction (which is not always supported by the evidence) that really important books do in the end find their audience. Some of these editors are highly valued by their employers, who recognize the usefulness of their contributions and who have seen that some of the writers they sponsor do eventually become popular. Others are embattled, at odds with the companies they work for; sometimes they become embittered, quit or lose their jobs, and leave publishing altogether.

It is not easy to be a literary editor in a commercial house; nor is it easy to become one. When the aspiring editor comes to publishing with the aim of being involved in the presentation of important new work, he or she is immediately confronted by the dominating profit motive of the business. From the outset, if he makes the mistake of revealing his ambitions to those he meets who are already in publishing, he will be discouraged from pursuing them. He will be told that publishing is commerce, that most of it has nothing to do with literature. He will learn that within the publishing industry the adjective "literary" is usually a synonym for abstruse, artsy, Brahmin, gnomic, high-falutin', or academic and that the highest praise which can be bestowed on a book is for it to be called "commercial". The would-be editor may be momentarily thrown by all this, but he will not quite be able to believe it, and if he perseveres in looking for work, if he is smart enough to stop talking about his more rarefied interests and concentrates instead on his enthusiasm for books of all kinds, eventually—if he is persistent enough—someone will give him a job as a secretary or an editorial assistant. And if he learns quickly, picks up on the politics of the business and shows an aptitude for the work and a willingness to do it, he will sooner or later find himself in a position where he is able to express his own interests and even at times to act on them.

80

And he will come to realize that, although the publishing industry is often suspicious of "literary" works, enormous prestige is still attached to their publication, and that this prestige, which is a commodity second only to money itself in the world of publishers, can be a most effective weapon; for many (though certainly not all) publishers still feel that the publication of an important book validates their existence to the reading public and their peers, and to themselves as well. Many of them still feel in some visceral way that the publishing of significant books is the real purpose of their work. Some deep love of books drew them to publishing in the first place; and though this love may have been thwarted by experience, and may even be the source of their cynicism about literary publishing, something in them still wants to be convinced of the importance of a new writer's work; for they know nothing is as thrilling as the discovery of a new writer of potential importance. There are scores of editors in commercial publishing today who have successfully learned these invaluable psychological lessons, and who have been able to make the trade publishing machine work to accommodate serious new work at least some of the time. In doing so they have contributed greatly to the liveliness and strength of American publishing.

What does it take to be an effective literary editor in a trade house? Apart from courage, tenacity, good humor and tact, the primary requirement seems to me to be an educated and well-defined taste. This does not mean a closed mind; obviously, the more wide-ranging and inclusive an editor's interests the better equipped he or she will be to respond to really good new work. But an editor should have ideas of his own about what he thinks is important and why. He should be aware of other cultures and traditions than his own and should constantly be replenishing his reservoir of experience through the exploration of new areas of interest. If his values are well grounded and well developed, he will not be duped by pretentious works that are neither saleable nor useful, nor will he lose touch with what he believes to be important when he confronts the skewed values of the corporate environment, where saleability is often the determining criterion of judgment. What passes for literature in the publishing house may at times strike the editor as high-class hackwork or worse; and what he feels is important or exciting may not always be seen as such by his confreres. Often he will have to keep his real opinions to himself. If he is sure of what he thinks, however, and is willing to trust his own instincts, he will be prepared to act when something of real value does come along.

This intuitive taste is the bedrock of the *yin* or passive aspect of an editor's job. Along with it should come something comparable to what Keats wanted for the poet: a kind of "negative capability", a capacity both to see the writer's work objectively, as it would be approached by a common reader, *and* to understand it subjectively, from the inside, as it must be felt by the writer. This dual way of appreciating the work—empathy with its creator combined with dispassionate critical distance—is the second intuitive quality necessary in an editor. If he has it, he will always approach a writer's work, even work which is not to his personal liking, with a respect for its particular integrity and an appreciation of its specific aims; he will not be tempted to re-fashion a writer's work to suit his own idea of how it should be written.

The complementary *yang* or active side of an editor's work begins with reconciling the writer's sense of his book with the reader's needs. If the editor feels changes are necessary to clarify or point up the writer's intentions, he must be able to persuade the writer of their advisability; he must inspire the writer's confidence and trust. And then he must be able to turn around and do battle for the book within the publishing house itself.

With the writer the editor is collaborator, psychiatrist, confessor and amanuensis; in the publishing house he must be politician, diplomat, mediator. He is a double agent. Since he represents the publisher (who employs him) to the writer, and the writer (to whose work he is committed) to the publisher, his loyalties are inescapably divided, for though these interests should ideally coincide they often appear to be or actually are in conflict. Within the publishing company the editor is in competition with his fellow-editors for the always-limited resources (time, money and manpower) of the organization. This is true for any editor; but the literary editor's role is especially tricky since the book he is interested in seeing succeed is often likely, because of the apparent limits of its potential market, to command the least degree of voluntary commitment from the publishing machine. Having agreed, often reluctantly, to take the book on, and with little hope for immediate financial reward, the publisher expects to spend as little effort and money on it as he can, imagining that the book will "find its own way"—*i.e.,* that its author and editor will go away and be quiet and not cause trouble.

Often the literary editor will have to be content with the very minimum of effort the organization is willing to spend on such books. In the publication of poetry, for instance, where the potential readership is small and dispersed, it is questionable whether a poet's work can be effectively promoted by a publicity campaign, and the most the editor can really ask is a few ads in literary reviews.

But there are other books which are more susceptible to a publisher's efforts, and in order to be effective in getting his company to work for these books, the editor must have the respect and confidence of his colleagues. He must be able to speak their language; he must make them feel that he is fundamentally one of them, and that his goals and theirs are actually the same, though they may assume different guises. The literary editor, if he is to succeed in his aims, must be seen as a significant, not a secondary, figure in the overall affairs of the company. He needs to master the financial and technical dimensions of the business; he should be able to carry his own weight, through the editing of other types of books if necessary; and he must be able to demonstrate to his superiors that the serious works he wants to publish will in fact benefit the organization: in visibility and prestige, as backlist properties which will sell well over time, as investments for the future. Sometimes, as a well-known literary editor once said to me, he has to lie, has to make claims he doubts will be proven true. But he cannot lie effectively unless his earlier predictions have been accurate at least some of the time.

Once the editor has established that his judgment is reliable and that the books he is interested in publishing do stand a good chance of being noticed, he will be in a much better position to wheedle, cajole, kvetch, scream, beg and plead for the kind of special attention that careful publishing requires. This involves painstaking consultation and checking with everyone involved in the process of publication: art director, copy editor, designer, publicity and sale departments, and, outside the house, with reviewers, critics, other writers, other editors, bookstore buyers—with anyone, in fact, who will listen. The editor who makes himself a nuisance—who is an agreeable but constant and demanding presence—is probably the editor who is doing the best job for his writer's book.

This can be lonely and frustrating as well as time-consuming work, and still the editor's best efforts can lead to disappointing results, for the truth is that much literary publishing is bound to fail in the short run (and the short run is how businesses measure success or failure). The argument that publishers' backlists are rich in works which sold slowly at first but have continued over time has been used again and again to convince a reluctant publisher to take on a chancy book, and I believe, as anyone must who is committed to this kind of work, that the relatively small risks that intelligent literary publishing involves do generally pay off in the long run. But there are good books which do not sell, even in the very long run.

Often when such a book does prove to be a modest financial success, it remains problematic for the contemporary commercial publisher, for the economies of scale of high-gear commodity publishing today are not compatible with the much smaller risks (and gains) a serious new writer's work usually involves. The most successful houses have developed efficient mechanisms for the distribution and marketing of their books, and the size and expense of these mechanisms require big, highly saleable properties to keep them occupied, and ever-larger revenues to justify their size. Expertise in marketing eventually brings these houses many excellent writers whose reputations have actually been established by smaller publishing houses, where the new writer's book represented less of a relative drain on the company's less sophisticated machinery. Thus the larger publisher, like any big business, tends to reap the fruits of his smaller, often more adventurous but necessarily less efficient competitor's ability

84

or willingness to take a chance on a new talent. The predictable consequence is that more and more of the smaller publishers are being forced by economic necessity to imitate the policies of the larger companies, or are themselves being swallowed up by them.

All of this seems to bode ill for the future of the literary editor in commercial publishing. And yet, as I have indicated above, I believe that the publishing industry will have to continue to find ways to encourage the new writer. The whole superstructure of publishing as we know it depends on this trial-and-error, this vital spadework of introducing new work, whether it is done by the smaller commercial publishers or by the even smaller small presses. The publisher relies in the end on the work of the serious editor, the person who is interested in books not as momentary properties, but as ideas with a future. The serious editor is the one person in the publishing organization for whom the long view is his basic stock-in-trade, and if he is perspicacious his employer can profit from his initially unpopular decisions a decade or a generation hence. If the publishing industry cannot find room for new writers eventually it will have nothing to publish.

This is why it seems to me that the doomsaying about the future of literary publishing is somewhat exaggerated. True, the immediate prospects for the publishing of serious books do not seem bright. But how easy has it ever been to publish such books? Literary history is peopled with great writers—Joyce, Frost, and William Carlos Williams, to name only three—who struggled for years to find publishers; it is crowded with great books—*Walden, Moby Dick,* the novels of Italo Svevo—which were virtually unread for years after they were published. In fact, it is probably easier for a writer to get his work published today than it has ever been. The number of poetry books published annually in this country, which is supposed to be hostile to or uninterested in poetry, is staggering. And the proliferation of writers (and of writing programs to "teach" them) seems geometrical. As always the number of the really talented remains small, but the fact that so many people in our visual culture still want to write seems to indicate that there are also still readers.

Certainly the audience for serious books is limited, and it

may be shrinking. Yet the market for commercial books has its limits, too, and recently the sales volume not only of hardcover books but of mass-market paperbacks as well has been declining, while sales of trade or quality paperbacks have risen. If it is true, as it seems to be, that literacy itself is on the wane, then commercial publishers are battling for shares of a shrinking market, and the effects should be felt more definitely in the sale of books for the mass of readers than among the much smaller but relatively more constant audience for serious books.

In fact, it seems possible that in time the market for the really commercial book—the suspense novel, the romance, the how-to manual—may shrink to a fraction of its current size. When recipes can be beamed onto the kitchen wall at will and the Regency romance and the thriller have been replaced by Huxley's feelies, the publishing industry as we know it today will have been absorbed by the bigger, more sophisticated mass-media entertainment cartels. Yet there will still be a group of hardy non-conformists who read and write fiction, poetry, biography, philosophy, criticism. And they will still have publishers, though they may have to work out of basements and sheds and do without expense-account lunches. Serious books may become a comparative rarity again, as they were before the invention of moveable type; they may once more be the habit of a passionate minority (as some feel they have always been). But they will not disappear as long as there are people who think.

For writing is simply the elucidation of ideas, the most complex, supple and sophisticated means of expressing experience that man has yet devised. The word remains our intellectual currency, our surest way of explaining ourselves to each other; and the publisher, the purveyor of ideas, remains fundamentally dependent on the man who can express himself on paper, who extends the capacities of the language and points the way. All the publisher can do is follow, with his bevy of interpreters, popularizers and rip-off artists. He may begrudge the truly original man a place in his scheme of things, because the truly original man is by nature ahead of his time, and therefore not immediately "commercial"; but if the publisher is intelligent he recognizes that the serious writer's work is the heart and soul of his undertaking. Everything the publisher does depends on the writer's gift, his inimitable spark of intuition, genius, creative intelligence.

This is what the serious editor makes it his business to recognize, to nurture, and to promote. And that is why I believe there will always be some kind of place for him in the publishing business as long as it survives. He will never be rich, and he may never feel really at home or appreciated, but he belongs and needs to be there, because he and the writers he devotes himself to will still be at work when the idea of books as entertainment and as big business has gone the way of the serialized novel and the illustrated weekly.

THE LIFE AND DEATH OF AN ACADEMIC JOURNAL
by Cleanth Brooks

Cleanth Brooks, the critic, author and educator, was a founding editor of THE SOUTHERN REVIEW.

I am too far removed from any active work in an editorial office to presume to tell a present-day editor how to cope with what seem to me the very formidable—perhaps even insoluble—problems that he now faces. Let me then move back into the past. I shall not say, as I recall the 1930s, "Bliss was it in that dawn to be alive." But it was exciting and it was even fun.

Now for a little history. I came back from Oxford in the summer of 1932 without a job and with small prospects for getting one. The depression was on, and without a Ph.D.—my degrees were an Oxford Honors B.A. and a B. Litt.,—neither the proper union card—and with no connections with a great mid-Western state university or with any of the older institutions on the East coast, my prospects were bleak, for there were very few jobs going, and I had little chance of knowing when the occasional one did open up; and if I did hear that door come ajar, little help in pushing it wide open for me. The Oxford English Faculty simply couldn't do much for me.

I was lucky, however. I was nominally, at least, a citizen of Louisiana, and the state had, under the impetus of Huey Long, begun to pump money into the long-neglected state university. Indeed, L.S.U. tripled the size of its faculty in ten years. During the depression, it was one of the very few universities in the country that was actually recruiting.

I was doubly lucky, for I had a friend at court, Charles Pipkin, a fellow Oxonian who had recently become Dean of the Graduate School. So I secured a lectureship a few months before the fall semester began. It was like catching the last train out of Berlin.

The Louisiana State University was in the process of acquiring a big-time football team, an opera department, headed, incidentally, by two men recently retired from the New York Metropolitan, and the President of the University was soon to come to the conclusion that the university also needed a university quarterly, somewhat on the order of *The Yale* or *The Virginia Quarterly* reviews.

By this time Robert Penn Warren had arrived at Baton Rouge to take a job as an assistant professor in the English Department. This would be the fall of 1934. At that time, the university took a first cautious step toward founding a magazine. It became a partner with Southern Methodist University in sponsoring the *Southwest Review,* long established but at that time in financial trouble. The President soon decided, however, that L.S.U. should have its own quarterly, and, having been apprized that Warren was a poet and biographer of consequence, approached him directly, asking him how much it would cost and how soon it would take to get a first number off the press. The university would be celebrating its seventy-fifth birthday in June of 1935. (When the President consulted Warren it was, if I remember correctly, already well into January of 1935.)

So *The Southern Review* was hastily set up, and a writers' conference was planned, at which the founding of *The Southern Review* was to be announced. We began frantically soliciting contributions from friends, acquaintances, and from people whom we had never met, but whose work we had admired from afar. We worked fast, but we didn't quite make our deadline. The first issue did not appear in June, as originally scheduled, but in July of 1935.

I said a few minutes ago that I was a lucky man, and I was indeed lucky. I felt a little like Ko-Ko in Gilbert and Sullivan's *Mikado*. You will remember that when Ko-Ko appears on the stage, he relates, in song, how "By a set of curious chances," he had been released from "Jail, without bail,/On his own recognizances," and had been "Wafted by a favoring gale/. . . To a height that few can scale." He had in a trice been removed from durance vile, where he feared the loss of his own head, to the post of Lord High Executioner, where he disposed of other folks' heads. I, who had made small head-way in getting published, was suddenly to have a say in who got published and who didn't. Warren, of course, had no reason to feel like Ko-Ko. He had been getting published for some time.

Before I drop this matter of how *The Southern Review* came into being, I think that I must take a moment to dispose of one canard. Some years later, a reviewer whom I shall not name elaborated what must have seemed a plausible yarn to some of his readers in *The New York Times Book Review*. *The Southern Review,* he opined, had been cleverly devised by Senator Huey Long to give himself a better image in the eyes of liberal intellectuals. Therefore, Long had imported three young intellectuals to run a magazine of high standards as a respectable window dressing for his own probably Fascist machinations.

In a sense, his plan had succeeded. *The Southern Review* had won respectability. Its standards were high. It had not stooped to propagandizing for its patron. But this was just the catch: By keeping its pages untainted, its editors were actually furthering the intending dictator's ambitions. The editors would have been obviously at fault if we made the review a house organ for Long, but we were also at fault in doing just the opposite, in keeping its pages clean and its standards high, for we had thereby improved Long's image. In terms of such a formulation of the issues, we couldn't win. Damned if we did and damned if we didn't.

The cream of the jest, of course, was the absurd notion that I had been accounted a valuable article of commerce. Huey Long, almost certainly went to his death without knowing that Warren existed—and certainly without knowing that I existed. I have good reason to believe that he did not even know that our university quarterly existed. Long had far more weighty concerns to occupy his mind. A more accurate account of *The Southern Review* is sketched in William Faulkner's novelette, "Knight's Gambit." In the passage I shall quote, Chick Mallison, Gavin Stevens' nephew, opines that, "Huey Long in Louisiana had made himself founder owner and supporter of what his uncle said was one of the best literary magazines anywhere, without ever once looking inside it nor even caring what the people who wrote and edited it thought of him . . . ." I regard Chick's surmise as quite sound.

I concede that Long might have looked inside *The Southern Review* had he lived long enough to see the second number, which was on the press when he died. For the second number contained an article written by one of his critics that might well have irritated him. But since he never saw it, we never found out whether or not we were really courageous in deciding to publish it.

The editors of the new quarterly were fortunate in the time in which their review came upon the literary scene. The recent folding of several quarterlies had created a certain vacuum. *The Dial* had ceased publication in 1929; *The Symposium* in 1933; and *The Hound and Horn,* in 1934. Here we were beginning in 1935 with, if not a clear, at least a clearing, field. *The Sewanee Review,* to be revived a few years later so brilliantly, was at this time still locked in its academic slumbers. *The Kenyon* would not be established for four more years.

The Partisan Review was alive and vigorous, but granted that it provided real competition in matters of literature, it had its own special political and economic program. As for the university quarterlies, there were then only *The Yale* and *The Virginia Quarterly* reviews, and they gave far less space to literature than we were planning to give. This state of affairs was especially true in 1935. Quarterlies such as *The Hudson*

Review, The Massachusetts Review, and *Mosaic* had not yet been born. It would be too much to say that we had for a time the field largely to ourselves. We certainly did not, but I think that we did enjoy a special advantage because of the limited number of places where certain kinds of material could be published. This was particularly true with regard to poetry and fiction. There, the pickings were good, not only in quantity but in quality.

For example, there was Eudora Welty, who had published one story in a very little, little magazine. She lived not too far away from Baton Rouge, in Jackson, Miss., and though we had never heard of her, her first submissions were the only recommendations she ever needed. Here was a young first-rate story-writer, and we profited immensely by the fact of early acquaintance. We published no fewer than seven stories by her between 1937 and 1941. A little later, *The Atlantic Monthly* "discovered" her, and whereas we were happy that her work would henceforth have a wider audience, we felt that by 1941 she was surely visible to any editor not quite blind as a bat.

On the other hand, Katherine Anne Porter did not come to us out of nowhere. She had published *Flowering Judas* and *Hacienda* in limited editions. A rather select group of critics and general readers were acquainted with her work. Warren knew of her through Allen Tate. Now she had returned to America after several years of residence in Mexico and Europe, and she brought with her a whole collection of stories in ms., a collection that she generously put pretty much at our disposal. Our first number contained one of her short stories, and in the next several years we were to publish one more of her short stories and three of her novelettes—a group that included those masterpieces "Pale Horse, Pale Rider," and "Old Mortality." We certainly did not discover her: she simply burst upon our sight.

I feel that I must mention one further episode in which Katherine Anne Porter was concerned. A popular magazine accepted one of her long stories. That magazine would pay far more per word than we paid, and Katherine Anne Porter in those years could have well used the money. But when she found that the magazine in question insisted on some cuts and, worst still, some alterations to make the story more palatable to its audience, the artist in her was affronted. She withdrew the story and told us that we might have it at our regular rate—as a policy we had from the beginning resolved never to pay extra sums because of name or fame. Our printer set it up in our font (Old Style No. 7), not from her typescript, but from the rival magazine's galley proof, for matters by this time had gone so far that the story was ready for final corrections.

Sometimes, of course, the young and unknown writer was no Welty or no Peter Taylor. Yet an editor worth his salt must take the gamble involved. If the editor insists that every plant to be set out in his chosen garden shall bear much fruit, then he will be safer to get established authors who have already produced a crop. The future is always uncertain. The unknown author may later run out of steam or acquire new interests, or just up and die. The editor who insists on a sure thing will simply market other people's notions of literature—not encourage experiments or develop new talents.

Besides, if a story or a poem is good, it is good. It does not have to be attached to a man or woman of distinction. I have no regrets that we published a good many stories by young and unsung authors who did *not* go on to glory. Indeed, in three instances, some of the most promising stories that we ever published turned out to be the only good story that the writer had in him.

The author of one such story later went into medicine and is now a practicing physician. Why he achieved nothing more, I do not know. Perhaps he simply became completely involved in his chosen profession. Another author has, so far as I know, not published a single additional story to put beside the one that we printed. But he was, and is, a perfectionist. I take it that he never could really please himself again and so refrained from making another offering to us or to anyone else.

I pause at this moment to allow editors to cry out with one voice: "Blessed Be His Name," for I assume that most editors have a backlog of stories that will last for years and that in every new mail fresh manuscripts are arriving. How extraordinary to find an author who exercises self-restraint.

The author of the third of those one-shot stories that I

have in mind—and his story is the most massive and perhaps the most brilliant of all—this author, I have never heard of again. I doubt that he is still in the land of the living.

I could add at least a dozen more such names of fiction writers alone. Reading the list of them now, some forty years later, I can see mistakes that we made, stories that I suppose should have been returned with a rejection slip. But not many, perhaps not more than two or three. The others I still think ought to have been published.

Fiction, by the way, was our heaviest editorial burden. Warren and I once calculated that we had to handle ninety mss. to find one that we could accept, and thinking of how much time the process took, I remember that I once suggested that we give up publishing stories and confine ourselves to poetry, criticism, and general essays. But Warren, quite properly, pointed out that a main part of our job was to provide a place for the young fiction writer to show what he could do. We continued to publish fiction, omitting it from only two of our numbers, those devoted entirely to essays on Thomas Hardy and on W. B. Yeats.

Poetry was easier to handle than fiction—more concentrated and, for me, at least, easier to assess. Moreover, we often had leads on the young poets, from friends like John Ransom or Allen Tate. But quite often unknowns sent in poetry and sometimes it was very good. Early in the career of *The Southern Review,* in our second summer, we held a poetry contest. We offered a prize of $250, no trifling sum of money in 1936. We received four hundred seventy-eight mss. and after sifting them through finer and finer sieves, we sent what we took to be the best dozen to the judges, who were Allen Tate and Mark Van Doren.

The shifting process itself told us something about the state of the culture, and certainly revealed how wide our net had been cast. I remember one suite of poems in particular, entered by a hopeful young man. He had painfully copied, with a lead pencil, on cheap lined paper, a dozen or so poems from Housman's *A Shropshire Lad.* So we read to each other in the office "When I was one-and-twenty,/I heard a wise man say," "In summertime on Bredon," "With rue my heart is lade,/For golden friends I had." And "Be still, be still my soul; it is but for a season." There was something refreshing about the whole performance—his ignorance, his hopefulness, his eye on the main chance.

The winner of the contest was adjudged to be Randall Jarrell and runner-up John Berryman. Not a bad catch for a fledging magazine trying to get established. Bear in mind that at this time they were *young* poets—Jarrell just 22; Berryman, just 21.

We did publish poems by writers who had already acquired their reputations; for example, several by Mark Van Doren, a couple by John Gould Fletcher, a half dozen by Auden, and exactly one by Allen Tate. Indeed, most of the contributions by poets like Tate and Ransom took the form of literary essays and critical articles. John Ransom, for example, during this period, was writing almost no poetry at all. We took what we could get from him—prose that exhibited his intense interest in criticism and critical theory, the interest that dominated the last half of his life.

As I look through the cumulative index of *The Southern Review,* I note, and take some satisfaction in noting, that most of the poetry we published came from people who were at that time quite unknown, such as Josephine Miles or Malcolm Brinnin or Richard Eberhart, or else the unknown poets who died early or sank beneath the waters of oblivion, leaving not even a trace. But as with the fiction, we did not gamble on a futures market: we chose, or at least tried hard to choose, poetry that we thought was in itself worthy of being printed.

Easiest to secure were good articles, and with some reservations, good reviews. For one thing, we could often commission them, seeking out a particular writer and suggesting that he really ought to do an essay on a particular topic. Thus, it occurred to us that Kenneth Burke, already so much interested in the way in which words work together to produce a particular effect, and so expert in semantics, ought to do us an article on Adolf Hitler's *Mein Kampf.* We made the request in 1938. World War II was already in the offing. Again, for an intelligent adversary review of W. J. Cash's *The Mind of the South,* we chose that thoroughly unreconstructed

Southerner, Donald Davidson, who loved New England dearly, but also had very stubborn notions about what was right and what was wrong with the South.

We tended to merge the review and the essay. The essay-review could provide a solution for problems encountered for such a deep-draft, rather unwieldy craft as a quarterly review has to be. We could fire our guns only four times a year. The aim must there be accurate, and our ammunition heavy enough to do some real damage to the target. (This idea was Warren's, though I must take responsibility for the metaphor in which I am expressing it. I must not foist my own metaphors on a distinguished poet who could devise better.)

The weekly magazine—even the monthly magazine—was much more maneuverable. But we had our own advantages if we worked within our limitations. We had room for more elaborate analyses of a problem and could develop an argument more fully and bring more evidence to bear on the issues.

Moreover, the long essay-review could, in the hands of an able scholar or critic, accomplish the kind of sorting and subordination that the longer view required: poor or trivial books could be mentioned briefly and dismissed; the more important ones could be given the attention they deserved; and if the individual items treated when placed in perspective, made a general point or illustrated a tendency, then the essay-review might approach the unity and coherence of a well-argued thesis.

Were we successful in applying this notion? Honesty compels me to say: not too often; yet, I think often enough to want to continue the scheme.

The more political articles were often tied closely to a specific situation, and when the situation altered, the article might retain little more than a slight historical interest. But a few of the longer essays are still, I believe, worth thoughtful reading. I have recently made the experiment: a number of them still hold my interest. But as one of the characters in Joyce's *Ulysses* remarks, "Sufficient [unto] the day is the newspaper thereof." Though a last quarter's number of a university quarterly ought to retain more life than yesterday's newspaper, time takes its toll even here. As I run my eye over the cumulative index of the original *Southern Review,* I am aware of how many of the essays we published are now out of date. The best of the poetry and fiction, however, has not been damaged at all by the passing of the years. Authentic literature is impervious to time. That is why we continue to discuss it, and that is the real justification for the ongoing discussion of literature and of literary quarterlies.

Thus far, I have stressed the good fortune that *The Southern Review* of 1935-42 enjoyed. But, of course, we had our difficulties—and ours, I suspect, were probably the difficulties that continue to dog every such magazine, down to the present day. The funding of such a magazine is nearly always precarious; and when the university suffers a financial pinch, the university quarterly is usually the first activity to be curtailed. It is deemed to be a luxury item, a showpiece, a decorative frill. Editors have good reason to worry about their magazines' being discontinued.

Furthermore, the editor of a university quarterly is bound to a sweatshop trade: he is usually underpaid and over-worked. In the 1930s at L.S.U., Warren and I were freed of one quarter of our normal teaching load as compensation for our work as editors. Since the normal teaching load at L.S.U. was then 12 hours, this arrangement meant that we taught three courses in addition to our editorial work. The load was too heavy. I would not want to do it again. What helped immensely was our good fortune in having in succession two extraordinary managing editors, Albert Erskine, now for many years a senior editor at Random House, and next, John Palmer, former editor of *The Sewanee Review* and for many years the editor of *The Yale Review.* They made the difference for us. We were also lucky in our secretaries. One of them was no less a literary figure than Jean Stafford.

Another of our problems was our failure to win a sympathetic understanding on the part of the faculty and administration, and of our having incurred real hostility. We had generated enough of this to insure our suspension when the entry of the United States into World War II provided a plausible excuse. The claim that it was necessary to save funds was proven untrue when it was divulged that the University had actually gained a million dollars through its wartime contracts with the Government. The real reason for cutting us off was quite different.

I mention this matter because it gives me an opportunity to salute the revival of *The Southern Review*, which came about years later through the action of a different and enlightened L.S.U. Administration. The present *Southern Review* has surely been a brilliant success under the able editorship of Lewis Simpson and Don Stanford. I am happy to claim at least a sentimental association with it, though I can claim no actual part in its distinguished career. Warren and I feel honored that in creating a new quarterly they chose to insist on a continuity with the magazine of the '30s and '40s and retained its name.

So much for the present *Southern Review*. But I do not intend here to make comparisons between it and the other half dozen or more university quarterlies. Comparisons are always invidious. Besides, I cannot claim to be a qualified judge of their merits. In any case, I don't want to judge. For one thing, I count as my good friends the editors of four or five of the other quarterlies, and I have had some pleasant associations with the editors of the rest. There are, in any case, enough honors to go around.

Let me conclude, then, by congratulating all literary editors but also by commiserating with you: How do you manage at all? How do you do your jobs so well? I wouldn't change places with any of you, not even for a king's ransom. Leaving out of account the nonacademic community, the academic community itself must exert terrific pressure on you. With some 2000 degree-granting institutions in this country alone, most of which urge their people to publish, and with a decently large number of them producing competent, able, and sometimes interestingly written work, are you not smothering under a load of paper? How do you find time to read the submissions?

The amount of material that you do accept and publish is itself overpowering. I find that I simply do not have time to read the magazines to which I subscribe. I must choose between writing and reading. There does not seem to be time for both. The result is that too often I read in snatches. I put a magazine aside, planning a little later to peruse thoroughly that obviously fine article that I have only sampled. But a dozen other things happen, and I don't get back to it.

Perhaps the answer for me, at least, is to stop writing the book that I am at work on, and to give my nights and days to the God's plenty that such publications (and others) set before me. If I did so, I am sure that I would be a quieter and a wiser man. Perhaps I shall do so, one of these days, and if I could induce enough others to do the same, your great pressing problem might be solved. You might have many more readers and many fewer submissions by would-be writers. For you are the primary victims of what I have to call literary inflation. And this kind of inflation I predict will be harder to control even than inflation in the economic realm.

THE
AMERICAN LITERARY SCENE
AS A WHITE SETTLER'S
FORTRESS
by Ishmael Reed

Ishmael Reed's most recent book is SHROVETIDE IN OLD NEW ORLEANS. *He is editor of Y'Bird Books and a founder of The Before Columbus Foundation*

In the 1960s, some Afro-American poets referred to whites as devils, the name which some eighteenth century whites called them. Fortunately, we've moved from the language of Cotton Mather to a language which may be a harbinger of a sophisticated discussion of a subject which often arouses disturbing passions, and incites usually sober and reasonable people to go out. Recent essays and interviews have referred to white males, white females, black males, and black females, so now in order to sound less strident one could, without fear of being called a racist, cite evidence to prove that white males have a considerable amount of power, and that those of us whose points-of-view are less well known don't always agree with the uses to which that power is put.

With only three percent unemployment in the midst of a

worldwide depression, it can be said that white males have accomplished what few classes in history have accomplished: a near economic utopia. Instead of using this power beneficently, as their classic philosophers say they ought to behave, they challenge even the right of minorities and women to sop up the leftovers with crumbs. Affirmative action is wrong because the rest of us don't achieve their "standards," and are incapable of creating meritorious projects. We are not qualified to them. One of their elitists, Thomas Hoving, who will swear to you up and down that Tut was white, said he preferred the National Endowment for the Humanities because, unlike the National Endowment for the Arts, they awarded grants on the basis of merit, and not on the basis of "democracy." The average untutored white person would simply say that niggers are getting away with everything.

A multi-cultural society where the cultural standards and tastes are dictated by one class—in this case a powerful white male class, is just as culturally undernourished as other societies where the tastes and standards are dictated by one class, Nicaragua under Somoza, Iran under different people.

What is encouraging about this picture is that some white male intellectuals—poets, novelists, artists—agree with my analysis. They too are deprived of the cultural exchange which created their great artists, Picasso, Stravinsky, and Beethoven, a German, who was influenced by Turkish march music. They agree that powerful white men control television, radio, publishing, newspapers, and the distribution of these media, often mere vehicles for white male aggrandizement— take a look at today's entertainment page, "White Publishers Weekly," or "The New York Times Colonial Book Review." They should be investigated by Betty Furness or Ralph Nader for consumer fraud.

Instead of continuing to wail about the situation, in 1971 I decided to do something about it. Al Young and I founded Yardbird Publishing Company, Inc. We published five Yardbird Readers which contained the work of scores of Asian- Hispanic- Afro- and Euro-American writers. Significant excerpts from those Readers appeared in *Yardbird Lives!*, published by Grove Press.

101

Yardbird Wing Editions published Toby Lawson's *Zeppelin Coming Down,* and *Changing All Those Changes,* by James Girard, a writer whose manuscript came to my attention while I was writer in residence at the University of Kansas, at Lawrence.

Reed, Cannon & Johnson was begun by Steve Cannon, Joe Johnson, and me in 1973. Unlike Yardbird Reader which was published in magazine format, and which, from the beginning, included Euro-American writers, though it was constantly referred to as a "minority" publication by the literary wholesalers—even though it published more whites than the publications they liked published blacks—Reed, Cannon and Johnson was devoted to publishing single volumes by individual authors. Between the three lists, we published points-of-view that the majority of the American reading public was unacquainted with, due to the monopoly over distribution by powerful white males.

When I came on the board of the Coordinating Council of Literary Magazines, an organization which conduits government grants to literary magazines, the board consisted of white males and one white female. It was a paranoid white settlers highlander's club at war with the magazine community which some members of the club referred to as "stupid." The current board consists of Chicanos, Native-Americans, Afro-Americans, as well as Euro-Americans, reflecting a wide diversity of American writing.

Since equal access to capital doesn't exist in this country (H.U.D. issued a report recently which concluded that American banks, subsidized by taxpayers, discriminate against blacks) I introduced, in 1976, a special assistance program, which provided for the funding of "ethnic" and regional magazines. As a result of that program, which has been adopted by the National Literature Panel, magazines appeared in communities where before there were none. As an answer to the charge of elitism, Maureen Owen, Eileen Callahan, and I introduced a resolution which would require the board to draw fifty percent of its membership from the literary community—a community dominated by white males, who derive most of the benefits from the organization; yet the absurd, irrational implication was made by a feminist editor,

102

and an Oberlin English professor that the minorities were making off with everything. No evidence could be brought forth to support such a charge. The feminist editor accused the board, which includes four women, of misogyny because no women received an editor's fellowship from the organization in 1979, a new program under which grants were awarded to editors of magazines to do with what they saw fit.

During the same year, no blacks, nor Asian magazines nor presses received grants from the National Literature panel on which women outnumbered men, and there wasn't even an appropriate word for this action since misanthrope could mean both men and women.

The whites at the Galveston Treasure Island motel stare at people different from them, those who don't wear Hawaiian shirts, golf caps, and shorts, because their educators, the purveyors of culture, keep them green and ignorant by controlling distribution similar to the situation in a dictatorship where one family owns all of the Mercedes Benz franchises.

With this in mind, poet Victor Cruz and I founded the Before Columbus Foundation in 1976. The name was dreived from our reading of American history, that American literature was at least 2,500 years old, and did not begin when the settlers arrived in New England, Alaska, Espanola, or California. That there were thousands of American poets before Walt Whitman and that three generations of American critics have been wrong: Moby Dick was the benevolent monster of Eskimo mythology who became enraged by whalers' gluttony.

Poets Bob Callahan and David Meltzer were elected to our board. In 1977 I introduced twenty multi-cultural magazines—Hispanic, Asian-American, Afro-American, and Euro-American—to a Sorbonne audience. It caused a sensation. Never before had the French audience experienced American literature in other than mono-cultural terms: white male writers.

Mostly white male writers or mission natives, those with the appropriate missionary sponsorship, are sent abroad to represent American society. Why the American government would want to project one class which subscribes to a cluster of similar aesthetic and cultural values is a mystery. They sent one to central Africa who returned to write a cliche-ridden satire about his hosts. An international audience desires American writing in all of its different shades and textures. With the attendance by Before Columbus at the Sorbonne we had violated the settler's literary curfew against us and introduced the true American writing to the world.

The Before Columbus Reading, held at Columbia University, in May of 1978, brought poets from all over the country to read their works before a Manhattan audience, a city isolated from the many cultures of the United States, those who've never seen the pirate's Galveston and know St. Louis only by the emblem on Lindbergh's plane. The Manhattan audience was fascinated as multi-cultural poetry hit them from the stage. The New York scene of academic monks had been shaken up by some invading gypsies, by people who move around.

In 1968 we sponsored fifty-eight poets in New York, New Mexico, Texas, and other states. Eight readings and book sales were conducted at the Oakland Museum and the San Francisco Museum of Modern Art. In 1978, Before Columbus co-sponsored the Big River Festival in St. Louis, Missouri. In early 1979, the Before Columbus Catalog was released, containing two hundred fifty titles from sixty-two presses. The more you view how diverse American writing is, the more you become more indignant to what amounts to a cover-up by booksellers and publishers who've kept the American reader in the dark, and increasingly incapable of coping with an international society. The tendency in American society can be traced to fear of change, political and cultural. The white settlers in their ghost dance, yearning for the lost days—days when all they had to do was make a bellicose speech to get the oil flowing.

They're ruining the universities and driving students away from literature as they use "Liberal Arts" as their tea party where they pine away about England, their "mother country," and our taxpayers' dollars pay for this decadent spectacle. They even got descendants of people who were enslaved by the British doing it. Like janitors in a dead villa polishing old marble. The students hate it. The students write themselves, but their writing is not taken seriously, even though some are as talented as the people who "teach" them.

There they are asleep over their port, shoving Tennyson and Suckling down peoples' throats. All the unoriginal stuff on Blake, twenty-five miles of library stacks.

The National Student Anthology, *Will It Fly,* now in its third issue, originated in one of my classes at the University of California at Berkeley.

The students copyedited it, raised money for it, and took it through to printing. Learning to do budgets, organize manuscripts, and publish magazines provided the students with an opportunity to examine one anothers' experiences, and to write with the possibility of publication. This is probably more useful than writing stories from the models of "famous authors." The taxpayers will soon discover the students will read and write by reading and writing, as opposed to some instructor boring the students, driving them away from the university as he prepares some dead travel brochure for the mother country. Jimmy Carter in England, snapping photos; this mah mutha country.

Millions of citizens don't agree.

SMALL PUBLISHING—
IS IT BEAUTIFUL?
by Simon Michael Bessie

Simon Michael Bessie was a founder of Atheneum Publishers and is now Senior Vice President of Harper and Row, Publishers, Inc.

In simple truth, I can think of no question more challenging to our society than the one of size. Listen to these words by E. F. Schumacher in his book *Small is Beautiful*—published, I am pleased to say, by the not small house to which I now belong:

"What is the meaning of democracy, freedom, human dignity, standard of living, self-realization, fulfillment? Is it a matter of goods, or of people? Of course it is a matter of people. But the people can be themselves only in small comprehensible groups. Therefore we must learn to think in terms of an articulated structure that can cope with a multiplicity of small-scale units. If economic thinking cannot grasp this it is useless. If it cannot get beyond its vast abstractions, the national income, the rate of growth, capital/output ratio, input-output analysis, labor mobility, capital accumulation—if it cannot get beyond all this and make contact with the human realities of poverty, frustration, alienation, despair, breakdown, crime, escapism, stress, congestion, ugliness, and spiritual death, then let us scrap economics and start afresh.''

This may seem a very high note on which to approach the subject of book publishing, but I suggest that we would not be publishing books—any of us—if we didn't want to play a role in the development of the ideas and insights which aim to make life more intelligible and more beautiful as well as more enjoyable. It also seems to me a good thing to keep in mind as we go through some thoughts on the business of publishing which, all together—the money value of the whole industry—is exceeded not only by many other industries but by more than fifty of the individual companies on the *Fortune* list. Small or large as houses, we are a small industry. I did not say we are unimportant; in fact, I am still surprised by the amount of attention devoted to us by such arbiters of the public agenda as the *New York Times,* the *Wall Street Journal, Time* and *Newsweek.* I am still astonished, if pleased, that the start of Atheneum in 1959 and its merger with Scribner's in 1978 made the front page of the *Times.* And with that semi-autobiographical note, let me start off by telling you a few things about my experiences as a small publisher—not because I think they will startle you, but because they may lead to some answers.

Why did we start a small house in the first place? My partners were securely fixed—Pat Knopf with his parents and Hiram Haydn as chief editor of Random House; I was in my thirteenth year as editor of General Books at Harper and Row. Perhaps each of the three of us had a reason or two of his own, but mine were these:

First, good as Harper was, it was quite large and owed much to the past. Could I ever say to myself, ''Here is something I've really helped to build''? Could I call myself a publisher if the ultimate responsibility for choosing and publishing lay elsewhere?

Second, how to resist the opportunity to participate in starting a new house from scratch, along with the opportunity to own a good piece of it and, thus, prosper, if it did?

Third, how to deny the attraction of working with two friends in building a *small* house, a list reflecting our own interests and tastes?

Those were essentially my reasons for grabbing the chance when it came.

Why did the opportunity arise? A series of accidents: Pat Knopf, Hiram Haydn and I were friends and each of us had a rich friend or two with some money to spare and an interest in publishing. As it worked out, our four backers included a distinguished academic who wanted to work in publishing, a bookseller, a Maecenas who had worked in publishing, didn't want to anymore but liked the idea of backing what might be a good new imprint, and, lastly, but perhaps most influential, a man who likes using his money to help friends do what they'd like to do but can't afford.

These four put up a million dollars which was what we figured we needed to launch a house that would publish twenty to forty general books a year, a similar number of children's books and, if possible, a small list of upper level college books.

Another accident, and an important one: At just that time, Sir Allen Lane, founder of Penguin Books in England, was looking for an American partner to develop Penguins in this country. There were numerous contestants for Allen's apple, but we got it, partly through friendships and partly because he was beguiled by our newness and its promise. That gave us a launching pad and lent reality to our hope of building a house for the times ahead, one that could publish hardbound *and* paperbound books and would have a foot in both the USA and Britain. Such was our design.

We studied other starts and agreed that we must keep our staff as small as possible and our expenses as low. We would keep the overhead down with modest quarters. What we couldn't do ourselves we'd get done outside—design and manufacture, selling on commission. For the first year, we'd distribute and develop Penguins while trying to get our hands on the books and writers for our own list. And so we started.

I should say at this point that I don't mean to drag you through twenty years of Atheneum history. I just wanted to show how we started so I could try to focus on the highlights of what ensued. I also realize this start may not sound as small as all that—one million dollars in capital, fifty to sixty books a year, Penguins—but I believe the essentials of smallness were there . . . and the problems. What happened? It divides into good and bad.

Perhaps the most important advantage we had we couldn't have known in advance: We picked a good time to start a publishing house. From 1960 to 1970, publishing in this country flourished. The whole economy was expanding but books benefitted from two special factors:

A big increase in government money for education in general and books in particular.

A notion among financial and industrial leaders that book publishing was a good place for investment; they were attracted by the promise of an expanding educational market and the idea that publishing's command of the 'software' combined with the new electronics hardware would produce a new Jerusalem.

As you know, both factors weakened by 1969, but Atheneum's first ten years were a period of prosperity for books. Even so, three years after we started we had used up our capital and had to ask our backers for another half million dollars, which they provided at the price of a very modest amount of our management stock. What had gone wrong? Essentially, we had calculated poorly and tried to grow too fast. And this, in turn, was partly the result of success.

Thanks to a mixture of good will and good luck, we had a pretty steady succession of bestsellers. Each of our first three lists had a national number one bestseller—*The Last of the Just* by Andre SchwarzBart, *The Making of the President—1960* by Theodore H. White and *The Rothschilds* by Frederick Morton. The children's book list under Jean Karl flourished from the start and provided volume and, in time, good profit as well as the most coveted prizes. But our growth was accompanied, of course, by a growth in staff and overhead. Before very long, we were sixty people producing each year about seventy adult books and fifty or so children's books. We had also acquired Russell and Russell, a distinguished producer of library reprints which, for several years, brought in a good flow of cash, but declined as that market declined and became saturated.

Possibly the worst thing that happened in our early years was the loss of Penguins. Since Penguins then went through several sets of bigger and better hands than ours before coming to its present situation as owner of Viking, we can't claim a unique failure. We have been assured that we were not at fault and I do believe that it would have taken a saint of patience, a seer of utter prescience and a devil of deviousness to stay in bed with Allen Lane, but the blow was a heavy one, depriving us of one half of our design and virtually removing us from the paperback field. We hastily constructed a paperback list by persuading the Harvard, Princeton and Stanford University presses to give us a first option on their books in paper, but by now we were far behind the paperback procession; and without the means for catching up.

During the golden (if you weren't in Viet Nam) 1960's, we received several very large—it seemed then and it seems even more so now—offers for purchase of the house. But our lists were doing well, our health seemed okay and our desire for independence strong; so we said thanks, maybe someday, but not now. By the early 1970's, as the economy sagged, we began to wonder. We were profitable, but it was apparent we had not built much of a backlist, except in children's books . . . and each season was a cliffhanger. We saw Knopf go to Random, Holt to CBS, Little, Brown to Time, Inc., Dutton to Elsevier, and so on. We also saw Farrar, Straus seeming to go on as a strong, independent, literary house but neither of us two remaining partners had private means and we wondered what would happen to our staff if either of us died. This meant we were open to an offer to get under a larger umbrella, but the world had changed and the suitors were less ardent. If you are going to give up your independence, you try for economic safeguards for yourself and your staff. They just weren't there, unless they have now been found in the merger with Scribner's.

Could we have carried on by cutting costs? Possibly, but that is a most difficult thing to do. It means firing people, publishing fewer books. We had arrived at a volume of about five million dollars a year—neither small enough to be flexible nor large enough to compete with the larger houses. In terms of what we were publishing, it meant—for the adult list—that we had to try harder for commercial books, go easier on literature.

Into this situation came an offer from my old house of Harper to buy us and continue Atheneum as a separate imprint, as they had done with Basic Books some years earlier. My partner Pat Knopf was not attracted to the Harper offer but wanted to hold on and see if something more appealing to him developed. I *was* attracted to Harper—partly by old attachments and partly by the opportunities there to publish the kind of books that most interest me . . . and I was reconciled to departing from the place I'd helped to start by the thought that I could no longer solve its problems.

This summary of sixteen years as a small, independent publisher obviously omits many elements and experiences for which there simply isn't space now. But it should include one or two observations. It was one of the most exciting and satisfying periods of my life. To be small, independent and literary—which we were for years—is a rare and wonderful condition for the likes of me. We published a number of books—both for adults and children, and both from America and abroad—which may find permanent places on the library shelf, and for all but one of those years, once we started, we made a profit. We gave several people an opportunity to express their talents as publishers. To mention only two: Harry Ford who has designed and manufactured all those handsome books since 1960 and who is solely responsible for the best poetry list of his time; could that have happened in a large, more structured house? And Jean Karl who started and developed one of the finest lists of children's books of her time. That, I suppose, could have happened in a larger house, but would it?

Obviously, no one person's experience can sum up all the problems and pleasures of small publishing and I'm sure that my experiences at Atheneum did not include much that has happened to a number of others but I trust that some of it sounds familiar. With apologies for what I've left out, I'd like now to explore the other side of the coin, large publishing, and then see if I can put together a modest picture of the whole.

The Harper to which I returned in autumn 1975 was not the biggest publisher in the US by quite a stretch, but it was a lot bigger than the 142-year-old house I'd left in 1959—1,400 employees as against 400; $80,000,000 a year of business as against, say $17,000,000 in 1959. In other respects, it was both similar and changed. *Similar* in that it was still a federal structure, a grouping of publishing units that operated with considerable independence within a corporate structure. *Changed* in that the corporate structure had developed much; there were now systems of planning, budgeting, accounting that were a lot more complex and sophisticated. Everything had grown—and spread. Harper was now publishing not only in New York, but also in Hagerstown, San Francisco, London, Australia, Mexico and Brazil, and distributing almost all over the world.

Old friends welcomed me back and one or two of them said: "You'll see. The Harvard Business School has taken over." Were they right?

Since I was coming back as a corporate officer and director, as well as an editor of books, I was officed on the corporate floor and spent much of my first weeks learning the new systems, while also working with writers whom I was going to publish. The systems soon became familiar and intelligible as necessary ways of managing that number of people and dollars. I won't say there has never been a moment when I longed for the simplicity of a place where only one voice (my own, of course) spoke for decisions, but it hasn't happened often. And I have come across virtually nothing that I *really* wanted to publish that I couldn't find a way of doing, and paying for. Which, of course, was not so often the case in the smaller house.

Just as I couldn't hope to cover all aspects of small house publishing, I won't pretend to do that for the large house. What I'm going to try to do now is examine the two and see how they compare.

What can a large house do that a small house can't? I suppose the most obvious item on this short list is the very expensive project. Examples: Only a large bankroll can enter the lists for something like a Kissinger memoir where the ante goes above two million dollars. The same applies to costly reference books such as encyclopedias and dictionaries, and I had an example of this at the very start of Atheneum: one of the projects which I obviously couldn't take with me was the *Encyclopedia of Science* which James R. Newman and I had then started at Harper and which was going to cost about a million dollars—the total amount of Atheneum's capital.

I also take it that no small houses can really compete in college or school text publishing where the costs of researching, producing and distributing have risen so high. Having said this, I should note that there are still some small houses active in this field and I suspect there continue to be opportunities for those smart enough to develop a needed or superior text. There are also opportunities in this field for small producers who generate a book or series in a sort of joint venture with a large operation. (As further evidence of this, I am impressed that of the ninety-odd member-companies that have joined The Association of American Publishers as "smaller publishers," some forty-two are involved in other than general publishing, including five in the School Division, seven in College and fifteen in Technical, Scientific and Medical. They must be doing something that the giants can't do without them—or that they cannot do as well.)

What about small publishers and bestsellers? As advances and subsidiary incomes have mounted, some have said that small houses will be excluded from this vital aspect of general publishing. Well, this week's bestseller list in the *New York Times* includes five or seven (depending on your definition of small publisher) books from smaller houses. In thirty years of publishing, I can recall very few, if any bestseller lists that had nothing from a small house. Fine, you say, but isn't it true that a small house may find or develop a bestselling author, but how to keep him against the greedy giants? Good question. In these past thirty years, we have seen the Norman Mailers, the Irwin Shaws, the James Clavells, the Joan Didions, and so many others leave the small houses where they began to follow what looks like the sight of gold. And I know no cure for this. I'm tempted to say that large houses are better equipped to *acquire* bestselling authors, but maybe small publishers are as well equipped as ever to discover and develop them.

What about the ultimate question, namely *existence?* Are small publishers less able than they used to be to come into being and to survive? Here we must turn to statistics. For the past forty-five years there has been a steady increase in the number of publishing establishments. Despite merger, strangulation and mysterious disappearance, there are now an estimated thirteen hundred separate houses, as compared with twelve hundred in 1972 and about four hundred before World War Two. The annual net rate of increase is about two and one half percent. And obviously, almost all the new firms are small.

We need no statistics to agree that the large houses are getting larger and, more frequently, owned by the public or by conglomerates. This is not my subject, so I'll spare you my thoughts on it.

What I do want to say now is that much attention has been paid to the mergers which have removed many of the outstanding houses from the independent ranks. Much less has been given to the continued presence and increase in number of the truly small houses who, today, share twenty-five percent of the total book market (I count the other seventy-five percent as covered by the fifty largest companies and, when you say fifty, you are coming down to houses which are not really very large). I am not saying it is becoming easier to start a small house or to survive as a small house, but I can't read the numbers any way that doesn't lead to the conclusion that it *is* possible and more people are doing it.

How are they doing it?

Small publishers, I suggest, are flourishing because they are focusing on two fundamentals of creative activity in a complex, industrialized society: Specialization and Doing Your Own Thing, the thing you care about and know about. For some it lies in subject, for some in regions, for some in ways of doing something better. It is no accident that most small houses are not located in New York or Boston or Chicago or even San Francisco. Most are in smaller places all over the country, places which allow a small publisher to focus on doing his thing and—important—playing a part in a community which is small enough to be intelligible.

I am told that some, perhaps many feel isolated and under-recognized. If so, I suggest they may have to accept this as part of their chosen situation. To be small, to do a small thing in a small place, is not likely to gain just recognition from a society that seems to have sold its soul to bigness. Well over a hundred years ago, when reproached for not seeing more of the world, Thoreau said: "I have traveled much in Walden." Viewing not simply the book industry, but the whole of the economy, Schumacher says:

"What I wish to emphasize is the duality of the human requirement when it comes to the question of size: there is no *single* answer. For his different purposes man needs many different structures, both small ones and large ones, some exclusive and some comprehensive. Yet people find it most difficult to keep two seemingly opposite necessities of truth in their minds at the same time. They always tend to clamour for a final solution, as if in actual life there could ever be a final solution other than death. For constructive work, the principal task is always the restoration of some kind of balance. Today, we suffer from an almost universal idolatry of giantism. It is therefore necessary to insist on the virtues of smallness—where this applies. If there were a prevailing idolatry of smallness, irrespective of subject or purpose, one would have to try and exercise influence in the opposite direction."

Does it not seem reasonable to say of book publishing in our time, that it can, indeed, be beautiful—large or small.

A QUARTER CENTURY OF THE JARGON SOCIETY: AN INTERVIEW WITH JONATHAN WILLIAMS

Jonathan Williams is founder and director of The Jargon Society, Inc. He was interviewed by poet and publisher William Corbett on the occasion of Jargon Society's Twenty-Fifth Birthday. The interview was produced in 1976 by Susan Howe, who also edited the transcript with Mr. Williams.

To start with, Jonathan, twenty-five years ago did you think you would still be doing Jargon Books twenty-five years later? Has anything surprised you by this?

Nothing surprised me. I expected to be doing it for twenty-five years, and I suppose if luck runs against me, I'll be doing it for twenty-five more.

Somebody asked you where you would have the Fiftieth party. I wonder had you thought of that?

No, not really. Well, I hope to have it at the Gotham Book Mart again. I'm sure Frances Steloff will still be there.

116

In twenty-five years you have done a lot of things, but what have you wanted to do that you haven't done?

There are still a lot of people that seem to need attention. I never run out. And they still live in these curious places. I mean for instance, I don't know whether Mason Jordan Mason is a figment of Judson Crew's imagination, but I like Mason Jordan Mason's poetry. I don't know whether he's a psychotic black man living in India, as Judson likes to tell us, or whether he really was somebody who came from western Louisiana. But anyway he writes a good poem. He's a man I've wanted to publish for a long time, so I'm going to do him. I've never got around to doing Bob Brown's selected poems. I still have Mina Loy to complete. I'm going back into the great days of the Moderns. This is a generation that now is rather disappearing from view. I don't know how many people listening would know about Mina Loy or Bob Brown at this point.

Of course one of the aspects of your work as a publisher is that you've had that kind of tenacity, that if you wanted to do it fifteen years ago, there is no less a reason you want to do it now.

We live in a society which wipes out as fast as it builds. Robert Kelly suggested one time to me, that the real misery of this country was the fact that just about the time somebody got serious about Edward Arlington Robinson, they would bulldoze him in favor of William Carlos Williams and, suddenly, Williams wasn't interesting anymore. So you'd go on to Robert Creeley, and then someone would say "Well, gee, Bob Dylan is really better than those people" and you wouldn't bother anymore.

But again to ask that particular question—has there been anything in the last twenty-five years that you wanted to do, and were unable to? Were there any dreams that you started twenty-five years ago that you haven't been able to make true for yourself?

117

I don't think so. It has never been gauged as, like they say, a success or achievement. Either under-achieving or over-achieving, Jargon has produced close to one hundred books by now. About four books a year. It is certainly adequate to the time I can give to it. After all, I have my own writing to occupy me. I have the traveling. I have the reading in public. I have those ways to make some money. I can't do more than four books a year. That's it really.

What has been the effect on your writing? This is perhaps a question you can't answer. I mean, do you think it would have been different if you didn't have all that traveling? If you didn't have to spend all that time with writers, as an editor?

It obviously changed my way of writing a poem. I know Guy Davenport said to me, it took about six months for him to get a few lines down on paper whereas, he said, "It's easy for you, you can stand by the fireplace with your elbow on the mantle, and write it with the other hand in thirty seconds." In a sense that's true. But you know, as I'm driving across Nebraska seeking out some peculiar bit of homemade architecture, one does think. The stuff is there. Cooking away quietly on the back burner.

How do you juggle traveling the way you do, and raising money?

That's the most tiresome part of it. The amount of time I have to spend with moneyed people, who are essentially disinterested in the whole business. But you ask for support from the people who have it. One is stuck with that.

Has it gotten easier to raise money?

Not at all. I think there is a certain irritation on the part of some, that this enterprise does persist. It does become boring to go back. I don't think I'll go back anymore to certain foundations in New York City for instance. I've been going for almost twenty-five years. It's never been the right time, or the right situation, and I suppose in a way it never will be. I've

118

always felt that foundations were responsible, themselves, to find what to do. Not the other way around. I remember . . . well, I think it might have been the Ford Foundation, I'll probably get it wrong . . . one of the large foundations announced that it was going to spend $450,000 in order to find out which painters in America needed to be supported. And of course they came up with a considerable number of painters who were living very well, to whom they gave the money.

They've just put $90,000 into compiling a list of magazines and then finding out how the magazines distribute books, then what needs to be done to help distribute books.

This is what Cyril Connolly long ago said: everything for the milk bar and very little for the cow.

Do you raise much money from the government? That's the way people for the last seven or eight years have been able to support themselves. The National Endowment for the Arts, Coordinating Council of Literary Magazine.

I was lucky because the Jargon Society was the recipient of three grants from the NEA back in the late 60's. That's money—I think it was $35,000, over a three-year period— which was crucial. Because private sources seemed to be drying up at that particular time. My own sources: as I say, you badger people for a particular time, I mean year in year out for fifteen or twenty years, they do get tired. But NEA was very helpful. That was when Carolyn Kizer was running the Literature Panel for Roger Stevens. Since then, there's been one more grant through the Visual Arts program, to do two photographic books. Jargon isn't simply poetry and prose. I've always had an interest in graphic arts and particularly photography. Such people as Doris Ulmann, and Ralph Eugene Meatyard, Lyle Bongé and Art Sinsabaugh. I hope to be able to continue to do that.

Have the books ever come close to supporting themselves? Everything you made twenty-five years ago is selling now at

119

the Gotham, or Bob Wilson is selling it for $35 or $40. Has it ever been a going concern in that way? Or have you always been thrust back on private donations?

Well it may be that I simply don't know how to manage money? That's perhaps part of it. Other people seem to be much more able in that respect. I gather John Martin of Black Sparrow seems to manage an operation that allows him to live largely from it . . . I do have this problem of being somewhat distracted by the demands of my own reading, writing, and traveling. We have a cooperative with Aperture and Corinth, and an office where we do shipping, invoicing, and so forth. But, as I say, the income is minimal, and I don't know what to do about that. I've done everything that I could possibly figure out, or that anyone has told me to do. I took on the basic American notion that if there wasn't an audience, you had to go out and find or make one. Actually *make* one, more than find one.

You used to travel around the country in a Volkswagen?

That's right. Earlier than that it was two beat up old Pontiac station wagons.

I once heard that you read in a gas station?

No no, Guy Davenport got that wrong. It was actually a train station that had been converted by the Maryland Institute of Art. He got that wrong. No, that's even far fetched for poetry! I used to take on forty thousand miles, year in, year out, back in the 50's and go everywhere. I remember back in '57, just when Ginsberg's *Howl* was published by Ferlinghetti's City Lights Press—I had about five hundred copies of the First Edition in the back of the old '50 Pontiac, and I was traveling through places like Tuscaloosa, and writers conferences in Biloxi Mississippi. You know, the Live Oaks Writers Conference, frequented by strange ladies from the bayous—

What kind of reception did you get?

Very little. Very little. But it's interesting. One doesn't think of the future. If I'd been clever enough I might have salted away one hundred copies of *Howl*. Last time I heard they were what, about $100.00. But you don't think of futurity. You don't think in terms of investment. I mean you're constantly using all, and you use it up. The books disappeared. I didn't keep one hundred copies of things up in the attic. I didn't think that way.

It was obviously necessary for you to travel around that way, to keep in touch with the kind of people you publish. I mean they're not concentrated in New York, they never have been. I always think of that Sherwood Anderson business, about the apples that fall on the ground in that story—even though they look—

That's right. I'm interested in the eccentric. The culls, perhaps, the ones that have the spots on them, the wrinkles. I'm not interested in the polished, packaged sort of supermarket poetry.

So the traveling did put you in touch with those people?

Of course it did. Certainly it did. There's a kind of network. There still is. And of course as you get older the names change, the places change. I'm sure that if I had the time and energy, that if I were to go across Kansas right this minute, I would find plenty to occupy my attention. If it were not a poet, it would be a photographer, or it would be a painter, or graphic artist, or as I say, some sort of strange whimsical architecture. You know: genuine homemade.

How do you find the people you find? Alfred Starr Hamilton particularly interests me, whom you've championed, written about, and I understand you even raised $10,000 for him after the article in the Times Book Review.

It's a typical case. You know it's not as if any one person can do this job. Alfred Starr Hamilton was first called to my attention by David Ray. David is a poet you may know, who is now at *New Letters*, University of Missouri at Kansas City. In those days David was at Reed College. I met him at a lunch table when I was reading in Chicago one day. We talked, and he said "Come to Reed." I came to Reed, gave a reading. He said, "I know this man who used to submit to *Epoch*. This is a man who lives in a furnished room in Montclair, New Jersey. He writes ten poems a day. He sends me shoeboxes full of poems, doesn't even keep the originals, just sends them out by the shoebox full." He also said that in his estimation, he was one of the most original poets that the country had ever produced. So I'd say to people as I traveled about, "Have you ever heard of a guy called Alfred Starr Hamilton?" Everybody would say, "No, never heard of him." I think he had only published in *Epoch*, which is not a magazine that, frankly, too many people saw. But you know how things are sometimes, I looked at the poems and didn't quite get it. David left it there. One of David's students, Geof Hewitt, came up to me two years later, after I was reading at the Maryland Institute in Baltimore, and said, "I don't like to bring this up at this particular moment, but do you remember anything about Alfred Starr Hamilton? David and I still think he deserves to be published." So I said "Well let me take the stuff back home to North Carolina, when I've got a day or two to sit down, I'll look at it." I looked at it and this time I could put my mind on it. This is one problem of course. That you are always traveling or talking. . .

There are a lot of projects proposed, and the time to focus and concentrate is limited. That's why I have to write short poems. But then—Catullus is still around, and he wrote short poems. So I'm hoping. But, back to Hamilton. It was not just *me*. I did not go out to Montclair, New Jersey and stumble into him. I was told by correspondence and by meeting with David Kay and Geof Hewitt. This is the way it is.

Have you ever on your own, stumbled across anyone? Without that network? Somebody you could say was a discovery?

I don't think so. Even before I was at Black Mountain college, I was being educated by people like Kenneth Rexroth and

122

Kenneth Patchen. More by Rexroth. Because he's a man who had a tremendous interest in what other people were doing. And then later of course Charles Olson, who had a literary program rather like Ezra Pound's. Many books, many people he wanted to call attention to. As far as he was concerned at that particular moment, there were about four writers he thought I should interest myself in. I can remember that two or three of them were Robert Duncan (whom I knew slightly before meeting Olson); Robert Creeley, naturally, and a man who, I think, became an archeologist and stopped writing poetry, Lawrence Richardson. And fourth was W. S. Merwin, interestingly enough. . . . Anyway, another instance. Robert Duncan was at Black Mountain. I knew him there, and then I knew him in San Francisco back in the mid-fifties, and he just sort of threw out one day: "it seems a shame that someone as remarkable and first class as Louis Zukofsky is sitting out there in Brooklyn Heights, and nobody is paying any attention to him." It doesn't take too much effort to get yourself to Brooklyn Heights, really.

There is something about the archeologist to your work. Or that enthusiasm of a child. You once said you were given by your parents L. Frank Baum, and fairy tales, and that you loved those books and you wanted to make books for your own shelf. That seems a constant concern.

Indeed. If they are not as interesting as the magic books of childhood then why should we bother? That's the way I read. Some of us read for *childish* reasons, hopefully. And that has nothing to do with making money. Childhood desires had nothing to do with making money.

Why do your books have to look so good?

Well, after all, I was brought up on Tolkien, L. Frank Baum, and Hugh Lofting, and Kenneth Grahame. That was a standard which I had to adhere to. It's my own foolishness, I suppose. I have been loudly criticized for making them precious objects. Some people say, well look, multilith is as good. Get it out for a dollar. Alas, I've never felt so abject.

You know there is an attitude in this country, a rather de-meaning one I think, towards poetry. That sure, anyone will buy anything that only costs a buck. Well that never occurred to me as a reason for *wanting* anything. Because it only costs "a buck." My books have often cost as much as a bottle of whiskey. And I've always felt that once in awhile you could forego the case of beer, or the bottle of Jack Daniels, and invest in Robert Duncan, or Ronald Johnson, or whomever it happened to be. A book may happen once every four or five years. I insist it has to do with desire. The desire that really excellent readers have, and the kind of enthusiasm and pas-sion that reading can inspire. Our friend Pound says, that the only reason he bothered was in order to *enforce* his desire. He was able to do a few things for a few people. Revive a few reputations. To *insist* that certain things be brought to peoples' attention. And this was all it amounted to. This was it. This is all one man can do. I mean you can make the books, you can write the poems, you *can't* necessarily go out and sell them to everyone in sight. It is a two way arrangement. There may be a response. Maybe in 2243 A.D.?

Are you proudest of any one book you've done?

No I don't think so. Certainly some of them have been happier than others, and the relationships with the writers sometimes have been unfortunate. There are so few people in this coun-try reading poetry, that it does begin to get a little bit on occasion like Miriam Hopkins vs. Bette Davis you know, fighting over the last seven readers of poetry. And some of the writers have not been kind to each other. Mr. Olson was not terribly keen that I publish Mr. Zukofsky, and the feeling was mutual. But this was none of their business shall we say. This was my decision. This was me, exercising what taste I had, what enthusiasm I had, and that was my responsibility.

Of course you've dealt with a great many strong person-alities—

Right. Jahweh is Doris Day compared to most of them.

124

Maybe because they were out in the thicket so long—and somebody finally comes along—

Yes, often they had been isolated from each other. Edward Dahlberg felt that every other person I published was a disaster. But again, that's Edward. That's not me. I'm fairly genial ultimately, and I like more things as opposed to less things. I don't like just one kind of writing, one approach to writing a poem, one approach to walking a landscape, or one kind of landscape. It's a fairly large world. What's the remark by the medievalist that Pound translated: Richard of St. Victor?: "There are more things to love than we could possibly have imagined." It's good to know, it keeps one as they say, *active*.

After twenty-five years, I assume you are getting more manuscripts in the mail. And, as people become more and more aware, and as the publishing scene seems to be drying up on the one hand, how do you deal with that? You must get a lot of unsolicited things.

I do. It's not that you want to wall yourself against outside possibility, but first of all are the letters I write, which year in year out number about fifty a week, when I'm not in an automobile every day. The letters keep the network going. There is more to do than I can do already without inviting the floodgates to open. Very little has ever come in unsolicited that interested me.

Have you ever published anything that was unsolicited?

Almost never. I guess maybe Harold Norse sent me his translations of G. G. Belli, the 19th Century Romanesco poet, and out of the blue Russell Edson, who had been at Black Mountain before me, and really had no contact with Olson and the people of that later period. Russell some years after the Black Mountain time sent me a book of his fables which I thought were excellent.

125

Have you ever turned down anything that you were sorry about?

As I recall, though I may be misreading history—there was even an opportunity presented to me by Allen Ginsberg to do, if not *Howl,* then something of that period. There was talk of doing *Naked Lunch.* But Burroughs realized at the time, that there were probably legal considerations there, that would have made it very difficult for somebody without any resources to take on a chance like that.

Have you stayed away from prose for any particular reason? I mean beyond the fact that to publish a two hundred page novel—costs a lot of money.

I've done Guy Davenport's prose—mostly his poetry, though. Paul Metcalf—I've published four books of his prose. But it's like my interest in photography, it's something marginal to the main stream that I'm swimming in. And also it's a question of ignorance. I don't keep up.

Do you have a sense of Jargon's impact on things. Of its place. I don't mean in a hierarchical sense of good, bad, indifferent. But has twenty-five years given you the idea that other people are picking up on your lead, and that there has been created out of Jargon, and out of what it stood for, a kind of following?

I suppose. I simply think of it in terms of a kind of continuity, a kind of tradition, which I imagine in this country started with Parson Weems, and the whole 18th century business of getting the books out in the provinces, out in the hinterlands. And then there was Whitman over there in Brooklyn Heights cranking it out for his phrenologists, and then you come on down to Pound and his effort, and Bob McAlmon at Contact Editions. James Laughlin is of course is an admirable case, running New Directions for over forty years. He is the man who has done more than anyone else. And I would like to think that Jargon is in this tradition. Jargon is a small effort.

Yet I think it stands for something. That's all that's important. . . .

This kind of effort has to be done every few years by new presses. Because after all I'm forty-six now and there are an awful lot of things that are done by people in their 20's that miss me completely. This is something that simply happens. And it's also true for younger people. The kind of work that older writers in the middle generation are up to is usually of no particular use to them.

There's that notion of keeping up with what's going on—

Well I'm not interested in keeping up. I'm just keeping on. That is the more important thing. And, as I say, it interests me. There is enough going on in Man and Nature to keep one alive and active, as Mr. Zukofsky said. That is really all one can hope for. Just to keep alert.

On the invitation you sent out for the twenty-fifth Birthday Party at the Gotham Book Mart there was a photograph of you taken in North Carolina. And then on the right, there is a photograph of you now, twenty-five years later, sticking your tongue out. I showed that to someone the other day, and they said "Is he a sorehead?" Have you become a sorehead?

Well I'm cranky. Like W.C. Fields, or H.L. Mencken, or Thelonious Monk. I mean cranky in a dazed, mildly eccentric way. But as I said, I think I have more friends than most people.

Being public in that way on an invitation—was that a spur of the moment thing?

Call it a quirk. I'm not a very public person in that sense. I'm, of course, liable to say anything in a poem because there it's required. But no, I'm not interested in quote "publicity" really. The whole concept of having an audience is quite beyond me. The whole notion of being a spokesman for one's generation is so much horseshit. The whole idea of having

127

followers is very antithetical to what I'm interested in. Only *I* can do the kind of thing that I do. I may do it badly or I may do it well, but it seems to me that this is what writing is for.

You also take photographs. When did that start? And I know you put on presentations of photographs—Lorine Niedecker, Basil Bunting, and so on—

I guess I'm brought up on a lot of classic notions, but Herodotus in one of his histories said something like—"the names of the three hundred I have remembered because they deserve to be remembered." I mean, you suddenly realize that there are only two pictures of Lorine Niedecker in the world. Or that nobody knows where Charlie Parker is buried, or that almost nobody has ever seen the Garden of Eden created by Mr. Samuel Dinsmore in Lucas, Kansas. I'm interested in plotting this entire continent. I'd love to have the fantastic energy required. Of course you can't. George Blanda is fading. We're all fading a little. We do the best we can.

Do you find that traveling around and giving readings, or showing photographs has changed during the past twenty-five years? I don't mean to put you in the position of being a pundit about student audiences.

If you go to a good school like Bard for instance, there are always ten or fifteen people who get very excited, which makes it fine. And I don't know what the other people are thinking. You really can't worry about everybody you meet. The same thing is true for one's poems. They are there for the ones that want them. And you can't worry about the other people, can you? You do the best you can, and assume they will meet you on equal terms. That's fair enough. "Poetry," as Dr. Williams used to say, "is for them what wants it." There are plenty of other things in the world that a lot of kids these days crave. They know eight hundred seventy-five rock records and have never heard of Franz Schubert. Which I think is, frankly, unfortunate.

Do you find it disconcerting or curious that a lot of the

audience you stand in front of are college kids? That is a student audience. Would you like it to be something else?

It's hard to imagine what it's going to be in this society. Where else can you go? You're not going to garden clubs. You're not going to bridge clubs. I don't think you're going to go to the Rotary Club. You go where you're asked, and where you think there's a possibility. Ferlinghetti used to say, "I want to take it out of the classroom and into the streets." The problem is, the better one learns to write, or the better one can write, it seems that fewer people are willing to go with you. I don't know whether you've ever noticed this, but it seems to be true. So you get a man like Zukofsky with a *prodigious* technique, almost nobody can read it at this juncture. They don't have the background, they don't have the *time,* as people say. Well we've got more time than not. That's never been an issue. There is plenty of time to do just about anything that you are really interested in doing. It's not that I have to give up writing poetry because I'm traveling. I get a few more poems written than perhaps one needs to.

How do you hear all the music you like to hear when you're traveling? Does the car radio have FM?

No. I listen to AM radio. It want to see what Carl C. McIntire is saying about the Catholics.

Billy James Hargis too.

That's right. The solid core. The dark heart of America's feelings, in case we suddenly have to leave.

You've done other things. Besides being a poet and publisher, and I'm thinking particularly of that attempt to build a concrete monument, or a poem in steel for Carl Ruggles' grave site in Arlington, Vermont. Did that come to naught?

Since David Smith wasn't around to make a sort of stainless steel piece in a field, that would suggest a white birch—something of that marvelous strength that Ruggles' music had—I

129

thought that I would try to make one and I approached the U.S. Steel Foundation which had money to put into such projects. Here it didn't happen. I'm not convinced that it's entirely hopeless.

Have you attempted other things like that?

Yes. There was one which I think may already have been accomplished. When I was at the Maryland Institute of Art in Baltimore, it occurred to a sculptor there named Tylden Streett, and myself, that Billie Holiday had come from just around the corner.

As Babe Ruth had—

Yes. I also tried to do a Babe Ruth poem. A kinetic poem that would light up—a neon poem where the ball would disappear but we couldn't get that one done because the city wasn't able to raise enough money. However, I think they might have saved the house he was born in. Anyway the last I heard, Tylden had been able to get the City Fathers to fork over. As I say, black people or white people either, nobody knew anything about Billie Holiday around there. I hope this is not just nostalgia, but someone as good as Billie Holiday deserves to be remembered. Going back go Herodotus—we cannot ever achieve what is called Civilization in this country as long as we wipe it out as quickly as we build it.

You have lived in England part of the past few years. Do you travel as much there? And are you as much in touch with things—you started to publish English poets like Simon Cutts in your new series.

Yes. There is a young Scottish poet I like very much named Thomas A. Clark, as opposed to the American Tom Clark who lives in Bolinas. I've published Ian Hamilton Finlay the Scottish concrete poet, though post-concrete poet by this time. Yes, I'm interested in several other people over there.

Has England been more amenable than America?

130

It's a more amenable country. It's not artistically a very active place. We have the best of it and the worst of it here. It's all *here*. I say this as an outsider and maybe it's a very silly thing to be saying. For American tastes there are only about ten poets over there who would stir us at this point. But certainly, they have a few very, very good ones, including Basil Bunting, who is one of the best poets in the world. And younger men like Roy Fisher, Gael Turnbull, Simon Cutts—very good.

Do you find things more or less active here after twenty-five years? I keep coming back to ask you to comment on the scene because you've passed through so much of it. Somebody once called you "America's only open air museum, a walking, talking Johnny Appleseed." Is there more activity now?

There's a lot more activity photographically than there was. In terms of the things I abide by in poetry half of the people and half of the things I was involved in have been obliterated. Either by death or by the bulldozer. It's not that one is left *entirely* with memories. I think it would be fair to note, in the case of James Laughlin of New Directions, you do tend to stay with your own avant-garde. Somebody once asked J. Laughlin who were the five young poets, and he said. "Let's see, Ezra Pound, T.S. Eliot, Wallace Stevens, Mina Loy, and Marianne Moore." They were *his* five young poets. Who wants to know the latest always? I'm not interested in that. I'd much rather hear sixteen performances of the D. 960 *Piano Sonata* by Schubert, than perhaps know what Kiss or the New York Dolls are doing right this second. None of us has the time for quite everything. That Schubert sonata is more important to me than most of what is going on. . . . You can't obliterate the lot. It's not that all those other things are useless or terrible. But you get stuck with a period. If you are brought up on jazz, or on Schubert, or on Tolkien, one abides with these things. And I think J. Laughlin is probably not prepared to be interested, any more than I am, in everybody who is twenty-five years old. Impossible. He put years into building the reputations of Pound, Williams, Kenneth Patchen, Kenneth Rexroth, Tom Merton, and Tennessee Williams and dozens more. We are talking about one-man bands. We're not talking about a whole cultural apparatus. All these presses are essentially the work of a solitary writer who is concerned with what his generation is doing. And maybe the one before, which is already being wiped out.

I wanted to ask you about music. You published a poem about Mahler's symphonies, and you were working on something in Ravel. Writing a poem every day for a year on Ravel?

Yes, but I couldn't handle it. The notion came from Emily Dickinson. In her best year she had three hundred sixty-five poems. I though I'd try. How many good ones you could get out of three hundred sixty-five is of course problematical. But why not? . . . We're playing childhood games like old ball players. But that's alright. I think I did about one hundred Ravel poems, and decided to print fifty . . . It's difficult for me to imagine poets who don't pay attention to music. But obviously there are some who couldn't carry a tune more than three feet. I can't read musical notation, but I don't think that much matters. I'm concerned with those sixteen perform- ances of the Schubert Sonata. I can hear the differences. I know more about that sounding than I do about the history of literature in English. One abides by what one cares for most. I've been listening to music constantly ever since my mother took me to "Fantasia" when I was nine years old, and I heard Sousa's band when I was four.

Not the Disney version?

Yes. It was 1939 I think, when "Fantasia" first hit the scene. And I'd never heard anything except Carmen Cavalero, "the poet of the piano," Eddie Duchin, Nelson Eddy, Jeanette Macdonald—all those great happy vacuous things that Middle America and all of our families loved. Why demean them . . . but I suddenly heard Bach, Stravinsky, Beethoven, and went on from there. Bought all the records and used to drive my poor father mad by playing "The Rite of Spring" when I was ten years old. He wasn't ready for that, even with the volume on the Philco low.

132

What are you doing now? Writing? Publishing?

Well the occasion of being in New York at this time is, as you said earlier, to celebrate twenty-five years of The Jargon Society. We just did a Paul Metcalf book, *Middle Passage,* we just did a Ronald Johnson book, and I'm very pleased about this because I published their first books. Paul's, back in the fifties. So I'm still publishing him . . . I've got a manuscript of mine to put on the desk of Grossman who's done my last three books. And I hope they'll hang in. It's a big one. Poems of the last five years. That's like two hundred pages. Essentially five books in one. Anyway, there is no shortage of things to keep me occupied. They feed each other and leave me to get on down the road to McDonald's or the Restaurant de la Pyramide.

THE EDITOR AS UNDERTAKER OR THIS WAY TO TEMPORARY IMMORTALITY
by James Landis

James Landis, a recipient of The Roger Klein Award for Editing, is Vice President and Editorial Director of William Morrow and Company, Inc.

Contributing a short piece to a long symposium like this places one in a box. Have terms been defined with any consistency? Or is there lack of consistency in such definition, and does this itself serve to enlighten the reader, or does it further frustrate her or him? I say "further" because I begin with the assumption that frustration is at least one of the impulses that would bring someone to read this book in the first place. Frustration over the current state of literature. Frustration over the current state of publishing. Frustration over the current state of literary publishing. And, at the moment, continuing frustration over the fact that terms may not have been satisfactorily, or at least consistently, defined.

What is publishing? So far as books are concerned, it is the printing, binding, distribution, and promotion of written words. Simple enough, at least as regards the printing and the binding. But what about the distribution and promotion? It is generally assumed that the "small press" publisher is not so competent or least successful in these two areas as the "commercial" publisher. But what is also assumed is that the serious small press publishes "literature" while the commercial publisher, for the most part, does not.

But what is literature?

Damned if I know.

Damned if Sartre knows. He writes in *What Is Literature?:* "The American writer . . . does not see in literature a means of proclaiming his solitude, but an opportunity of escaping it. He writes blindly, out of an absurd need to rid himself of his fears and anger . . . He muses less about glory than he dreams of fraternity . . . He rarely appears in New York . . ."

Damned if you know.

And what, then, is "literary publishing"?

God only knows. (Though a God-fearing literary editor would have made the transposition in that little phrase eons ago, so it would read: Only God knows.) And God is not in the habit of enlightening us about anything, let alone such punditary concerns as we are engaging here.

But if you are prepared to admit that there are no satisfactory answers to any of these questions and are willing still to permit the use of such terms as "literature" and "literary publishing," then you are equipped to continue your quest for enlightened ignorance with the requisite open mind.

As I write this, here, in order, is the current *New York Times Book Review* best-seller list for fiction: *War and Remembrance* by Herman Wouk. *Chesapeake* by James A. Michener. *The Far Pavilions* by M. M. Kaye. *Fools Die* by Mario Puzo. *Bright Flows the River* by Taylor Caldwell. *Illusions* by Richard Bach. *Evergreen* by Belva Plain. *The Empty Copper Sea* by John D. MacDonald. *Second Generation* by Howard Fast. *The Silmarillion* by J. R. R. Tolkien. *Prelude to Terror* by Helen MacInnes. *Scruples* by Judith Krantz. *Wifey* by Judy Blume (Wifey! Sounds ironic. Tough publishing decision: whether to go with such an obscure title). *Eye of the Needle* by Ken Follett. *Thursday the Rabbi Walked Out* by Harry Kemelman.

Well, fellow pushcartelists, what are we to make of that?

We can dismiss the list as not being typical, but of course we would be wrong, for it is both typical of itself at any given time and, by its very nature, typical, statistically representational, of what America is reading at this very moment (and will be reading even more widely next year at this time, when these same books have been released in paperback).

We can say that there is not a single work of distinction here (though some adolescent-minded might argue the Tolkien), but then we're going to have to distinguish between distinction and distinction, for there can be no question that a novel that has made the List and is being so widely read—and these books *are* being read—has attained a very real distinction indeed.

Or we can conclude—avoiding the intermediate argument that the public doesn't know its ass from its elbow when it comes to "good books"—that books of real distinction, real "literature," are not widely read and that even when they are widely purchased (*Ada; Daniel Martin; The World According to Garp*) they are not read *through*.

But what is literature anyway? Having concluded that even God doesn't know, we can push Him, in His divine ignorance (perhaps the only thing we share), aside and get on with our search for an answer.

Literature is books that last:

Like *The Prophet?*

Literature is books that move us to joy, tears, and a feeling for the eternal evanescence of human life:

Like *Love Story?*

Literature is books that are well written:

Like *Remembrance of Things Past?* ("And the others too were beginning to remark in Swann that abnormal, excessive, scandalous senescence, meet only in a celibate, in one of that class for whom it seems that the great day which knows no morrow must be longer than for other men, since for such a one it is void of promise, and from its dawn the moments steadily accumulate without any subsequent partition among his offspring." You can accuse Proust of being a lousy writer, but don't say he had no sense of humor, for he went on to write: " 'My dear,' she had said to Mamma, 'I could not allow

136

myself to give the child anything that was not well written.' ''
You can bet that kid didn't get a copy of *Swann's Way* in his
stocking.)

Literature is books that are well written:

You are spared here quotes from the work of Henry
James, whose editor had an opportunity, in advance, to make
Maxwell Perkins look like the kid in the mailroom.

Literature is books that get good reviews:

Like *The Women's Room?*

Literature is books that not only get good reviews (''women's novel of the year, perhaps many years''—John Bark-
ham Reviews) but take a political stance and speak to the
most important issues of the day:

Like *The Women's Room?*

Literature is books that don't sell:

Like . . . but that's the point, perhaps.

Aren't we really talking about books that don't sell (and
that rare book that, against all odds, though seriously conceived and written in a style in which the placement and sound
and look and feel and even smell of words are important and
right, does sell)? Aren't we really talking about books that are
at one and the same time successes (literature) and failures
(literature)? About good books of which no one has ever heard
but the frustrated author, the forlorn publisher, and the
fickle critic (who loves to turn against a writer he ''discovered'' once other critics settle comfortably in the writer's plot
and rob his grave)?

When you try to attain a definition of literature, and you
try to attain a definition of publishing, and then you try to
define the two together (''literary publishing''), you end up
talking about the indefinable if not the ineffable. You end up
viewing things wall-eyed through the side of the telescope.

For publishing itself affects the way in which the literary
value of a particular book is assigned. If the publishing of a
particular book is highly successful—in publishing terms, if
the book ''really *sells*''—it is unlikely that the book will be
considered literature, or at least serious literature. Con-
versely, if the publishing fails, the same book is much more
likely to be hailed as a masterpiece long after it ceases to be
available except by special order.

Who can doubt that *Ragtime* would be taken at least a bit more seriously today if it had been taken less seriously and, more important, had sold less well, when it was published? There is no pure judgment of anything once the public at large has committed its checkbook criticism. And we all of us tend to shoot from our swiveling, envious hips at the work that too many others have fastened their small minds upon and praised.

There are, in short, no standards.

For the editor in a publishing house, or at least for the editor who aspires toward the publication of literature, this means merely that he or she tries to do the best with what he or she has upstairs (I use that word in at least two of its meanings) and with what the book in question seems to offer, in both aesthetic and pecuniary terms, upstairs. It isn't always easy. To take two aforementioned examples, *Ragtime,* I have been told, was nearly rejected by its publisher as unsalable if not unpublishable when it was finished and submitted under contract, and *The World According to Garp was* rejected.

In my own experience—to get to that, as I have been asked—at the time I was editing Jacqueline Susann (who *did* consider herself the Dickens of our times, and was charmingly demure about it), I was taken to task at a cocktail party by an editor from *Cosmopolitan* who asked me how I could live with myself for having unearthed such dreck. In a rather pure self-defense, larded with a healthy glop of self-righteousness, I asked her if she had read *Time of Parting* by Anton Donchev, *Palace of Ice, The Birds, The Bridges, The Boat in the Evening,* all by Tarjei Vesaas, William Harrison's novels and collection of stories, the early Margaret Drabble, the early and thus far only Su Walton, R. M. Koster's *The Prince,* the first five books by Harry Crews, the work of Nicholas Delbanco, of Paul Scott, of Monique Wittig . . .

"No," she said.

"Then don't talk to me of Jacqueline Susann," I replied, hoping she'd see the tenuous connection between what she had read and what she hadn't, and be chastened.

"I haven't even *heard* of those books," she said, with more accusation than apology.

"Well, we published them all," I said proudly.

"I haven't even heard of those *authors*," she replied.

"Exactly," I said, hoping I'd made my point (that she was not qualified to speak of what she considered bad books until she'd read what I thought were good books; that we were a good publisher).

I hadn't. "I knew you were a lousy publisher when I heard you brought out Jacqueline Susann," she said. "Now I know you're an even more lousy publisher when I hear you publish people that no one knows diddly about."

That hurt. It always hurts more not to be noticed at all than to be noticed and maligned. It is especially painful for a published writer to receive that particular blank look of ignorance and barely withheld contempt when he answers the question, "And what are the titles of your books?" It is not much less painful for the editor of that writer's books and the no doubt equally obscure work by many other novelists he publishes. No one seems to know what an editor does anyway, but most people have at least some idea of what a book *is*. When no one's ever heard of nearly every book you've edited, you begin to think they're looking at you as if they believe you can't possibly be earning an honest living. As a result, even the most literary of editors tend to mention only those books of theirs that sell, and this leads further to the emphasis on sales in the publishing business. It is just plain embarrassing to tell people that you are responsible for nurturing a child who seems to have chosen to spend his entire life in a closet with a bag over his head.

A very intelligent, well-meaning editor friend of mine said recently to me, "You ought to get rid of Delbanco. He's the one blot on your career. You publish book after book by him, and none of them sells. It's embarrassing. You're getting a bad reputation."

And there all along I had thought that my reputation was, if anything, *salvaged* by the fact that the house and I had stuck by Delbanco from one book to the next, seven in a row (his first two having come from Lippincott) over ten years, with the newest just out (and getting its very first review from Elliott Anderson in *Book World*: "There are a handful of novelists who have published a substantial body of work and have attracted considerable critical attention, but who have not, for one reason or another, established much of a popular following, certainly not the following that their work deserves. I'm thinking not of the experimental novelists . . . I'm . . . thinking of Nicholas Delbanco, who must, on the strength of his most recent work, rank among the overlooked talents of the decade. He is, in my opinion, as fine a pure prose stylist as any writer living. His gift for narrative is considerable, and his characters are as strong, as true, and as original as any that I can think of. His talent is major and deserves a major public reputation.'').

Is this vindication? First of all, earlier books of his have received similar reviews, and these have caused no ''major public reputation.'' Secondly, if he gets, finally, just such a reputation, his subsequent books, which may be even better than this current one, *Sherbrookes,* will very likely be maligned in the review media precisely to the extent that *Sherbrookes* is celebrated. Thirdly, it's just such exuberant encomia as this that often drive away prospective readers, who confuse good writing with difficult writing (I have learned to be very sparing in my reading of a novelist's good reviews during our company's sales conferences, when new books are presented to the salesmen; who in turn are even more sparing when taking advance orders from wholesalers and bookstores: the dominant thinking in the business is that, for fiction, the more a writer is praised in print, the less likely he is to be appreciated by the book-buying public, which is terribly insecure about what is, or passes for, literature). Fourthly, there is no sense talking of vindication; writing, and the publishing of writing, ought to be free of competition, of the weighing of values other than those aesthetic (including monetary), and of the nonsensical pain involved in justifying a book, or a life, or a way of life, to others whose praise or censure derives more from what they expect to find than from what is delivered, whole, to their conniving sensibilities.

There are no standards.

But there are books, thank God. And there are readers. There are good books and good readers, and there are bad books and bad readers. The good reader, reading a good book, says, ''That's a good book.'' The bad reader, reading a bad book, says, ''That's a good book.'' The good reader, reading a bad book, says, "That's a bad book." The bad reader, reading a good book. says, "That's a bad book." It all evens out. But the eveness is only symmetrical. It is not balanced. For while there are enough good books to go around, there are not enough good readers. Their small number influences the publisher, who loves nothing more than to sell books and sooner or later panders to the general lack of taste and critical faculties among the public he serves and services. Sartre, wisely, quotes Paulhan: " 'Everyone knows that there are two literatures in our time, the bad, which is really unreadable (it is widely read) and the good, which is not read.' "

But why write if not to be read? Why publish if not to have read what you publish? I have never yet met a writer who didn't write for public consumption, *wide* public consumption. I have never yet met a writer who, sharing his or her fantasies on the matter, didn't, in this day and age, muse about glory, envision earning with one book a lifetime's money and at the same time enough critical praise to feed his ego and his family's ego for at least the day and a half that it takes a healthy ego to absorb and digest and eliminate all the world's praise, before hungering for more. I have never yet met any writer with the least bit of confidence that justice would be done.

It won't be done. You're damned from the moment you pick up a pen with the presumption that you have something true to say, something new to say, damned because you probably can't say it well enough and damned because the only people listening, reading, will betray you one way or another before it's all over. If they love you, you will write to please them, and the pleasure will come too easy. If they hate you, you will write to please them, and the pleasure will come too hard. If, on the other hand, you write to please only yourself, one day you'll find your audience has shrunk and there's no one listening, reading, and your pen will squirt only loneliness and self-pity.

As for the publisher, literary and (predominantly) otherwise, he'll box you up and ship you off and pray you find a hundred thousand homes. There are, after all, worse coffins for your ideas and your life than books.

ON EDITING
THE ONTARIO REVIEW
by Joyce Carol Oates
and Raymond J. Smith

Joyce Carol Oates and Raymond J. Smith are married to each other and to THE ONTARIO REVIEW. *He is editor of* THE ONTARIO REVIEW *and she is an associate editor. They are currently organizing The Ontario Review Press, which will soon publish its first list of books. Part One of this essay is written by Ms. Oates and Part Two by Mr. Smith.*

Part One

The artist, as John Stuart Mill once observed, is not heard but overheard: he addresses the world but he must address it indirectly, and his work, when completed, when sent out from him, must make its way as if no one, no explicit being, had created it. Has anyone ever considered how strange this situation is, has anyone (including even the artist himself) reflected upon its perverse maddening cruelty, its *injustice* . . . ? To be an artist, then, is to freely surrender not only a part of one's self but to surrender (unless one is exceedingly brash) the very temptation, perhaps even the very instinct, to protect and define and argue for and exhibit any signs of affection for that self.

But to be a critic, or an editor—!

An editor, then. An editor speaks directly: he may actually address his readers in the pages of his magazine, if he wishes;

he certainly addresses them by way of the material he chooses to publish. He is a kind of god. He arranges everything. A four-line poem in the lovely white space at the end of a long story—a poem that beautifully expresses the hidden spirit of that story—what a joy it is to discover the connection, and to set the poem in place! *Art-work. The arrangement of.* Does a photograph on page forty bear a secret connection with an image in a poem on page eighty-five? Does the very color of the cover relate to the tone of the issue . . .? Does it mean something that three stories are arranged in a certain order, with certain poems between them to set them apart, and certain drawings as well . . .: Certainly it does, and the editor knows it; no one else will 'know' it but he might sense it if he studies an issue with care. All issues of *Ontario Review* are arranged in an order the editors consider—after many hours of brooding, talking, and contemplation, and perhaps good luck—the absolutely perfect arrangement of that particular body of material. I am inclined to think that this mysterious process of arranging disparate works of prose, poetry, and art is the most gratifying aspect of editing a magazine: but one cannot comprehend by being told of it, one must do it. Start making plans to edit you own magazine.

*   *   *

Baskerville, Caslon Old Style. Centaur. *Centaur* (almost unbearably lovely in italics). And then there is Chisel: costly, elegant, almost *too* elegant. Cochin bold. Copperplate bold. COPPERPLATE GOTHIC BOLD. Copperplate Gothic light. Freehand. Futura. GARAMOND BOLD. And *Goudy,* hand-tooled costly lovely *Goudy.* Huxley, Libra, Paramount, Park Avenue, Twentieth Century bold . . .

The artist very rarely chooses his type face; he is not even supposed to know about that sort of thing. Innumerable intermediaries deal with his work, once they decide to publish it: theirs is the exquisite pleasure of determining the type face, and theirs is the pleasure of determining the kind of paper that will be used, and the kind of cover, and the design . . .

The editor quite freely does all these things. He really *is* a kind of god. He knows that a poem set in delicate Centaur will be a quite different poem from the same assemblage of words set in heavy-footed Bank Gothic. He knows that a group of words, however fastidiously chosen, set in Engraver's Old English, will be irresistibly funny; just like a contributor's note set in Tango Swash Initials. A masterpiece set in 5-point Baskerville is not quite the same as a masterpiece set in 14-point.

Then there are those staggeringly lovely colors for one's cover. Some four hundred eighty-seven of them. Yes: four hundred eighty-seven distinctive colors. And even some special colors, if you can believe it. (*Black Plus. Super Warm Red. Black on Black.*) . . . The more one considers the editor's work, the more astonishing it is that anyone wants to be an artist, a writer, at all.

*   *   *

Literary creation is a solitary activity: by the time the work is actually gone from one's desk it has eased out of one's soul, and a new project, a new ecstatic torment, has replaced it. As Conrad once observed, perhaps crankily, the writer only wants to hear sympathetic remarks—'criticism,' however well-intentioned, comes too late, and is anyway beside the point since (as few non-artists know) the work is almost always as close to perfection as the artist could make it, and that's that. *Don't* take me aside and say, "May I speak frankly . . . ."

The editor, however: he is not at all a solitary person. He is gregarious. He is warm-hearted. He is always ready for a luncheon, a telephone call, a batch of free reviewer's books. If the artist is an albino violet, the editor is a huge glaring grinning healthy sunflower. He craves remarks—of course he prefers good ones, but others are halfway welcome too, for he wants to know *that his magazine is being read.* (The artist, the writer, may sometimes hope in secret that his work isn't being read—by too many people, anyway.) The editor, far from being displeased by well-intentioned criticism, or confused by irrelevant praise, is eager to talk; he loves the company of other editors because they can compliment one another on their most recent issues, trade anecdotes about bizarre sub-

144

missions or printers' idiocies or that one indefatigable poet in Bad Ax, Michigan, or Black Fly, Ontario, who sends hundreds of poems out everywhere with a covering letter badly photostated. . . . The only thing the editor does not care to hear is that a library, somewhere, claims never to have received the most recent copy of his magazine. And perhaps he does not care to hear that the poem he has just published on page 105 has also just been published on page 87 of a rival journal.

*   *   *

But before I was initiated into all these secrets, before I could have guessed what lay ahead, I was simply intrigued by the idea of a little magazine. Not a glossy magazine— never—but a *little magazine*. (Not too little: the original *Kenyon Review*, say. Remember those gorgeous covers?) I was fascinated from about the age of eighteen onward by the notion, the abstract, almost Platonic notion, of a physical thing that was at the same time a communal phenomenon. That is, one picks up a magazine, weighs it in the hand, it appears to be a *thing,* but in fact it isn't a *thing* at all. It's a symposium. A gathering. A party. Open the cover and look inside and there (if I leaf through an issue of *Ontario Review*) are Elizabeth Spencer and John Updike and Fred Morgan and Robert Phillips and Reynolds Price. . . And in another issue, Margaret Atwood and William Everson and Lynne Sharon Schwartz and many others whose names might someday become well-known. The artist creates a single, a singular thing, out of his solitary labor; but the editor creates a small unanticipated community that has never existed before and will never exist again.

Writers, poets, and artists meet one another in the pages of magazines, in the warm confines of this unique community which, apart from its covers, its editors, its print, would never have come into being. We all remember the contributor whose poem was discovered on the back of our first off-print, and the quizzical concentration with which we read and reread his poem, no matter that it was truncated abruptly. Difficult to believe that there was not some arcane meaning behind the fact that we shared a single sheet of paper and that our destinies were not, in some tantalizingly obscure way, irrevocably linked. . . .

* * *

Why else edit a magazine? Because we are insatiable readers. Because we hope to 'discover talented young writers,' conventional as that might sound. Because people have been very generous to us, in the past. Because we know people, gifted people, who cannot always get their work published. And so on, and so forth.

Most of all, because a magazine is a *we*, and one can get somewhat tired of *I*.

—*Joyce Carol Oates*

PART TWO

A distinguishing feature of *The Ontario Review* is its character as a North American journal of the arts—"North American," I say, though for purely practical reasons it focuses mainly on the English-speaking cultures of the continent. As Americans teaching in Canada, in the border city of Windsor, knowledgeable about the literary traditions and in contact with writers of both countries, Joyce and I felt that we were in a fine position to start such a journal. While it has never been unusual for Canadian authors, like Earle Birney, to appear in American periodicals, and while some Canadian journals, like *The Malahat Review*, have long had an international scope, to my knowledge *The Ontario Review* is the first literary magazine to concentrate specifically on North American writers and artists and to try, with intercultural articles and reviews, to create a kind of dialogue between the two cultures.

We did this partly as a corrective to a tendency toward cultural chauvinism in Canada, despite our fundamental sympathy with the grievances of the Canadian nationalists, and partly to present more systematically to an American audience some of the products of a Canadian literature that has achieved its maturity during the past two decades. We did this, deliberately risking the ire of the ultra-nationalists and rejection by those Americans (and there are many) who might have no interest in the culture of a country whose existence for them was at best hazy. But so far the venture has worked; *The Ontario Review* has been generally well-received in both countries, and Joyce and I generously supported by writers and artists on both sides of the border.

One of the initial problems was finding a printer. A competent printer, whose galleys never contain more than two or three mistakes each, whose type fonts include accent marks and italics, and who has the equipment to do something more than wedding invitations, is imperative. When I asked one of our local printers what the biggest job he had done was, he proudly showed me an 18" x 30" menu for a Chinese restaurant; another wouldn't work without cash in advance, since a neighboring church group had recently neglected to pay him for printing a cookbook. Nonetheless, our first printer was a local one, with plenty of good will but without the necessary resources—typesetting was done in London, Ontario, the book was put together in Windsor, the binding was done in Hamilton. And he wasn't really equipped to collate the magazine; pages were often missing, or sometimes duplicated or even triplicated, and often showed signs of handling—wrinkles, smudges, and once a bloody fingerprint! (I realize now, too late, that the latter would have made a wonderful collector's item some day.) The climax came with the third issue, which the printer assured me would have no bad copies since he would hire a college student to go through each book page by page before it was sent to the binder. The student dutifully paged through them and inserted a folded piece of yellow paper to indicate missing pages. I could hardly believe it when, checking one of the contributor's copies about to be mailed to a distinguished poet, I opened it to find in the place of his poems a folded piece of yellow paper bound into the magazine. After that *The Ontario Review* was printed in Victoria, B.C., two thousand miles across the continent.

Printing, as most editors know, does not constitute publication; adequate distribution of the printed material is what really matters and is one of the editor's primary obligations to his contributors; it is also crucial to the economic solvency of the magazine. Step one for journals is to send a flier to the bigger libraries in North America—a sample of your product which may include, as ours did, the front cover and several pages from the first issue may be a better idea. Many of those libraries will subscribe through subscription agencies like Ebsco/Canebsco. This is the best way to handle subscriptions, since the renewals are automatic, invoices are unnecessary, and payments come in lump sums. Distribution is not really adequate unless the publisher supplies the bookstores, and this is where the major problem lies. Canadians seem to be starting to solve it with the help of the Canadian Periodical Publishers' Association, an organization which differs from its American counterpart COSMEP (Committee of Small Magazine Editors and Publishers) in several significant ways: membership is restricted to periodicals, mass-circulation items like *Saturday Night* are not excluded, and literary magazines constitute a minority of the membership. This kind of cooperation has been highly beneficial to little magazines like *The Ontario Review*.

With the *widest* distribution, a little magazine isn't going to break even financially, and that's because it is usually priced unrealistically—as if competing with the mass-circulation periodicals that get most of their revenue from advertising (an inconsequential source of income to the average little magazine). To help compensate for this, most literary journals are subsidized by government funds, foundations, and/or sponsoring universities. The role of the CCLM (Coordinating Council of Literary Magazines) in America is played by the Canada Council in Canada. The generosity of governments and foundations should not be an excuse, however, for deliberate underpricing. Not only have most little magazines been unrealistically priced from the beginning, but editors have been slow to raise their prices to help absorb growing printing, paper, and mailing costs—for obvious reasons.

As for content, we have always relied upon both submissions and solicitation. The little magazine exists partly as a vehicle for struggling new talent, and it's one of the editor's chief responsibilities and pleasures to be on the lookout for new voices, to encourage them, and to help them in their development. Solicitation, too, is an important part of the editor's job—asking writers and artists whose work he values to send something his way. We have been pleasantly surprised at the generous response to our requests, and we owe special debts to people like Margaret Atwood, John Updike, Philip Roth, Irving Layton, Colin Wilson, George Woodcock, and Saul Bellow. Soliciting material, however, can create its own problems if someone submits something that is obviously inferior. Some years ago, a long-established American writer upon solicitation sent us a critical essay that I wouldn't have accepted from one of my undergraduates. Joyce and I were faced with the dilemma of either publishing it, which was unthinkable, or rejecting it, which in this situation would have been particularly ungracious. Fortunately, the problem worked itself out without embarrassment to either party.

While special issues featuring a particular writer or based on a particular theme are often valuable, this approach (especially in the case of themes) can become mechanical—a theme for its own sake to suggest unity and especially relevance, as well as a controlling editorial consciousness. We prefer the miscellany, though we are not intractably committed to it. We work with what we have—the best that has come in since the previous issue—with an eye for balance: balance of material (fiction, poetry, criticism, graphics, reviews) and balance of tone (maybe a touch of "comic relief" for an otherwise too somber issue). Our editorial aim is to be interesting and to avoid the kind of pedantry that sometimes enervates the scholarly magazines. So far we haven't published many critical articles, though we would like to do more of the intercultural kind, like Ann Mandel's in Number Three, and more of the interdisciplinary kind, like the essay by Arnold J. Mandell, M.D. in Number Two. Reviews are generally assigned, with an attempt to balance prominent titles with those from small presses. A special feature on small press publications appeared in our Spring-Summer 1978 issue.

I have mentioned some of the problems facing a little magazine editor; now let me name some of the rewards. I see editing a magazine not as *compiling* but *creating*, and the finished product as a work of art in its own right—the book itself (its cover, stock, type, layout, etc.), as well as that unique whole that is formed by the magazine's many parts (stories, essays, poems, etc.). The rewards of the job are many—discovering a well-shaped and compelling story or poem by a previously unpublished writer, watching hitherto disconnected material gradually assume a focus, designing the next cover, paging through an advance copy of a new issue, getting some positive reactions from people you admire. Finally, the editor, for better or worse, contributes (no matter how little) to the shaping of a culture. He need not, and perhaps should not, be doctrinaire; nevertheless, he will have values—aesthetic, cultural, even moral, that will be reflected in what he chooses to publish. I have never thought of it this way before, but I suppose that *The Ontario Review*, whether quixotically or not, is tilting with the dragon of anti-art— resisting the deadening commercialism of modern Western civilization.

—*Raymond J. Smith*

THE FALL
OF LIVERIGHT
by Saxe Commins

Saxe Commins was the senior editor, and in the words of Bennett Cerf, "one of the great men of Random House," from 1933 until his death in 1958. The following chapter discusses his final days at Liveright, where he was an editor from 1931 until that firm's reorganization in 1933.

When I brought the completed manuscript of *Mourning Becomes Electra* to the Liveright offices in 1931, there was a general dismay over the title. The then editor-in-chief, Thomas R. Smith, looked at the sheaf of papers, concentrated on the title page, played for a while with the long black ribbon on his spectacles, cleared his throat as a preliminary to uttering a shattering profundity, shook his white-thatched head and exploded the word "meaningless" with an implied exclamation mark at the end of it. As on cue, the editorial assistants and the publicity director embellished the verdict with even stronger adjectives, both commercial and semantic.

Not until patient explanations were offered that the verb in the title was a synonym for "suits" rather than the active word for coming into being, were they relieved of their perplexity. Even then they grudgingly admitted that it made some sense, but not enough to identify such an exploitable property. They insisted, as publishers habitually do, that a book title must smite the beholder in the eye, whether it applies to the contents or not, and must, above all, be easily remembered.

The Liveright firm, as everyone knew but would not openly admit, was teetering on the brink of insolvency and it was hoped that the publication of the new O'Neill play would postpone the disaster for a while.

Fighting for that postponement with every stratagem at his command was an accountant, the new owner of the Liveright publishing company, Arthur Pell . . .

Pell counted heavily on the sale of 100,000 copies of *Mourning Becomes Electra* and not without reason or precedent. If this could be accomplished, the plus would replace the minus . . . . *Strange Interlude* had been one of the most phenomenal commercial successes in the history of modern play publishing. Approximately 110,000 copies, in the trade edition alone, had been sold, a figure no play by anyone but Shakespeare had attained until then. *Mourning Becomes Electra* became Pell's hope of coming out of financial mourning known by its mournful color as in the black. His subordinates merely hoped that the play would produce a lighter shade of red.

I had been working with O'Neill in his home in Northport, Long Island, and in subsequent visits worked on the galley proofs of *Mourning Becomes Electra,* omitting any mention of how much the publication of the play meant to the survival of the Liveright company. The reticence was not so much discretion as it was the lack of certainty about the danger signals; it would add to his anxiety on the eve of the publication and production, to learn that the work on which he was engaged so long might be jeopardized. So the matter rested.

Mourning Becomes Electra was produced and published in November 1931. Its immediate success eased the financial difficulties for a time. Alas, the earnings from the publication of the play were not enough to prop up the tottering house indefinitely. Matters went from bad to worse in 1932, after the

152

brief respite provided by O'Neill's play, but we struggled along on its momentum until another stroke of publishing luck made a national best seller of *Washington Merry-Go-Round,* a savage critique of the Hoover Administration which at the moment was in as perilous a state as our own little regime, since both tried to ride out the depression.

In 1933 as that depression was approaching its nadir, our salaries were cut in half and from all sides creditors were clamoring for some sort of settlement from Pell. [Insolvency was imminent.] There was only the question of how long it would be postponed.

As O'Neill's editor I was very concerned about the large sums of money due O'Neill in royalties from *Mourning Becomes Electra* and his other plays. Worry impelled me to call a meeting of the principal stockholders and to place an ultimatum before them. Either a certified check covering all of O'Neill's royalties would be given to me within twenty-four hours or I would announce on the book pages of the *New York Times* that O'Neill had decided to transfer his publishing program to any one of the five leading publishers of the country.

It was a staggering threat which . . . could be carried out, for I had a virtual power of attorney in O'Neill's behalf and had been authorized specifically to exercise my own judgment, as his editor and in the protection of his royalties.

Late that afternoon a certified check for the full amount due O'Neill was on my desk. The reason for the alacrity with which they submitted to my seeming blackmailing threat was that an announcement of O'Neill's intention to change publishers would precipitate bankruptcy proceedings among the many creditors . . . .

With the check safely in my possession, I took the train for Sea Island, Georgia, where Gene and Carlotta had established themselves in manorial style in Casa Genotta, a large home, architecturally Spanish, near the Atlantic shore, its name compounded from the given names of its owners to sound somewhat Iberian. On my arrival I merely turned over the check to Gene, saying as little as possible about the circumstances under which it had been obtained.

My visit was brief but pleasant. Gene brought a football

and we spent many hours on the hard crusted beach throwing it back and forth. We swam often, I near the surf and he far out of sight in the ocean. We went for long walks along the shore, reminiscing about the old times and old struggles and a now romantically recalled poverty. Our companion on these walks was Blemie, a Dalmatian of aristocratic canine lineage, idolized and pampered by Carlotta and protected by Gene. Blemie's food was shipped from New York after consultation with animal dieticians. Special steel instruments were made for scaling tartar from his teeth. He slept in a made-to-order bed in the upstair hallway. Sheets on the bed were changed at frequent intervals and a monogrammed blanket was provided for his comfort.

When I walked alone on the beach with him, it gave me a perverse pleasure to see him stick his aristocratic nose in the debris washed up by the sea or the offal of less privileged dogs. Years later, when he died in Danville, Contra Costa County, California, where the O'Neills were living in Tao House, . . . (then it was the oriental period of their constant migration, after they had abandoned their French chateau near Tours), Blemie was buried on the estate with ceremonial grief and heart-rendering wailing. A tombstone with a touching inscription was erected over his grave and Gene wrote an elegy in very lyrical prose for the departed dog.

From the isolation of Casa Genotta on Sea Island, with all its opulence, I returned to New York and its anxieties over little more than survival. On my arrival it was all too evident that the Liveright creditors were organizing to deliver the coup de grace. The blow came with suddenness and a fierce bitterness in April 1933, when Van Riis, the printer who staggered under a load of $280,000 due him, Herman Chalfonte, the paper supplier, and the Ace Paper Company, constituting the necessary legal triad, filed suit. The sum due authors in unpaid royalties added up to more than $150,000.

Pell could not stem such a tide of debt, although he marshalled all his forces . . . .

Arthur Pell emerged from the reorganization in control of all the remaining assets of the Liveright Company. In that list of assets was one item that provided an ironic note to the death scene. To particularize on this single item requires a

154

discursive section characteristic of the writer who was involved. He, Theodore Dreiser, owed the decomposed company $17,000 for unearned royalties. These, by way of explanation, are monies advanced to an author until he can complete a work . . . . The weight of evidence was in favor of Pell and against Dreiser.

In the decade of the 1920s, when Horace Liveright was in possession of his senses, or more particularly his flair for sensational publishing, . . . virtually every best seller list was crowded with titles published under the Liveright imprint. In a single season Gertrude Atherton with her *Black Oxen* jostled Emil Ludwig and his *Napoleon* for national leadership. *The Story of Mankind* by Hendrik William Van Loon was cheek by jowl with Anita Loos's *Gentlemen Prefer Blondes,* and *Flaming Youth* by Warner Fabian (who in real life was Samuel Hopkins Adams) was compelling nationwide attention. Into this mixed company of successful writers came Theodore Dreiser who hitherto had to console himself for the apathy of the public with the approval of a few critics. His *An American Tragedy,* to his great surprise and profit, became a sensational best seller.

In one of his inspired moments, Horace Liveright had suggested to Dreiser that he write the story of a murder committed at Saranac Lake by one Chester Gillette, a lad grown up in abject poverty. Young Gillette had fallen in love and impregnated a girl from his own social and economic stratum. When he caught a glimpse of life a reach above his own position and dared hope to win the love of a maiden with a little more grace and a great deal more money than his first girl could even hope to possess, he was confronted with the problem, so to speak, of evading the issue. His solution had the fault of simplicity, he merely induced his first love to go with him for a canoe ride on Saranac Lake and there he hit her on the head with a tennis racket until she fell overboard and was drowned.

To Horace Liveright this was the perfect if bare outline of a plot that would reveal the predicament of the most ordinary of young men trapped in a common but all-too-human situation which would end in no other way but tragedy. What was the background of this young man? What was his psychological and social conditioning? Dreiser, taken by the idea, was confident that he could answer these questions in full and unsparing detail. He set to work in his lumbering manner to write the long, relentless, and powerful novel, in his unrelieved, naturalistic manner, about the simplest of American men in one of the oldest of the eternally human plights that brought in its wake his downfall and his death.

Upon its appearance, *An American Tragedy* immediately became a huge critical and financial success. Dreiser had the grace to inscribe one of the first copies to come off the press to Horace Liveright. Over the autograph he wrote an acknowledgement of his indebtedness to his publisher for providing him with the central theme and plot and outline of the novel. Horace was of course touched by this evidence of generosity.

As time went by and the book became more and more popular, Dreiser approached Liveright and asked him whether he thought there would be a possibility of selling it to a motion picture company for twenty or twenty-five thousand dollars. Liveright promised he would try, but instead of asking that sum he would attempt to get forty thousand dollars. Dreiser was elated and loudly sang the praises of his publisher—for the moment his agent.

Liveright, a shrewd trader, succeeded in raising the price not to forty thousand, but to ninety thousand. The contract for *An American Tragedy* was drawn up. But before the picture could be ready for production, a revolutionary event occurred in the movies. *The Jazz Singer* by Samson Raphaelson, with Al Jolson in the leading part, was made and shown; it was the first talking picture and, at a stroke, the silent movies virtually became obsolete.

Never having foreseen the possibility of talking pictures at the time the contract for *An American Tragedy* was drawn up, the so-called party of the first part had failed to mention this in the agreement. Because of this lapse, the motion picture company was obliged to buy the rights to the property all over again.

Dreiser was not only jubilant, but he was also very rich. At a luncheon to celebrate his newly acquired wealth, Liveright reminded him of the first modest proposal and his reaction when Liveright suggested the doubling of the original price. Now it had multiplied almost eight times. Calculating what the agent's commission would have been, if there were an agent, Liveright laughingly said Dreiser's debt to him would easily run into five figures. Thereupon Dreiser picked up a cup of coffee and threw it into Liveright's face!

Before this time, while *An American Tragedy* was at the height of its popularity, Dreiser proposed a new novel to Liveright; its was to bear the title *The Stoic*. Arrangements were immediately made whereby the author was to receive a stipend of $100 per week as an advance against royalties ultimately to be earned by this embryonic but still highly putative novel. Announcements of its forthcoming publication were printed in catalogue after catalogue, season after season, but no manuscript was in existence. My conscience is still disturbed because I wrote an announcement describing a book no one had even seen. In 1947, fifteen years later, *The Stoic* was published under the Doubleday imprint as a posthumous novel, born two years after the author's death.

In the early 1930s, however, the weekly payments of $100 had accumulated until they aggregated $17,000—and still no manuscript. Promptly and conscientiously, Horace Liveright had paid the weekly sum and it was continued even after he was . . . out of the business he had established and conducted so brilliantly, if erratically. After the Wall Street crash of 1929, broken in spirit and in health, his money lost and his prestige faded, humiliated and abandoned, Liveright was forced to relinquish the publishing house that bore his name . . . . Wild ventures in the stock market, the theater, in Hollywood—all went against him and brought about his downfall. His friends ignored him, his flair was gone—he was unwanted and dispossessed. Within a few years, he was dead.

In 1933 . . . all the assets of the reorganized Liveright firm was bought for five cents on the dollar. One of these assets, now transferred to the new owners, was the $17,000 advanced to Theodore Dreiser for the still undelivered manuscript of *The Stoic*. The foremost American realist could discharge this obligation in one of two ways; he could repay the money or submit the new novel. Unfortunately for him, no new manuscript was then in existence. Accordingly, Pell sued and asked in his bill of particulars for the money or the novel.

157

The court having learned that there was no manuscript, had no alternative but to order Dreiser to meet his obligation and turn in $17,000.

Dreiser set up a hue and cry, wrote articles on the infamy of the courts, stooped to virulent anti-Semitic attacks and let himself be used as a figurehead by American communists. His appeals to the public and more persistently even to the courts were unavailing. The verdict stood and he had to pay the full sum. He could well afford it. His income and investments were enormous!

At that particular time Dreiser was at work on a book that in a manner reversed the title of his most successful novel and was published as *Tragic America*. Working with him was not exactly a rewarding collaboration. He was obstinate, truculent, and totally lacking in courtesy. There was always the dread of what he might say in a moment of pique and, afterwards, the even greater dread of what the critics were always certain to say about his inaccuracies, his ponderousness of style, and his juggernaut assault on the simplest of declarative sentences. Grammar was violated and syntax slaughtered.

Insistence upon realism does not preclude carelessness. While editing *Tragic America* I flagged twenty-seven references that were either manifestly or suspiciously libelous. It is part of my job to call such passages to the attention of the author and publisher, so that they would at least be aware of the possibility of law suits and perhaps heavy damages. The usual procedure in such cases of possible libel is to consult a lawyer expert in the field of literary infringement and learn from him whether the questionable reference comes within the meaning of the law. Generally his decision is based upon his own confidence in his ability to defend what might be considered libelous in a court of law. Damage done by a word or phrase or a passage or even the entire context is difficult to determine, but an egregiously harmful statement is usually omitted or modified. Even the truth under some circumstances can be libelous.

When Dreiser saw the twenty-seven passages I had marked for possible libel, he erupted into a volcanic rage, demanding that I be dismissed at once and calling me names that even he wouldn't allow to be printed in his novels. My only defense was that I would have been remiss if I had not at least marked the dubious passages which might or might not cause trouble and that no harm could come from being cautious or even captious.

Then I suggested that, to be on the safe side, we should submit the manuscript to Gustavus Myers, author of *History of the Great American Fortunes,* from whom Dreiser himself had obtained much of the material for his book. Myers, a gentle and meticulous man and the author of many books that undermined the reputations of numerous men in high places, had never been involved in a libel suit, in spite of the explosive nature of his revelations.

Dreiser was amenable to the suggestion and we arranged with Myers that he examine the manuscript for libelous statements, for an honorarium of twenty-five dollars. His report uncovered not twenty-seven libels, but thirty-four, seven of which I had overlooked. As anybody could have foreseen, *Tragic America,* when published, received a well-deserved chastisement from the critics and a shrug of indifference from the American public.

There is no gainsaying that Dreiser was a pioneer in the American literary movement in realism, even if this movement arrived in our country twenty-five years after the battle for it had been fought and won in Europe. His *Sister Carrie* certainly marked a decisive event in the history of the native novel at the turn of the century. Against the stern taboos and prejudices of that time and even against the attempt at censorship on the part of his own publisher, more to the point the publisher's wife (Mrs. Frank Doubleday), Dreiser struggled almost single-handedly for the right to interpret through the novel a truthful, if stark, reflection of human experience.

It is possible that Frank Norris, if he had lived longer, would have earned the honor of freeing the American novel from its heavy burden, for *McTeague, The Pit,* and *The Octopus* prepared the way and gave direction to Dreiser's work. It would be difficult indeed to dispute Dreiser's earnestness of conviction and his clumsy but irresistible power. It does not follow, however, that a novelist of historic importance and a writer of great influence does nothing else for an editor, it shatters the romantic illusion that a writer must perforce be an able thinker and a discriminating critic of his own or other's works. Association with men whose gifts outweigh their mentalities or characters raises many marginal queries about the sense and sensibility of some men of letters.

It was in this atmosphere of tension, suspicion, and conflict that the Liveright insolvency proceedings reached their climax. Just before the end came, all employees were given notice of dismissal, salaries were abruptly stopped and the seemingly rational activities required for giving form to ideas in books came to a dead end.

I consoled myself that O'Neill had collected all his royalties just before the debacle and that Dreiser would have to pay the $17,000 he had garnered on the promise of producing a manuscript that was still the figment of a blurb-writer's imagination. Unfortunately for all the other authors under Liveright's banner, they were able to realize only a very small percent of the royalties due them.

To a writer whose earning powers at best are meager, such a settlement is just short of a catastrophe. Most severely punished were Drew Pearson and Robert Allen, authors of *Washington-Merry-Go-Round*. Their topical political book, published toward the end of the Hoover Administration, had had an enormous success. It caught the public fancy because it reflected the nation's dissatisfaction with a regime that compounded its ineptitude with indifference. More than 100,000 copies were sold to a public avid for revelations about the powerless party in power. The authors received approximately one-twentieth of the money due them.

Quite as severe was the penalty imposed on the Liveright staff; it was disbanded. T. R. Smith, editor-in-chief, an old man now, still believing in the genteel tradition of publishing, was shorn not only of his security, but also of his dignity. Without any financial resources or prospects, he could only look to a bleak future; he was unwanted. For a while he subsisted on the sale, item by item, of his library, preponderantly volumes of erotica. All the passion spent, he died in loneliness and abject poverty.

Julian Messner established his own publishing company and Leane Zugsmith devoted herself to free-lance writing.

Louis Kronenberger, by far the ablest member of the group, became drama critic for *Time* and the author of many distinguished books on some principal figures of the eighteenth century. It was my good fortune to work with him several years later in another place and in happier circumstances. His many-faceted, sparkling mind earned my profound admiration.

Aaron Sussman, that anomaly in advertising, an idealist, established his own agency and is now the representative of the world's leading publishers. Albert Gross, Liveright's production manger and the most companionable of men, created a place for himself with the firm of Coward-McCann and continued his interest in Yiddish literature as critic and translator. He died of a heart attack only a few years after the reorganization.

My own outlook was somewhat brighter. Virtually every publisher in American hovered over the Liveright legacies, eager to inherit whatever of value of the company's assets. The most desirable of these reside in the continuing contracts with established authors and this property, so called, becomes free under bankruptcy. That is to say the writer is then at liberty to choose a new affiliation. Existing contracts are abrogated and the author can seek the shelter of a new home.

The most highly coveted "property" at that time and under those circumstances was Eugene O'Neill. Out of generosity and loyalty he made it plain that he would sign no contract without my counsel and consent. Furthermore, he wanted it stipulated in writing that no arrangement to publish his plays could be made unless the agreement included a clause which guaranteed me a job as his editor and a general editor of the company of his choice for the duration of his contract. To this latter condition, I raised an objection on the ground that I might conceivably embarrass him and that he should not under such circumstances be bound to me or I to him. O'Neill saw the reason of this precaution and agreed that a literary alliance is, at best, a hazardous venture. He insisted, however, that I remain his editor.

At once virtually all the publishers in New York began to court me. I went to Sea Island to lay before Gene all the offers that had been made and tried to assay their worth in terms of advantage. My preference was for Bennett Cerf and his company, Random House and the Modern Library. The reason for that choice was that I had known Bennett professionally during the Liveright days and recognized in him the potential of an imaginative, resourceful, adventurous and most trustworthy publisher. From my first meeting with his partner, Donald S. Klopfer, I was impressed by his quiet competence, his reliability, and his good sense. Subsequently, through a quarter-of-a-century of daily association I was to learn of his many attributes, not the least of which is his complete selflessness.

O'Neill suggested that Bennett fly down to Sea Island to consummate the arrangement and this was done in an atmosphere of mutual trust and friendliness. With the signing of the contract, a separate agreement was drawn up which provided for my employment as a general working editor for Random House for a three-year period, and I began my work on 9 July 1933.

Thus was born the trade publishing activities of Random House and thus began a relationship that endured for twenty-five years, a time of struggle and passion and growth, until the infant, come into maturity, is now a formidable figure in its field.

PIECEWORK
by Len Fulton and Ellen Ferber

Len Fulton and Ellen Ferber are editors of Dustbooks and specialize in small press and little magazine information.

There are no secrets to making a publishing venture work, nor any magic either. Publishing is entrepreneurial, whether you use your own money or someone else's, and it combines many of the more interesting—and risky—elements of creative enterprise and capital adventure. It takes a certain quantity of luck, some simple but imperative knowledge, and the rest, say something like 90%, is a willingness to work virtually every waking hour, and dream about it the rest of the time. You simply have to believe you will have your share of the luck. The knowledge can be learned. But, particularly for the small publisher, who cannot afford to hire technicians and experts, the knowledge required for publishing is an odd marriage of disparate fields, from manufacturing, retail sales and packaging, to postal laws, copyright and sales taxes; from typefaces and typesetting hardware to binding chemistry; from advertising layout and book design to a fairly solid, general awareness of what other publishers are doing. No publishing is tougher than *literary publishing,* for literary publishing makes all these same demands and adds one more: a knowledge, obviously, of literature, and a sensitivity not only to the creative product but to the creative producer as well, to the artist.

Because at Dustbooks we handle enormous quantities of publishing data for our string of small press information titles, we witness every conceivable sort of operation. No one operation yet—including our own—by its form of publishing and the content of its published material, has disposed us to predict it will either succeed or come a cropper. And, though they fail no more nor less often than the non-literary, the literary publishers are the hardest to predict of all. For while poetry, for instance, is often considered an odds-on favorite to sink an operation before it gets started, there are unique advantages in poetry publishing—enthusiastic authors, grants, a limited financial investment and generally low cost production—that presses like Copper Canyon, Black Sparrow, Crossing, and The Smith have seized upon brilliantly, and stayed in business. The one human characteristic that seems to predict success more often than failure is the capacity to *stay,* whatever the real or imagined forces against you (and there are both), and to put up with the antimonies to which literary publishing is particularly heir: willingness to learn and arrogant confidence, innocence and cynicism, austerity of lifestyle and a flamboyant readiness to risk all, a sense of the hard realities of the literary marketplace and the belief, with no catches, in the capacity of a short work to go a long way.

The founding and operant commitment for Dustbooks is to modern, contemporary literature by *living* artists. There is no half-way business to this commitment; it is the consumate force, with several lines of energy. First, we write it, novels mostly. Second, we teach it. Third, we publish it. Fourth, we seek to track, describe and promulgate its existence and progress worldwide through what we call our "skein" of small-press information publications. And fifth, we distribute it, through both the Dustbooks list itself, and through the Small

Press Book Club. We also try, within the realities of our human limitations and the demands of the five items above, to take an active role in organizations and institutions which are themselves committed to small-press literature: e.g., the founding of the Committee of Small Magazine Editors and Publishers (COSMEP) in 1968. Between us we have served on a half dozen or more grants committees for the Coordinating Council of Literary Magazines (CCLM), the State of California's Arts Commission, the Literature Advisory Panel of the National Endowment for the Arts; and served on panels and in conferences for the American Library Association, the American Booksellers Association, the California Library Association, and countless other organizations and institutions throughout the United States.

For a small literary publishing company to support itself and the people who make it run, it must, more or less, be a pieced-together operation. Particularly when you lack grants or what is known in corporate circles as "capitalization", the piecing process becomes critically important, on the theory that when one piece is not working out, another is. For Dustbooks this is in reality a very complex process involving many connected but separately functioning pieces, allowing for the cycling or phasing of our limited time and energies. There are four identifiable phases: editorial, production, promotion and distribution, in that order, and we try to have at least *some* of the pieces up to each of these four stages at all times, evenly dividing our energies among them. It is not until you get a project well into the third phase (promotion) that you stop spending money on it and start earning. Because our main support title, the *International Directory of Little Magazines and Small Presses,* is also the most expensive in its editing and production phases, we have a 2-3 month sag every year while the outgo of energy and money far exceeds the income, a phenomenon that profoundly affects everything else we're doing at that time, too. We have sought to prop the operation up during this period by putting on an advance-sale promotion just prior to the editing and production, and we've also attempted to shorten the time of these two phases by using computers to process and typeset the data, and fast-run printers to manufacture the book. But for every one of the fifteen years we've been doing the Directory we've had a rites-of-Spring crisis that shakes the whole operation.

Of the gross money it takes to live and run Dustbooks, about 25% comes from what the two of us can generate from *outside* the publishing operation (teaching, lecture, reading and consultant fees, royalties) and 75% is generated by Dustbooks itself. We figure that 15% goes to living costs, so that the publishing runs at about a 10% deficit annually, made up from the outside income. We work out of our home, which has been almost totally turned over to the operation (and its 20,000+ volume small press library). On the property, too, is a small print shop, which also houses a second office, and only quite recently were we forced to acquire off-property commercial warehousing for the book stock. All the packaging, shipping and mailing is done here (we're the biggest single customer of the local post office), as is the printing, assembling and mailing of the *Small Press Review,* monthly, and the many brochures, flyers and other material we release to both the small presses and our customers annually. Virtually all of the design, editing, paste-up and proofreading is done here as well. We employ one full-time person: an office manager; and one part-time person: a shipper, who also checks in and maintains the library, and helps us sort through the four hundred to five hundred books and magazines we receive every month, for review and Book Club prospects. Here's a list of where we spent our money, and in what proportion, in a recent year (rounded):

Salaries	11%
Postage	14%
Printing	22%
Supplies/repairs	5%
Typesetting	7%
Travel	3%
Fees/royalties	8%
Advertising (space)	1%
Data Processing	18%
Fed/State taxes	3%
Books for resale	8%

The pieces *within* the publishing operation (i.e. exclusive of our outside earnings) are several but far from disconnected. In fact, we are always amazed (and sometimes chagrinned) at how connected they are, and we're always reworking certain policies, designs and procedures to make them more independent. First, in the interest of our founding commitment, we publish four to seven titles of creative work annually—one or two novels, a couple of poetry collections, some criticism or essays, and an anthology or two. Only the anthologies (and only one of those) have ever shown any signs of earning back the production costs, but all of these titles, once they're in print and in stock, produce *some* annual income, and as we add more and more such titles to the list that income gets to be more and more significant. Of the thirty-three titles currently in the Dustbooks catalogue, twenty-two (or 66%) fall into this creative-work category. These titles generate about 10% of the Dustbooks gross income.

The second piece is what we call the "skein" of small-press information publications—three annuals and a monthly. While the creative work is the *spiritual* centerpiece of Dustbooks, these information titles constitute the *fiscal* centerpiece. First and foremost among them is the *International Directory of Little Magazines and Small Presses*, now in its fifteenth edition. This is the title around which the company must function if it is to remain solvent. This Int'l Directory lists over two thousand five hundred small presses and magazines worldwide and gives thirty-odd items of profile information about each of them. The *Directory of Small Magazine/Press Editors and Publishers* is an editor-alpha spinoff from the Int'l Directory, and helps locate editors by name and their associated presses and magazines. The third annual is the *Small Press Record of Books in Print,* a listing of ten thousand titles in-print-and-available from one thousand small presses worldwide. We have put in an enormous effort on this title, creating, starting with the sixth edition (1977), full access via four indexes: author, title, publisher and subject, and we hope the Record will become the standard Books In Print for the small presses. The monthly magazine is the *Small*

Press Review, which we've been publishing for ten years, and which as this writing is combined with the Small Press Book Club (see below). SPR reviews small press books and magazines, updates the annual Directories, runs news notes on small publishers and their projects, and for many years devoted a considerable proportion of its space to listing all the books and magazines received each month. The *Small Press Record of Books in Print* was in fact an outgrowth of these "received" listings in the late sixties, and is now the only running record of small press activity in the world. The huge cost of doing these information titles, particularly the annuals, is reflected as much in the data processing portion of our budget (18%) as in the printing or typesetting portions, for we use a computer to mount the information in machine-readable form, from which the typesetting onto galleys is only a matter of a few hours. And those few hours are the last ones before press time, allowing us to make last minute changes and corrections. The information titles, particularly the International Directory and the *Small Press Review*, generate about three quarters of Dustbooks' gross income, from sales, subscriptions, and advertising.

There are two other pieces in the Dustbooks pie, a string of how-to books on publishing and bookselling, and the Small Press Book Club, which together produce the final 15% of the gross income. The how-to books are designed to help prospective small publishers and self-publishers get started, and to help those already going to enhance production, promotion and distribution. For about half these titles on our list Dustbooks is only one distributor among many; for the other half Dustbooks is the original publisher. The how-to books help to fill out our commitment to small, independent publishing, while also promoting it.

We bought the Small Press Book Club from its ingenious founder, Robert Miles, in part because we were seeing so many extraordinary books published by small presses and wanted to get them a step beyond the review stage and into the hands of readers. It seemed a good way to test the distribution trail, and we hoped to piggyback much of the labor on the Dustbooks fulfillment set-up. We also had an invaluable source for selection in the books we were receiving for review in the *Small Press Review,* and, finally, we wanted to see why distributors, who should be the answer to the small publisher's prayers, were so often their purgatory. We bought the Club to see if we could make money and still pay our publishers, and we learned some interesting things. We did not, in our first year, make money, but we profited from the cash flow the Club provided. In small publishing one book often finances another, and the larger the publisher the less direct that relationship is. Thus, the Club is one of those pieces by which Dustbooks manages to keep on publishing without having to wait for each book to finance the next. It is one of the ways we manage to keep all of our titles in print—and for one full year we never missed a monthly Club consignment payment to our publishers. We also learned that, in this book club anyway, literature sells better than anything else, and certain careful and imaginative marketing gets response. On several occasions we paired up similar but previously hard-to-move titles offered a slight discount and some good descriptive copy, and sold out our stock. We've sold literary criticism and modern experimental fiction this way, and in the case of the latter reordered and sold that, too!

Aside from cash flow, then, the Book Club provides us with the opportunity to see how well we score, to match our tastes and preferences and, yes, our second guesses with our membership of about one thousand five hundred. In 1978 we tried another combination of separate parts, and merged the *Book Club Selectionlist* with the *Small Press Review*, giving us a new set of Club selections monthly instead of the previous bi-monthly selection lists and a faster turnover. It also permitted us to save the cost of a separate mailing. We hoped to increase both the subscribers to the magazine and the members of the Club, and to expose both groups to both reviews and books they can order directly from us. The combination has produced interesting results—neither ruinous nor particularly remunerative, but interesting. Subscriptions to SPR have increased, automatically increasing membership in the Book Club, but sales of books are smaller than when we did separate mailings to a separate list of members. We sell fewer copies of more books to a larger number of subscribers. We are able, however, to maintain the Club because of the combination, and to do so without the massive investment in advertising that traditionally sustains any book club against the ravages of attrition. We have also discovered that there is a serious interest among our readers in single issues of literary magazines, so much that we have been offering five books and five magazines a month for some time now, and the magazines often outsell the books. This is especially true of the "special issues" of literary magazines that are becoming more and more frequent.

The Book Club will, for the time being, stay in SPR where it can be maintained at its present level. If there is one lesson to be learned from small press literary publishing, it is that enduring is an alternative to the initial splash of success. You can gain attention and establish a reputation with massive investments of advertising capital, but you can also do it, and gain sales, simply by being around, publishing consistently and with taste, wearing down resistence with a steady stream of small successes.

For us editing is two processes. In the first we accumulate, attract, gather; in the second we select, discard, polish, hone. In our how-to and information publishing we often conceive of projects ourselves and find someone to handle them, or respond to ideas, plans, rather than full-fledged manuscripts, and help finance the completion of the book. We have published several extremely successful double issues of the *Small Press Review* built around a particular theme on which we invite input. One of these issues, on reviewing, got over a hundred very substantial comments from the small press world, and over $4,000 worth of advertising. For the magazine we maintain a list of reviewers we can count on, and accept unsolicited reviews as well. But in our literary publishing it is the second editorial process with which we most often contend.

Most small presses whose editorial predilections are formed around a precise nucleus, a style, a school, a genre, a subject category, use only solicited manuscripts, which generally tends to determine the realtionship between writer and editor from the beginning of the writing. Sometimes it is already formed by a ready set of mutual sympathies. At Dustbooks all the literary manuscripts we read and publish are unsolicited. The editor works on a manuscript without personal knowledge of the author. Unquestionably the process of selection and rejection is affected by economics. How big a production project is it? Does it have any chance of sale? What is selling now? But if we had to characterize the basis on which the editorial decision is most frequently made, the biological reaction that says *go*, it wouldn't be the Hemingway *gut* but the Dustbooks *ear*. We like a high and original style, and felicity of language is our idea of virtue. Literary publishing, in the Dustbooks canon, affords some decent luxuries, but it draws the reins on other indulgences. We publish what we like, what pleases and excites our ears, and that is the most selfish and self-indulgent luxury a publisher can enjoy. But we cannot, as we most certainly do with other publishing, calculate how much we will make, who will buy it, or whether it is a profitable venture. The literary publishing philosophy is like the attitude that refuses grants or awards. It is an attitude you act on because you can afford to. And so far, though we've made some mistakes, we can afford to.

What that philosophy requires of us is first to do justice to the work we choose by giving it all we can afford in production, and that necessity requires that we do much of the work ourselves. We often enlist the aid of the author in finding a cover design, in finding an illustrator, and in getting some of the promotional material ready. There is an extra effort to bring the book to the attention of the media, the middlemen, and the readers. Instead of publishing a seller, we publish a book and work to make it sell, reversing the process governing our information publishing. The effort here involves using all of the resources we have developed through the success of the information titles.

Once we have accepted a manuscript the major editorial work is done, largely because we accept what we like. There are, however, some editorial possibilities left. We sometimes return a manuscript with a report suggesting what we like, and what we don't like, and hope for a revision. We have suggested deletions, or additional inclusions, and have requested additional material to consider for this purpose in, for example, a manuscript of poems. We spend this editorial effort in an attempt to become sensitive to what the author has done, has tried to do, and to try to perfect the congruence between them. Sometimes there is also some mediation between writer and reader, as in the case of our suggesting an index/glossary for a modular science fiction-fantasy novel.

We can and do work with our authors through revisions, but in our literary publishing, the initial investment is time, rather than money. We generally offer no cash advance on literary titles, but do pay a respectable 15% of the annual gross sales. We keep these titles in print virtually forever, and even if some of them don't sell well, we still believe in them. And when their share of luck is parcelled out, the account books may add their chorus to our faith.

"Distribution" is often cited as the ineluctable barrier to small publisher success. That may be true, but the ineradicable nightmare is printing—and printers. This, we're convinced, along with other maddening details of the production process, is what drives small publishers to quit—not the inability to sell books. Printing can take *all* your time, and though you're paying him handsomely, you cannot depend on a printer to feel that mere payment is cause enough to lift any of the production burdens off you as a publisher. Most printers think they're publishers, see little more in publishing than printing, when in fact printing should be less than 20% of what publishing is all about. We have not beaten this punishing syndrome, but we've developed a three-level approach that spreads out the nightmare. First, we have our own print shop in which until very recently, we produced the *Small Press Review* monthly, and where we still make all our flyers, forms for gathering small press information, letterhead, envelopes and so on. We do *not*—and this is critical—print anything for anyone else for money, nor do we play in the print shop, or do much experimenting. It is important to us that the equipment be in operation only 10-15% of the time—any more than that and we're becoming printers, not publishers—and that we maintain a serious, businesslike and utilitarian attitude toward the hardware. In the half-dozen years we've had the shop we've saved ourselves the original price of the equipment ($5,000) three times each year. If we did not have the shop that 22% of our budget that now goes to printing would be 40%—except that we wouldn't be around to *have* a budget.

Though some of our output is a bit second-rate, and there is often a sameness to our forms and flyers, that step away from our own shop is the one that would break us as a literary publisher.

Our second level of printing is the use of short-run experts, medium-sized manufacturers set up for book runs of five hundred to ten thousand who do quality work at such competitive prices that they can produce a book for you in both cloth and paperback almost cheaper than you yourself could buy the paper for it. There are dozens of these now in the United States, and when we have the specifications together on a given book (size, pages, colors, print run) we release such specs to as many as are on our bid-list—and take the best deal. Since 1970, when Edwards Brothers of Ann Arbor, Michigan, pioneered this short-run concept, these small manufacturers have become so competitive and efficient that no book takes longer than twenty five days from camera-ready copy, and there are few hitches. *Caveat:* It is tempting to develop a "working relationship" with a single printer, and much of the time this is good, for they learn your inclinations and tastes as a publisher (and these guys *know* the difference between printing and publishing). But we've found that this makes us something of a captive account, and as such there is the danger of being taken for granted. We now make it clear to every printer we deal with that each job is a new one, to be subjected to competitive bidding. We also make an effort to continually use new manufacturers (new to us), and to add and subtract names from our bid-list. On the other hand there *are* times when a "proven" printer should be used even though his prices may be higher for a given job. We learned not to experiment with our must-get-out International Directory in the summer of '77, when we tried a new manufacturer who promised a twenty-five day turnaround—and delivered in sixty, upsetting our operation for two years hence.

The third level of printing for us is local printing, jobs which we either do not have time for in our own shop, or are slightly too big for us while being too small for the larger manufacturer. Here again we resist becoming captive, and we've found that the existence of our own print shop, and our knowledge of printing, has a significant effect on the service and pricing we get from the locals, for they know we are, in the last analysis, independent of them.

As with printing, we have come to think of the final marketing of our books as a multi-level process. The small press destiny lies with mail order, first and foremost, and at Dustbooks we spend great time, effort and money on the maintenance of a file of eighteen thousand names which we've collected over the years. Within this file are ten thousand names of people and institutions who've bought something from us in the last eighteen months, and at present we are busy redesigning our programs to cut the list to just those names. For us a mailing list is too large when it becomes more than 50% non-responders. We've also built what we call "product codes" into this list, so we can sort it by type of purchase and find those who've purchased our literary titles, our information titles, and our how-to titles. We can also tabulate the codes *and* the money each has earned in a given period—something that helps us pay royalties and know what we're doing. We use this mailing list two to four times a year to release catalogues and flyers, and this constitutes our major promotional effort.

At the next level for us are book jobbers, middleman dealers who sell to libraries and even (as with Baker & Taylor) to bookstores. We deal with about a hundred of these, and they are a good, steady, single-title, short-discount market. They generally pay within sixty days, and respond accurately and quickly. They buy copies of virtually all our literary titles, and are in fact responsible for the sale of 75% of the hardback copies sold for these titles. Though they occasionally order in large lots, most of our business with jobbers is in small orders of one to fifteen books which stream in steadily, often several a day. The best of these jobbers—Baker & Taylor, Blackwell, Eastern Book, Coutts, Midwest Library Service—seem perfectly suited to small press literary publishing, and our guess is that the future of the small publisher is more closely tied to these bookdealers than to vans and bookfairs. We've bet on jobbers and lost, too. Richard Abel was the biggest, a $30-million a year operation in Portland, Oregon, that went bankrupt. All of which illustrates that the jobber swims in corporate channels and occasionally loses a fin to larger sharks.

We classify *agents* as those who advance cash for either long-term subscriptions (one year plus) or on a prepublication basis for our annuals. These outfits, like Ebsco, MacGregor, are all computer based, take about 15%, and buy only periodicals of one kind or another. We have developed sliding price scales to encourage them to take longer-term subscriptions for their clients (mostly libraries), and we do a significant business with about fifteen of them. They renew automatically, often for two or three dozen of their customers at a time, always with up-front money—which can give you a boost on a dry day. A large bloc of the subscriptions to the *Small Press Review* is held by agents, as are several hundred on-going prepub orders for our information annuals.

Next level down for us are the wholesale distributors and bookstores. We work with a couple dozen wholesalers who, instead of regular small orders at short discounts, take large quantities of stock on consignment at anywhere from 40% to 51% and report and pay quarterly. We work regularly with Bookpeople, and cooperate with the small press distribution organizations set up by programs sponsored by the Coordinating Council of Literary Magazines and the National Endowment for the Arts. We've found this business, along with bookstores, to be the least suited to small publishing, because it ties up huge amounts of stock, takes deep discounting, is subject to inordinate returns, and pays off so slowly that inflation all but absorbs any profit you might make. Often, to get paid at all, we have to exert energy we cannot spare, so that it negatively affects other phases of our publishing. Still, to have the books out in the stores is important, especially for an author—who tends to think the publisher is remiss when he can't find his book on the shelf. Wholesalers and retailers work better for a larger publisher who can exert economic pressure. For the small publisher economic pressure is a scarce commodity, and were it not for our International Directory, which has some demand, Dustbooks would have a very limited leverage for payment of accounts. And all it takes to kick the wholesale/retail profits for a small

175

publisher into the loss column is for one wholesaler to go bust carrying large amounts of that publisher's stock, for then the money *and* the stock are gone. In a recent year Dustbooks, though it holds its wholesaler/retailer business to less than 20% of the gross, lost about $5,000 to bankruptcies, disappearances and inflation by late payment. Most recently we have joined the Small Press program initiated by Ingram, the largest paperback distributor in the U.S. Though the program requires some investment of capital by the publisher in advertising through their catalogue and microfiche listings, Ingram pays for its stock. We hope that the program may solve the problems of payment and bookkeeping inherent in handling individual bookstore accounts, and difficult for a small staff. If so, it will be well worth the deep discount. Whatever else, it is an opportunity to present our titles to a large number of bookstore buyers who would be otherwise inaccessible.

For two years we had an independent bookstore salesman on the road representing Dustbooks along with a couple dozen other small publishers. He opened up about three hundred fifty bookstore accounts for us, and in fact was the prime mover of our literary titles. His name is Leonard Smukler, and his technique was to read excerpts and poems from the books to the bookstore managers. He is so effective at this that he often doesn't even need copies of the books with him, and in fact sells books in advance of publication as readily as after. This, of course, does not help sell the book once it's in the store, so Smukler developed yet a further plan: a lecture/reading series (paid) for the authors of the books he handles, in the hope of generating enough interest to get people into bookstores to buy the books. Unfortunately, as is true of many distribution efforts, Smukler's did not adequately meet his expenses in travel and promotion. He stopped selling in 1978.

The author's willing energy is really the key to the sale of a literary title, particularly for the small publishers, who tend to publish unknowns. If an author will not acknowledge or promote his/her own book, that book is dead before it starts. When Fulton's *Grassman* was published by Thorp Springs Press in 1974, we embarked on a ten thousand mile trip, selling the novel directly to bookstores, visiting reviewers, and doing readings and lectures across the country in twenty-five states. After that trip we wrote a book about it, *American Odyssey,* and were more convinced than ever that a novel or book of poems requires the author's energy above all else, that an author can no longer "just write" if there is to be any distribution of his/her book. Incidentally, we lost money on the trip, but the longer range effect on *The Grassman's* sale was profound, and it has now been sold to the movies. And furthermore *American Odyssey* has itself, as a book, made money, and is still a steady seller for Dustbooks.

We've had a million special marketing ideas over the decade and a half of Dustbooks' life. Most of them haven't worked, but some have, and we keep on getting the ideas whether we like it or not. Occasionally you can dovetail a good marketing idea with a good editorial idea—and sell some literature. Back in '75, when we first brought out *American Odyssey,* and with the Bicentennial staring at us like a ghost from something past, we thought to make a series of our literary titles. We called it the "American Dust" Series, and each novel, book of poetry or collection of essays we've done since has been numbered into the series, which now has thirteen titles. As the idea of the series outlived and outgrew its original occasional origin, its shape also began to grow and change, so that now it continues by adding books not *like* the others but unlike them, chronicling the geographical, stylistic, ethnic, and genre diversity and richness of writing in the contemporary Americas. The Series has taken its time catching on, but more and more now we see orders from faraway places asking for the title *and* its number in the "American Dust" Series. We have even acquired some standing orders for all future titles in it. It has been a way to give some quick, early identity to new literary books and authors, and it is also a way to keep a certain amount of buying attention on the older titles in the series. And just to show you how *not* to miss a chance to promote your books, we will list the "American Dust" Series herewith:

#1 *American Odyssey* by Len Fulton with Ellen Ferber
#2 *Moving To Antarctica,* edited by Margaret Kaminski
#3 *Captive Voices* (Folsom Prison anthology)

Finally, there is something particularly American about this patchwork approach we take at Dustbooks. And from Melville's Ishmael, the jack-of-all-trades, to the quilting bee, Americans have covered ground by extending, joining, taping, stapling together. It's colorful, if not perfectly matched, and whole if not perfectly unified. At Dustbooks, at least, it is very functional. It keeps us warm.

POOR AND PURE
by William Phillips

William Phillips is editor of PARTISAN REVIEW.

One day in 1947, a letter arrived at the office of the magazine, signed by Allan Dowling, a poet, and a partner in City Investing Company, asking us whether we would be interested in enlarging the scope and increasing the frequency of the magazine. Dowling said *Partisan Review* was the only magazine which could continue the great tradition of the *Dial,* and he would be glad to help financially to make this possible. One reacts on such occasions with very mixed feelings. We were, of course, elated, but we were not sure it was not a hoax, and we had all the anxieties aroused by the prospect of unknown changes. For whatever else it meant, such a move suggested that the magazine might leave the world of the "little, littles," in which poverty was a guarantee of purity, and literary magazines were sustained by a community outside the cultural marketplace. We would be entering a world, we feared, dominated by considerations of circulation, publicity, the size of authors' fees, budgets, salaries—that is, the normal world in which enterprises live. This shift to entrepeneurial normality was accentuated by the fact that Dowling wanted *Partisan Review* to become a monthly.

But you do not say no to progress, expansion, financial stability, the opportunity to pay higher fees and presumably to get contributions that could not be had at the old, low rates. Part of the problem of non-commercial literary magazines—as of most non-profit cultural activities—is that in our society they constitute a form of mixed economy. Half a magazine is purely literary, having to do only with questions of quality and cultural interest, and is entirely impractical and utopian; the other half, however, is submerged in business, a losing and not very dynamic business, to be sure, but still it is occupied with such things as income and expenses, insurance, salaries, tax reports, distribution, subscriptions—with all the machinery of profitable capitalist enterprises applied to unprofitable ones. The result is that the purely editorial activities of a noncommercial magazine tend to get mixed up with the business operations. In commercial magazines, the confusion is normal, for the need for sales and advertising naturally affects the editorial side. In fact, the so-called editorial side is a packaging enterprise, in which considerations of quality and those of sales are permitted to be merged, though editors often maintain, partly out of habit, partly to keep their self-respect, that they publish things only because they are good. This state of affairs is as it should be in a mass culture that plays the numbers game and prides itself on the number of people who buy paperbacks, go to concerts and museums, and get through college. But the drive for quantity—which is essentially a drive for profit, despite all the rationalizations celebrating the spread of culture—is infectious, and little, literary, noncommercial magazines get bitten by the commercial bug, and get involved in promotion and distribution schemes and in trying to balance the budget. Even if some editors are aware that these considerations are transplanted from commercial magazines, still they are under pressure from foundations and individual donors to try to increase circulation and reduce the

180

deficit. Many years ago, a large foundation invited several writers and editors to discuss with the directors the problem of financing literary magazines. At one point, one of the directors asked us why we could not make a profit or at least break even. I thought of the character in Dostoyevsky's *Possessed,* who, during an argument about the existence of God, said "There must be a God, otherwise how could I be a Captain." I was about to say that if non-commercial enterprises, like literary magazines, could make a profit, there would be no job for the directors of the foundation. But I did not feel such a remark would be appreciated. The obvious solution—too obvious to be followed—would be for foundations and the government to support completely the leading non-commercial ventures in all fields: the leading operas, theatres, dance groups, museums, literary magazines, etc., with a supplementary fund for new and experimental ventures. This is, in fact, the procedure in many European countries, including the communist ones, where the government supports magazines as well as other cultural activities, and editors are concerned only with the contents of their publications. I know there are many arguments against such complete financing, but they all seem spurious, and based on the myths of capitalist incentives and individual initiative.

Anyway, being human and children of our time, we jumped at the chance to put out a magazine without constantly worrying about money, and to do the things we were prevented from doing for lack of money. Since Dowling wanted a monthly, this meant a larger office, a bigger staff, and a much faster pace. We figured out how much we needed in our own amateurish fashion, which always led to underestimating expenses and overestimating income, and Dowling agreed to put in forty thousand dollars a year. We moved uptown to Forty-fifth Street and Broadway into a building that Dowling owned. The office was comfortable enough and not too posh, but the neighborhood seemed grotesquely out of place for us, as though to remind us daily that this was not where we belonged. Most incongruous was to see Delmore Schwartz sitting half-dazed and uncoordinated in his own office, like some comic version of a midtown executive, or looking distractedly out of the window at a world as foreign to him as

181

Disneyland. But we did learn to have lunch at Lindy's, with its famous cherry cheese cake, or at some of the sumptuous cafeterias that were still going at that time. We hired a managing editor, an assistant editor for production, a business manager and a secretary, and we were in business. The production editor was Boden Broadwater, Mary McCarthy's husband at that time, who had a sharp tongue but was very competent and efficient. I have never been very astute in hiring people, but Boden was by far the best of the staff we chose. The secretary was unusually advanced. One day I discovered that her letters had no capitals, all lower case, including the addresses on the envelopes. When I told her this was not the usual practice, she said she used *avant-garde* punctuation, which she thought appropriate to an *avant-garde* magazine. Delmore Schwartz and William Barrett were not exactly what would now be called working editors, that is, editors who work on manuscripts, deal with writers, and generally press for new ideas and pieces without themselves being pressed. Philip Rahv would say that they were not really editors, though he said that of almost everybody who ever worked on the magazine. Perhaps they could be described as intelligent and gifted writers who supported the chief editors, gave excellent advice, and corrected their mistakes.

Putting out a monthly, compared to a quarterly, was almost full-time work. We came to the office every day, and thought about the magazine constantly, and, as a consequence, had less time to write ourselves. How good was *Partisan Review* as a monthly? I think it was still very good, probably the best literary and cultural publication around. In addition to the writers already associated with the magazine, we published in this period such new figures as Leslie Fiedler, Wylie Syper, Hans Meyerhof, Paul Bowles, John Berryman, Nicola Chiaromonte, Irving Howe, Isaac Rosenfeld, Bernard Malamud, Weldon Kees, Anatole Broyard, Vernon Watkins, Robert Warshow, Richard Ellmann, Robert Gorham Davis, R.W. Flint, Elizabeth Bowen, Tennessee Williams, Joseph Frank, E.E. Cummings, Richard Chase, Milton Klonsky, Francis Fergusson, Raymond Aron, Dudley Fitts, Philip Toynbee, Cyril Connoly, Arthur Mizener, Karl Schapiro, Marius Bewley, James Baldwin, Parker Tyler, Henri

Michaux, Vladimir Nabokov, Jose Luis Borges, Karl Jaspers, Wallace Markfield, Arthur Schlesinger, Patricia Blake, Angus Wilson, Allen Tate, Niccolo Tucci, Oscar Handlin, A.J. Ayer, Paul Tillich, Erich Auerbach, Albert Moravia, Diana Trilling, Isaiah Berlin, and others. The list is a long one, but I cite it mainly to indicate that as a monthly the magazine continued its earlier momentum. Because it was possible to pay more for contributions—the munificent sum of two cents a word—and because of the general acceleration, the contents probably had greater variety. We tried to maintain the earlier polemical spirit, which was one way of relating to and affecting the cultural atmosphere of the time. Clement Greenberg's strong art comments appeared regularly; there were pieces about atonal music by René Leibowitz and Kurt List; and the shifts in the cultural scene were examined in lengthy symposia on *The State of American Writing* and *Religion and the Intellectuals*. But the change from a quarterly to a monthly was more than a change of frequency. It is probably impossible to document my feeling about the change, but I feel that the stepping up of the tempo produces a greater emphasis on topicality, on journalistic interest, and something called readership, which involves both the size and the nature of the audience. A monthly is also usually closer to the world of the commercial publications, not only in content but in a concern with circulation, distribution, promotion, and advertising. The slower pace of a quarterly permits it to be content with publishing things that may not be popular, and to rely on a smaller, devoted audience of writers, teachers, and sophisticated professionals who identify with the aims of the magazine. In this respect, and quite unconsciously and without design, we were moving into another era, one in which, as writers and readers were slowly being homogenized into a more general culture, writers were becoming divided into those with academic and scholarly interests and those who were adapting to the need for writing for a larger market. This is why, in my opinion, so large a gap has developed between the literary magazines, particularly the quarterlies and those devoted mainly to criticism, and the more popular monthlies, like *Esquire, The New Yorker, Harpers,* and *Atlantic.* It is also why today students of a subject become specialists,

183

leaving the intellectually exciting but risky task of generalizing to the cultural journalists. There are, of course, other compelling reasons why this has become an age of specialization—not the least of which are the complexity of knowledge and the feeling of helplessness in the face of the overwhelming problems confronting us—but the fact is that the academic climate has become generally conducive to intense work within narrow limits.

Partisan Review's life as a monthly lasted three years. It was pleasant, relatively carefree, much like a cruise in which you left behind familiar routines and worries and got a glimpse of other worlds. We learned something about Madison Avenue techniques, and we learned something about advertising, promotion, and distribution. And we also learned something about the relation of a literary magazine to its potential audience. We reached a peak of about thirteen or fourteen thousand buyers—readers are calculated differently, usually for our kind of publication, about eleven readers per copy—which probably represented as large a circulation as was possible then without radically changing the contents of the magazine and without spending hundreds of thousands of dollars. There has been considerable speculation about the size of the potential audience for a serious literary and cultural magazine, and I have thought about this question which is constantly posed by naive editors and people who contribute money to these magazines, who have absorbed the American ideal of increased sales and balanced budgets, and I am convinced that the question posed in a simple, abstract form is a non-question, a belief in size and numbers put in the form of a question. For the answer depends on how much money is spent on promotion. If we could have spent, say, a few hundred thousand dollars on promotion, I do not know how many copies we would have sold, but I have no doubt it would have been enormously larger. On the other hand, it would have been a thoroughly wasteful and irresponsible act, based on the false analogy with commercial magazines. The economy of commercial magazines rests on the simple principle of buying circulation, which then pays off in increased advertising which depends on the size and exploitability of the circulation.

184

In 1951, Allan Dowling told us he had to cut down his contribution—which had risen to over forty thousand dollars a year—because of his own financial troubles. He was getting out of a difficult marriage and into a divorce from a Bulgarian opera singer whose tastes, I was told, were expensive. We cut back the magazine to a bi-monthly and Dowling cut down his contribution to twelve thousand dollars for a year. After that he said he could no longer afford even this much, and *Partisan Review* became a quarterly again, moved back downtown, and resumed its old pure and marginal existence. We took a little, dark office on the ground floor on West Twelfth Street, reduced our staff to one business and production manager and one secretary, and occasional volunteers from women's colleges during work-study periods. That office was most notable for being the place where Saul Bellow met his second wife Sandra, who had come down from Bennington.

A REVOLUTION
OF TWERPS
by Felix Stefanile

Felix Stefanile is editor of Sparrow Press

Though a few editors, like me, enjoy publicly tweaking the
noses of the public officials of the Literature Program of the
National Endowment for the Arts, with sometimes humorous,
never corrective, outcome, the general principle followed by
most serious little magazine editors I know remains stern and
simple: one gets on with the work, without distraction, without the waste of time of vain polemics. As this essay will go on
to indicate, much of the small literary publisher's work is
lonely drudgery. The work gets done despite today's hoopla
and hype about a poetry renaissance, the ever-burgeoning
creative writing courses, the reading circuit of Spasmodic
performers of verse, the so-called awareness explosion, the
"I-want-to-be-Me" mobs that have infiltrated the university
system and made the Language Learning Arts revolt a favorite
fraud and grants-game. It becomes difficult for the genuine

186

article, the poet-publisher, to resist developing, even against his or her will, a Siege, or Burning Citadel mentality. Taste, sure taste, by which I do not mean a secret formula, but vision, in the company of courage, has never been so important to our letters as it is today. One must *resist,* but one must also keep up with the current, no matter how miasmic, nor how cacophonous, the surrounding tide. A sense of humor helps, and a steady head. One perseveres. I urge the reader who follows what I have to say to accept me at my word when I state that I hardly take myself as seriously as my at times cavilling tone may lead one to consider. My correspondence, and my acquaintances bring me many a belly-laugh, and a few warm friendships. The enemy I write about is most frequently a fool, not a villain. The "revolution" I constantly refer to is largely a revolution of Twerps. As for poetry, the Muse has always been, at least since Plato's time, under siege. She will perdure, beyond the present age, even as Penelope outlasted the Suitors and the sycophants. What a lovely thought.

I prefer the use of a term like little magazine, or small publisher, to today's in-phrase, small press, to describe what I do. Little is honest, publisher is neutral. Small press has developed an organizational connotation I do not wish to be associated with, and is, besides, Federal grants jargon. It also smacks of tired Sixties nostalgia: small as opposed to big, with, of course, the big press as capitalist ogre, and confrontation implicit with the small press, the white offset Pegasus. At one time there was talk of a small press revolution. The revolution, as usual, took place somewhere else. The young conspirators applied, instead, for Federal grants, and got them.

Small press makes all sorts of pretentious claims. The little magazine has always been a publisher of books, as well as issues. In my youth there were scores of magazines like *Kaleidograph,* or *Wings,* with their prize volumes, some pretty good, presenting the work of a single poet. There were charming book, and booklet magazines, some monthly, like the splendid New Directions Poet of the Month pamphlets. How about the Work in Progress issues, so common in the past—of Joyce, for instance—that were published by the reviews? The truly small literary presses we have—as contrasted to the little magazines—depend for their currency on little magazine activity. It is not the other way around. The irony of bandying these terms about, of course, is that the modesty I seem to be so loudly proclaiming, has its own built-in time-bomb. A pretty example would be Vassar Miller's magnificent sonnets, "Bout with Burning," and "Ceremony," which originally appeared in my magazine in an edition of two hundred copies, and went on to become two of the most anthologized poems of the Fifties and early Sixties. I am not saying we must keep our light under a bushel, but I am urging we stick to straight talk about the kind of publishing we do, and avoid cant.

I have never deluded myself as to the importance of *Sparrow*. I have never wanted to compete with Random House, or Doubleday. For philosophical reasons I shall go into later I believe such a fanciful contest is absurd to contemplate, and foolish to propose. And I have never thought of poetry publishing as an ideological crusade, or revolution. My motivation for entering the field was, in truth, quite personal and selfish. I wanted to live the life of poetry. In the marvelous Italian-American neighborhood where I grew up and lived (Corona, Queens) my relatives used to refer to the poems I wrote as "stories," my dates were likely to be stenographers, not muses, my best friend and beer-buddy was a rug-salesman at Macy's. I was a civil servant. I was surrounded by love, and the aroma of good cooking, but my life was as far removed from Letters as though, at birth, I had gotten off on the moon. I had attended John Malcolm Brinnin's poetry workshop at the Y in uptown Manhattan. I had discovered James Boyer May's intriguing and permanently unreplaced "evolving directory" of little magazines. My poems were beginning to circulate. It didn't take me long to realize what I could do to commit myself to poetry. The idea, in 1954, of starting a poetry journal immediately drew my wife Selma's enthusiastic support. We went into our savings, applied for a vacation loan, and started planning issues. In those days there was no thought of grants, but some people quite literally found us out, and became patrons. Let me gratefully acknowledge the earliest ones: Richard Ashman, Americo Giannicchi, Lawrence Lipton, William J. Noble, Helen M. Rainsford. And, of course, my mother, who stuffed a ten-dollar bill in my lapel pocket whenever I visted, "for the magazine." She made me feel like the local bookie, and I liked the feeling well. Soon Selma and I were in deep, swimming in poetry.

My perfervid correspondents during my editorial novitiate were Cid Corman, of *Origin,* and August Derleth, of Arkham House. As I have written of Corman in another essay, and paraphrase here, they wrote letters the way the experts move pianos. Their communications had scope and versatility, their probes were full of force, they bound their arguments in all sorts of strong connections, and they never let go. They wrote in the old manner, page after page, and they shot their answers back, usually in two or three days, like a dare. Two of the most valorous and cantankerous individuals I have ever known, full of high prejudice and unstinting devotion, they never patronized me, and—what I prize just as well—they never returned to my mistakes, but continued the barrage of admonitions, suggestions, observations, reminders, discoveries, introductions. Derleth is gone, and with the passage of time, Corman and I seem to have stopped corresponding, but nothing can dim the glamor of those years, and I count myself fortunate to have had access to the wisdom of two such rigorous and sensitive poet-publishers.

They were worlds apart in taste and practice, enjoyed different kinds of "success." Corman's stance has not wavered since his youth: solitude, buttressed by vivid, important friendships, and a search for excellence in his own work and the work of others that has earned him solid, international esteem, especially among fellow-poets. Derleth prided himself on the fact that he wrote both for the slicks and the little magazines, and was able to earn a pretty good living. Certain poets were staple items of derision in the cranky column he wrote for the Madison *Capital-Times.* Both men stand, however, for the American mucker tradition—immense talents refusing careerist bondage, scorning professional protocol, and often—at great, personal sacrifice—breaking new ground, and along the way, sometimes, old friendships. Such writers will have their way, and we are all richer for their stubborn independence.

All the more interesting to relate is that they often,

unbeknownst to each other, concurred in their ideas. For instance, each insisted on the importance of the backlist for me. They warned about getting rid of "old" copies of magazine issues, or chap books. Here is a profound little magazine irony. Warehouse costs for slow-selling items can whack the big publisher. He has to pay rent, he has to worry about spoilage, he becomes involved in an intricate web of fulfillment and transport exigencies. Sometimes, out of "financial necessity," he remainders his books, and even pulps them for re-use. (The reader will agree that this is a helluva way to encourage literature.) To this sad tale what has *Sparrow* to add? Only that without the backlist, we would have been hard put to survive. We are still selling books that did not sell ten years ago. We are still providing libraries with replacement copies for past issues. We have a random, but rewarding collector's trade, including some publications listed in the Serendipity catalogue, and elsewhere, that now command a price in the $85-$100 range. We do not set out to perform any of these functions deliberately, and we most certainly do not consider ourselves exquisite producers of precious volumes to be cherished like expensive china, but we know our job, and such things happen. The backlist is but one example, of many, of the spuriousness of making comparisons between big and little publishing. The two are different worlds, and to brand whatever we do, either in concert, or against each other, by the name of competition, is naive. This fact of life brings into focus one of the unsubtler aspects of National Endowment for the Arts error. Government support of poetry, through its various grant-programs and projects, (PITS, CCLM, COSMEP, Literature Panel, etc.), has persuaded too many small publishers that with "more" they can reach audiences "now"; I mean the day after yesterday. The result is a steady lava-flow, often in unreasonably large, unpriced and "FREE" editions of poetry books sent streaming through the mails and flooding the arts festivals and poetry readings of the nation. It is an assault impossible to dodge, like a saturation terror campaign. I have even noted such NEA-financed broadsides (dreadnaughts) stacked on the counter, and "free" of course, at our local delicatessen next to the candy jar. These books, the whole paraphernalia of

190

happy art, are quite, quite frequently unreadable, so that along with the contemporary phenomenon of the Published Poem, we have the wasteful monstrosity of the Unread Book. We have come to the age of fast-food poetry. What all this frenzy has to do with the concept of great audiences I don't know, but I relish the thought of the problem it creates for the kind of grant-applying little magazine editor I have in mind. Like a hyperactive child, he has to have the hype, he has to go big, he has to throw his bombs. Exactly like Big Brother, he has to get rid of his warehousing problem and stay in fiscal line, in his case the next round of grants, which work by schedule and deadline. The Published Poem in the Unread Book has to be gotten rid of in a hurry. The answer: poetry dumping. A generation of young readers is being trained not to buy books, but to wait for their free copies in the mail!

Up until the Sixties little magazines were generally of two modes. There were journals like *Origin,* or *Black Mountain Review,* for which the guiding thrust was the editor's search for poets of a "shared aesthetic." He was determined in what he wanted of excellence, deliberately exclusive, and actively went after material. The Cormans, the Creeleys, solicited work, often from specific poets, like Charles Olson, or from a specific band of poets. I do not mean to give the impression that this type of editor labored with blinders on, immune to new talent. Quite the opposite is true. But operating as he did with certain tough ideals in view, a writer had to be pretty well on the mark, and within the editor's consuming field of vision to receive any real encouragement. (It is of interest, and to the point, to note here that at the height of his popularity in our country, among Dylan Thomas's severest critics were several editors of the "shared aesthetic" camp. Thomas's work simply didn't fit, or didn't always fit their idea of what a poem was supposed to be.) The best example of success among this group remains, to my thinking—I use the inexact but stubborn term—the Black Mountain poets. The "shared aesthetic" mode is in an honorable tradition, surely dating at least from the period of Dante Gabriel Rossetti's *The Germ.*

The other prevailing mode for little magazines used to be the "eclectic." The eclectic magazine is anathema to the "shared aesthetic" group because it emphasizes not so much vision, as faith, faith in the variety of poetry. In a true sense the editor waits for the material to come in, and ideally has no preconceptions as to what he will take, aside from his own personal taste, and an amicable ego. *Poetry,* under Henry Rago's direction, was a generally lively model of eclecticism. There were also, of course, some magazines, like the splendid but short-lived *Poetry-New York,* which attempted the best of both worlds, sometimes emphasizing specific critical themes, as when it printed Olson's essay on Projective Verse, alongside its miscellany of poems by people like Richard Wilbur. Often, as even today, the two groups fitted well together.

The shared aesthetic editor has a strong soul, on the heavenlier side of bigotry. He will nurture his poetic charges, bully them, plan whole issues around a group or an individual, and proselytize for his wares like an old-time preacher. He is more likely than the eclecticist to be holding forth on an FM radio station, gathering cohorts together, shooting off the guns. Filippo Marinetti, Wyndham Lewis, Ezra Pound, are all progenitors of this visionary mode. Like Robert Bly later, they conquered for art. The eclectic editor has a strong stomach, which he masks behind a faint, occasionally bilious smile. If his fate is anything like that of the editor of *Sparrow* he knows that before the year is out he shall have read over three thousand five hundred manuscripts—perhaps twenty thousand poems—90% of which will be pure, unadulterated, triple-threat junk. He is panning for gold in a muddy stream. The former type of editor is often accused of elitism—today, my favorite dirty word—the latter of moral slackness. Both do their work, and let me hasten to add that the miscellany is of noble lineage too, and performs its own valuable task, being more likely to reach to poetry societies, the club groups, the "appreciators." To cite another eminent graduate of the little magazine, William Stafford, we can be sure his early career was helped by exposure in the eclectic magazines of his youth. History proves we don't all write like Charles Olson, or Allen Ginsberg, or J. V. Cunningham.

It should be obvious by now why I decided in favor of an eclectic magazine. In the first place, I knew few poets, and was hardly a leader. In the second place, I knew little enough

about poetry: *Sparrow* was to become my research commitment. Also, like an energetic novice, I was greedy for con-
tacts. *I was making friends*. I didn't choose *Sparrow*; *Sparrow*
chose me. A roster of our contributors in those early years
would read like an honor roll of the newer poets of the Fifties,
and most of them are still around today—John Tagliabue,
James Schevill, Harold Witt, Barriss Mills, Gael Turnbull,
Felix Pollak, Vincent Ferrini, Charles Bukowski, James L.
Weil, Leah Bodine Drake, Gil Orlovitz, Sheila Pritchard,
Lloyd Zimpel, Theodore Enslin, and so on. Selma and I had
put our money down and come up with a rainbow! I have
come to realize a generation later, that there is such a thing as
a *Sparrow* poem, and image, but the unity did not happen
overnight.

In the Fifties one could have asserted, with little fear of
disagreement, that the three most important events for the
poetry of the time were the crumbling of the New Criticism,
and the rise of those special phenomena Ferlinghetti-and-
Ginsberg, and Robert Bly. In today's anarchic situation the
question of modes and poetries, of aesthetics and language, of
an advance guard, while as important a critical question as
ever, is no longer the *raison d'être* of the little magazine
movement. We now have Black Poetry. We now have the
feminist movement. Most powerfully, I fear, we now have the
National Endowment for the Arts. We now have access to
lesbian journals, homosexual journals, scores of journals devoted to the writing of children, and at least a dozen other
social categories of what, for lack of a better term, I call
"guideline publications," by which I mean quite literally
magazines published by Washington fiat and ukase,
magazines enlisted from the American populace by advocacy
or affirmative action guidelines. Where there used to be a
hundred reviews initiated by some perhaps vague, but
nevertheless ineluctable poetic impulse to publish, often re-
gardless of the state of one's own personal finances, we now
have hundreds and hundreds of magazines, mostly ephemeral,
often ideological, whose only reason for being is the
availability of government money. This motivating factor of
government money is not vision, but strategy. We have come
to the time of politics, of revolution. Poetry now has another

New Deal, and another NRA. And under the rubric of a monolithic "totalitarian" democracy the "silenced" are commanded to be unsilenced. The perennial tug-of-war between the reality of a minority of talent, and a plurality of groups demanding a voice is unleashed. Note Robert Brustein's ominous emphasis, from an article in the *New York Times* "Arts and Leisure" section for December 18, 1977:

When the twin Endowments (Humanities and Arts) were first created, many of us had hopes that America had come of age culturally, that it could support the minority of talent, that the imperative of intellectual excellence would no longer be overshadowed by the democratic demands of political necessity. For 12 years these hopes have been more or less sustained. Whether this condition will continue to prevail is an issue now shrouded in serious doubt and considerable uncertainty."

Men and women of good will and a correct passion can be found on both sides of this issue, but I state flatly that the *condition,* "the imperative of excellence," has not prevailed in the Literature Program of the National Endowment for The Arts since around 1970. What we have, instead, is a Malthusian nightmare of poetry publishing, a Vanguard of mediocrity. How all this will affect the little magazine as I understand it, I cannot at the present moment guess.

The main problem for the small publisher—he knows how to get the poems—is *finding readers who buy books.* The little magazine consumer—that hardy soul willing, especially in these free hand-out times, to take the next dreadful step and part with a buck—is a rare customer indeed. After twenty-five years *Sparrow's* subscription list still consists 60% of libraries, schools and other institutions. I estimate that the failure to renew rate among our individual subscribers is close to 80%. The average flesh-and-blood subscriber is the poet who tries us for one year. (He or she usually follows up with the submission of a hefty manuscript, has the work returned, tries maybe two or three more times, and then gives up on us. Renewal, in such cases, is hardly ever forthcoming.) At the latest count, the number of "people" who stay with us, year after year, comes to about two hundred. If it were not for the libraries, we should be hard put to explain our activities.

I do not offer these paltry figures out of a desire for sympathy, or out of frustration and anxiety. Literary publishing of the kind we do is hardly a millionaire's game, and we count ourselves lucky if we break even. For those whom such facts may fascinate, I can state that *Sparrow* last registered profits in 1976 and 1974. I have no patience with those high-minded people who scoff at my bookkeeping cautions, who view poetry only as a kind of proselytizer's arena in which the details of where, and how the money goes, are relatively unimportant. Whether we like it or not, we live in a business culture, and we are obliged to make an impact, however small, on that culture *in its own terms*. The fact that *Sparrow* can sell five hundred copies of a poet's book, pay royalties of a modest kind, and go on to another book, and pay royalties again, means a great deal more to me than those secret feelings of superiority as sweet as guilt, that assail too many of the *norodniki* in the movement today. I want to know, and it is important for me to know, that people are responding to my commitment with a commitment of their own. In our society one does that with money: as the saying goes, you put your money where your mouth is. I can believe such people, I can trust such people. When our magazine is late, a common failing here, some of our readers write anxiously to learn what has happened. They *want* the magazine. The establishment journal speaks to the network, the little magazine to the tribe. It is this tribal feeling, this sense of news from home, that any decent little magazine engenders. Such correspondence is scarcely effected by overloading the mails with "free" copies dispatched to the winds. It is a *dialogue* that usually takes years to develop.

The bibliographies are full of examples of one-shot, two-shot, three-shot journals that explode on the intellectual horizon, and then quickly fade—*Blast, Tiger's Eye,* etc. Research will reveal that most of the brief effulgences were really manifestoes, of special intent and effect. Often, I am sure, the explosion is precisely what was wanted. Also, quite frankly, some magazines go broke. By and large, however, I refuse to believe most editors willingly see their magazines fold. Little magazine annals are rich with the record of superb reviews that had their own staying power, and lasted as long as their editors wanted them to, even, in some cases, into old age: *Furioso, Poetry Chap Book, American Weave, Mother.* Harold Vinal's beautiful *Voices,* which published a gamut of writers, from Wallace Stevens and Tennessee Williams to Allen Ginsberg and his father, survived for close to fifty years and one hundred eighty-eight issues! The type of little magazine I am discussing, the magazine that makes the tradition—a tradition now under assault—takes time and experience. Both of these factors militate against the cult of youth being foisted upon us by the present NEA-NRA enthusiasm, which would have us believe there are some ten million mute, inglorious Miltons in the country, all probably under twenty-five years of age, and all in need of only the money the government can provide in order to be enabled to spring forth on the proscenium of the ages, and change our lives, expand our consciousness, increase our awareness, liberate our psyches, clean up the neighborhoods and turn the country around. Cant, I say. (The irony of this NEA-inspired propaganda about the generationally or experientially young who have been "exposed" to the arts, as to some silent, beneficent atom-bomb radiation, is that most of the grants-slicksters, the winners, the officials, the spokesmen of the committees and councils are refugees from the Sixties, activists in their middle Thirties, or dismally coping with their Forties.)

Here, of couse, I have been alluding to another type, almost a genre of little magazine, developed in the maelstrom, that comes and goes depending on the grant money. Happily, it often disappears. Though it constitutes a majority today, in terms of number, as any glance at grants-disbursement rosters will show, it is a majority of a peculiarly shifting character; sometimes, as in poets-in-the-schools, it can draw from a large surplus-army of college kids, changing from year to year. Even COSMEP (Committee of Small Magazine Publishers and Editors) seems to be breaking up—a consummation devoutly to be wished—into regional organizations, an impulse probably spurred by the twin pressures of the ever-increasing surplus-army, and the influence of the new regionalism

196

everyone is talking about. The traditional little magazine, on the other hand, a review like *Shenandoah,* or the *Beloit Poetry Journal,* though seemingly in the minority, quite simply stays. In terms of history the latter kind becomes the true majority. Another irony. The latter kind of magazine, though it may also use grants, *does not depend on them.* And then there are magazines like *Sparrow,* which refuse to apply for grants. Ten years from now, I have no doubt, there will still be a *Shenandoah,* a *Hudson Review.* As usual, and something the government seems constitutionally—no pun intended—incapable of understanding, faith in numbers is a spurious faith. As for excellence, that uncanny virtue, so far as I can determine it has never been delegated, or awarded by law, or voted. Mostly, all we can do with excellence is strive to recognize it when it glitters before us, something the Literature Program of the NEA has been trying to duck away from ever since the bona fide, if imperfect, prize system was abolished several years ago. It is with this parting shot at entrenched and officially sanctioned hypocrisy that I now turn to my closing remarks. These are directed to the genuinely interested, and genuinely "new"—whether young or old—little magazine editor who feels, perhaps, after my long cavil, curiosity as to what advice I can give.

I can only start by stressing the cornerstone of my own personal policy, translated into the simple dictum: get a job. Years ago the wonderful Bird Stair, of the CCNY English Department, who knew I wanted to be a writer, told me this. He told me too many young people thought the literary life was a relatively simple matter of hiding out in a garret, and writing. He described, in passing, the busy careers of authors like Dickens, Trollope, Stevens. He offered, out of his own vast personal experience, the conclusion that more often than not the writer who is "free" is free to worry about the rent, or to develop an anxiety about his support sources; that freedom, not built upon a clear, honest sense of personal security, may actually get in the way of his vision as a writer, and distract him with worry, and fear. He mentioned that the independently wealthy writer was rarer than the Dodo bird, that "nobody" gets a Guggenheim, that grants, fellowships and scholarships are unpredictable, and temporary. He went on to say that working for a living, in the context of a writing career, separates the sheep from the goats: if one sticks to it, if one makes a start on building a life, the very perseverance will contribute to the commitment all true writers have to write. On the other hand, if one is self-indulgent and a procrastinator, sooner or later one will fall into the comfortable round of movies, new suits and vacations in the mountains, and the ambition to write will eventually fade away, like a dream one forgets on awaking. And he said, that is all right too, that writing is a twenty-year bet with oneself, and that if things don't work out, we may as well have a job to fall back on.

Fifteen years later, in 1960, William Carlos Williams gave me similar advice. I was working, I was writing, I had *Sparrow*: *my job was simply in the way.* I was extremely discouraged. Like Professor Stair, and making no bones about it either, he stressed the importance of having one's own money. He said too many young poets he knew were bitter, invidious, and—the word he used—"scattered." He said, with a relish for the irony, so many of them were careerists without a job! Then he mentioned, with a smile, that when he had delivered his thousandth baby, the staff at the hospital he was connected with bought him an electric typewriter to commemorate the event. He told me, without too much pity, to budget my time better. I have been trying to do so ever since.

Get a job. The advice is about as inspiring as the sight of the sweat stain around the band of my old fedora, and just as up to date. And yet I suspect the best kept secret in these hype times is that most writers work at something else for a living. They are teachers, framemakers, mail clerks, accountants, gardeners. And they are busy writing, and—the poet-publishers among them—busy with the magazine. They are not pinning their hopes on the next grant. The information may be old, but isn't it still relevant? In a recent issue of the *Publishers Weekly* the novelist Reynolds Price complains that young people today are being encouraged by NEA policies to think they can make a living by writing, when, in fact, they cannot. Authors Guild statistics prove this year after year.

For the new poet-publisher my advice is equally as simple: hang on. Having a job, of course, will help you to hang on. Don't listen to the siren-songs about now, innovation, small press revolution. Just hang on. Building the tribe takes time. You have to become a habit. Come out regularly. Be not predictable, but expectable. Deliver the goods. Have no faith in the expansion gimmick of getting bigger and better, issue to issue. In fact, do the opposite: look the *same* from issue to issue, same number of pages, same color paper, same masthead. Look permanent. Notice the fine old staples, *Hudson Review, Poetry, Beloit,* etc. They haven't changed, even in pagination, in years. Look not like *now,* but like forever. Ignore the claptrap about multi-color printing, the hotsell cover that grips the eye, the zippy drawings. You're not selling cigarettes, but poetry. Don't be trendy, because in this country trendy is always yesterday; be you. In the best sense of the admonition, *imitate your betters; imitate what works!* We all need models. Select a couple of magazines you admire tremendously, and make a study of them. Steal ideas. If you can, steal their poets. And hang on, wait the wolf out. Plan—even if it means, horror of horrors, getting a loan, which you'll be able to do if you have a job—to *last* for at least six or eight issues. Don't think your fate on Olympus is going to be decided in one year. Leave that kind of speed-of-light thinking to the grants slicksters. For our first four years *Sparrow* never had more than 54 subscribers; then things started to happen. The libraries finally heard about us. A couple of the more reliable bookstores, like the fine Asphodel Book Shop (Jim Lowell), started to send in orders. Poets are a notoriously niggardly lot, but a few, like Barriss Mills and James L. Weil became our active supporters and advertisers. A few teacher-poets, like Ron Bayes, sent in class orders, money on the line. In due course Selma and I became as busy as we needed to be. Today we have a hard-core list in the few hundreds, and this core ramifies, and generates single sales. Depend on no one but yourself, and hang on! As you develop this stance of independence you will generate trust, and make real friends, and this friendship, this community, this tribe, will help you push on. You will expand in the only way that counts, inside your head.

Learn to respect time, and your life. When I use the term budgeting I mean nothing cold and automatic. I mean develop self-discipline. Respect what you are doing, learn to recognize the importance of things, and the budgeting will pretty well take care of itself. A good night's sleep usually helps. This respect and recognition will lead you, with some luck, to the right choices, as, for instance, if you *really* want to operate your own offset press. Do you like getting your hands dirty? Are you strong, and healthy enough, to lug all that paper around? Are you good at fixing things? Do you have the patience for working at paste-up? Right choice is often a matter of self-knowledge: do you have the time, or can you afford the time, to set your own type? Can you afford a magazine? (If you're working, there's a good chance you can.) Respecting the whole work will enable you to make distinctions, say, as between poet and poetaster. You'll soon learn the difference between the inquirer and the cadger, the frump, the vaniteer, who is pestering you for a free copy of your magazine, or to take his or her lousy poems. Soon, miracle of miracles, you will be recognizing your mistakes, in judgment, in intentions, before you make them, and start teaching yourself.

I can say little about the *business* of the little magazine. I keep good books, as the saying goes, not only out of a cautionary attitude towards the IRS, but because the practice helps me to know, often at a glance, how the money is going. I'm a fairly decent clerk, know how to bill a university in triplicate, how to maintain a subscriber's list. I've learned, over the years, and much to my surprise as I survey my small, but sunny study, that I'm usually neat about paperwork, files, bookshelves, etc. Order helps me think. I've taught myself, through sad experience, to save money, as well as time, even in such seemingly unimportant items as scratch paper, stubs of pencils, old tables. I'm not a miser, and my publishing has never cost a writer a red cent, but I adamantly refuse to pay postage to return a manuscript. I never accept postage due manuscripts. I reserve my charity for the United Fund, my church, a few other worthy causes. I receive my share of what I call Grue Mail, the angry, threatening kind. I never answer this, and thus save time. Basically I would have to say, about the business of the little magazine, as many individuals wiser than I have said, that if it were a business I wouldn't be in it.

Every little magazine editor likes to know how other people distribute their books. I estimate that *Sparrow* sells about 85% of its wares by mail. I suppose we have a modest, yet solid reputation by now. There are a few, very few bookstores I trust. (In the old days I used to put a collection agency on the delinquent ones, and still would, if the need arose. However, I pick and choose very carefully now, and have no complaint.) Fortunately, some of the larger jobbers and library buyers know about us, and order from us. We've also had good luck with Ed Ochester, poet-proprietor of the Spring Church Book Company. We also do business with a couple of other trustworthy little magazine dealers. We usually turn a deaf ear to the fly-by-nighters in the field who claim they mean to "bring" the little magazine before the public. I may be a bit cocky, but, over the years, I think I have learned to judge a person's potential for performance by even the way his flyer looks. I ship, on a consignment basis, to only a rare few, and I hereby warn the novice against the practice. I should like to find time to do more with college bookstores, which I have found to be prompt and efficient. The kids are still among our main readers, and are more likely to buy from such bookstores, than through the mails. I have had almost no success with my few ventures into national advertising, including space, as well as classified ads. I have never been able to afford repeat-ads, which may be the answer here, but I just don't know. As poetry-sellers we are in a non-field and it's difficult to generalize. Recently *Sparrow* was the beneficiary of two really long reviews in large, esteemed publications, with big readership—there were no dramatic increases in book sales. On the other hand, one of our poets was mentioned in his fraternity bulletin, and we received something like twenty-five orders in two weeks from the date of the appearance! Of all the directories, our listing in the *Writer's Market* has been our greatest boon, and we number our sales from this one source in three figures annually.

One thing we do that, we suspect, not enough little magazine editors do is work our poets. During the publication process, for either our pamphlet series or our chapbooks, we set them to building up their personal list of friends, mentors, loyal relatives, teachers, peers and colleagues, etc. We compose a flyer with, where possible, mention of previous reviews, editorial matter of that type, pertaining to the poet and the work. Then we persuade the poet—as politely as we can, and as firmly—to write letters, send notes, drop a line, to the people on the list, and include the flyer. Simple, but it works. The flyer is a mail-back form, and we pay postage, though only on pre-paid orders. This little campaign is probably the closest the little magazine editor can come to the posh autograph party offered by the big publishers. Readings help, but except for "Indiana Indiana" we've never published a poet within three hundred miles of us, and then, of course, we are not exactly asking the poet to become a "salesperson." Of our last three books, including one just out since last November (two months ago as of this writing) the following figures reflect current sales: five hundred fifty, four hundred seven, one hundred twenty-four. Let me add one final caveat: we never accept orders from individuals not accompanied by money!

What else is there to say? Read. Writers read. Writers always read, though not all writers admit this. Reading is the writer's, the editor's way of staying in touch, of keeping ready, of being alert. Read for the love of it, for the fun, and for the challenge. Read, and for heaven's sake, buy a book once in a while, and support the other fellow. Reading is a good way of occasionally getting away from your own poems. All poets need this break. And once in a while chuck it all, and go for a walk with the wife, the husband, the dear friend. Have a beer. Pretend you're an ancient Chinese poet, look at the moon, and have a laugh, or shed a tear. If you still want to publish a poetry journal after reading all this, then you are as mad as I, and as blessed.

CHEEK BY JOWL: ON READING, ANGELS, AND THE THREAT FROM WITHIN
by Elliott Anderson

Elliott Anderson is editor of TRIQUARTERLY

The easiest part of any good small magazine editor's job is the reading part, and what goes with it, the editing. In this sense, the business is really fairly simple, and without becoming tediously specific, rather unremarkable. There are difficult authors, just as there are certain kinds of editorial experience that can be trying—working with a collection of foreign literature in translation, for example—but by and large for me the business of editing, as distinguished from the business of publishing, is raw pleasure. Once the reading has been done, the thing is out of my hands until the truck arrives at the warehouse and the books come out of the cartons. Between times, for this part of the job, I'm pretty much free to contemplate future editorial projects. But then *TriQuarterly* is fortunate as few magazines are: its founding editor, Charles

Newman, established a pattern of consistent excellence; its chief patron, Northwestern University, is generous; and its professional staff, its executive and managing editors, and its art director, are among the best in the country.

About reading and editing, how to—even why to—I have very little to say. For me, it's mostly a matter of instinct and taste, recognizing what's good in what I don't care for as well as in what I do, and in conceiving particular identities, concepts and themes for the various issues we publish. But then in most respects, I suppose I am not a typical little magazine editor. Until coming to *TriQuarterly* I didn't read little magazines, I still don't read very many, nor am I much interested, except for certain historical reasons, in the so-called little magazine community. What I am interested in is good writing and good fiction in particular. Contrary to what many little magazine editors and an ever greater number of unpublished writers like to maintain—usually in opposition to one or another myth of a New York Publishers Conspiracy— or in an attempt to solicit private or federal support for their work—I find that such good writing is in relatively short supply. *TriQuarterly* publishes each year on the average of four to five hundred pages of short fiction, from forty to fifty stories, and under the circumstances—we see approximately five thousand manuscripts each year—we find that we don't reject much for want of space.

The argument for *TriQuarterly* that interests me more has to do with its capacity for invention—in small part editorial, in larger part physical, that is, fiscal—and for its place in a culture that can no longer much afford to pay attention to serious, noncommissioned writing. If there is a publishers conspiracy in New York worthy of the notion it is more likely one of economic survival. I find it difficult to fault the editorial director of a publishing house who declines to publish work that won't sell in sufficient quantity to pay its way for whatever reason. I may fault the economy, or the book buying public, or even an antiquated book-technology and its attendant book-psychology (hard cover means good), but not the man in the business of publishing and selling books for profit. But then this is my interest in *TriQuarterly,* and in a rather perverse sense it pleases me to think that as so-called quality

204

fiction declines in value as a commodity on the various commercial exchanges, it becomes increasingly valuable on some of the better non-commercial exchanges. Although I am saddened by the news of the demise of a magazine of the quality of *American Review,* I am also delighted that the competition has diminished. As T. S. Eliot was rumored to have wondered when informed of the death of Sandburg, "How do you suppose Frost is doing?", so *France Soir* proclaimed in boldface on the death of Churchill: "DeGaulle Seul a l'Europe!"

For most literary publishers, whether commercial or non-commercial, selling the product is the most difficult business of all. Unlike the audience for other book or magazine commodities for which certain market-audience research and promotion techniques have been developed, the audience for literature is a regular Diaspora. We're told that more people read on the east coast from Boston to Washington than elsewhere, that Jews read more than non-Jews, that college professors don't read at all. By read here we mean buy, but from what we know about the buying-reading habits of people for whom literature may be intended we conclude nothing. How such a market might be measured is difficult to say. How to imagine the statistical variables, and how to conjure the economic circumstances under which research and development funds to provide alternative book making technologies might come to exist is even more difficult. So long as there are telephone books to make up the business, companies with the r & d resources of an R. R. Donnelley, the world's largest printer, can hardly be expected to leap into the breech. Meanwhile, most of us are left with ordinarily marginal returns on direct mail and space advertising investments.

After fifteen years and with a tri-annual circulation of roughly five thousand, *TriQuarterly* ranks as one of the larger little magazines in the country. Because its issues typically run from two-hundred fifty to three hundred pages, and because the quality of its design is consistently high—and because it pays its contributors, not as well as most of the consumer magazines, but very well by non-profit standards— it has become an expensive operation. With discounts, and providing no margin for overhead, the magazine would currently have to sell for around nine dollars per copy, or twenty-seven dollars per subscription, to break even. This as opposed to the $5.95, $12.00 current pricing. The difference is loss and an occasion for angels.

Whether the angel comes in the form of a university, as is the case for *TriQuarterly,* or a wealthy heiress to a condiment fortune, or even a disc-jockey turned middle-level arts bureaucrat, the editor-publisher-angel contract is fundamentally the same. The editor promises something—usually prestige association, the sort of good public relations that money invested otherwise won't buy—in return for something—access to the money he needs to cover his losses.

The most desirable magazine-editor relationship in my experience is a one-on-one between a magazine and a non-profit institution. *TriQuarterly* has this sort of relationship as do a handful of other magazines around the country. Even though questions of overall budget support-versus-content-versus-growth can be complex, the university-magazine relationship offers me editorial freedoms that would be difficult to obtain under other circumstances. For-profit institutions typically make poor bedfellows, if only because the standard of literary quality against which non-profit publishing performance is measured has little necessarily to do with a bottom-line. Of all angels, however, the most difficult tends to be the individual, especially if his inclinations and ambitions tend toward literary expression, or if what he's really after is a paid personal friendship.

Several years ago my wife and I were invited to what I had been led to believe would be a fund-raising party for *TriQuarterly.* Our hosts were the Smythes, an elderly couple living in one of the more elegant high-rise buildings along Chicago's Gold Coast, just north of the Drake Hotel. Their southern view from the twenty-fifth floor took in the northern-most throat of Michigan Avenue, the throat down which most of the city's money travels each morning. I suppose because I'm something of a provincial—I was raised in Idaho—I often find myself under such circumstances thinking like a cash register—you know, for what this piece of real estate is worth we could do one hundred fifty six pages six

206

times a year for the next fifteen years; for what that one's worth we could get it promoted and sold. But as I say the occasion was money. For it I'd had my hair cut and put on a necktie.

Soon the Smythes spacious living room was filled with smartly dressed men and women, each of whom I presumed had been invited for their lively interest in the literary arts. I don't know, because I don't think I gave the matter conscious thought, but I imagine that I also presumed that a lively interest in the literary arts meant a lively interest in books and literary magazines, *TriQuarterly* chief among them. Well. After a half hour of canapés and circulation our hostess made a little introductory speech and I got up to make my pitch. *TriQuarterly,* I told them, was a magazine of some recognized excellence; it published important new work by established authors and younger authors as well; it had won more design and graphic arts awards than any literary magazine in history; nevertheless it consistently lost money, and without the support of kindred souls, . . . and so forth. Following my pitch the crowd thinned at once. Toward the end of the evening, which came rather suddenly, only two guests remained: a computer softwares magnate who had just purchased a fifty-foot sailboat and wanted me to tell him why he should read when he could have more fun on the water, and a retired physician who said that quite frankly the evening had been a disappointment since he'd expected some wild eyed person in denims. To the computer softwares man I replied somewhat lamely that he could always sail out to the middle, drop anchor and read; to the physician I apologized and promised next time around to come as myself. My wife, who had endured in silence since the passing of the canapés muttered an obscenity and that was it, or nearly it, because at the elevator down the Smythes told us that since we reminded them of their own children we really should come back for a chat sometime.

I learned two lessons from this evening. First, the association the Smythes had in mind wasn't really literary but social, or literary but only insofar as literature might serve as a field upon which other sorts of play could occur. To have secured from this group anything like the support I had in mind—a willingness to assume responsibility for a certain portion of our annual operating budget—say $15,000-$20,000—I should have been prepared to offer a variety of services, not the least of which would have been appearing from time-to-time in full battle dress, wild eyed and denimed. Second, there is a difference between a *thick* culture—one in which a man might have a new boat and never read and support the literary arts for tax reasons, or because it pleased him, or even because in some dark recess of his imagination he perceived alternatives to the cash-register of his soul—and a *thin* culture—one in which, if you want to get next to the man's money you get next to the man, and stay there for a while.

It was with these lessons in mind that I arranged to have breakfast some years later with another patron of the arts, also a midwesterner, a pharmaceuticals baron I'll call Jones. I had met Jones through a friend and had been informed that he might well take an interest in *TriQuarterly*. I had also been warned that Jones was a very particular fellow, not given to spending freely, and that should I make an association with him I might be prepared for much backing and filling before realizing a return on my investment—time in this instance. For breakfast I came attired in hand tooled buffalo jacket and beard, denims too, and when I made my pitch I merely wondered if we might not have an area of common interest. No mention of money, but more directly, and more to the point, wasn't there a project maybe? Well as a matter of fact, and this not over breakfast, but the course of several months, subsequent breakfasts and lunches and exchanges of letters, there was an area of interest, a certain foreign literature. No thick culture marriage of convenience here, at least not in the genteel sense, but a marriage nonetheless, and one moreover leading to the eventual publication of a volume of some distinction.

The point, it seems to me, is to suggest that there are angels and there are angels, and that the base motivation for certain editorial considerations needn't always have an end product in mind. In other words, when I went to see Jones that first morning I went without a proposition. I was merely curious to know if between us we couldn't get from A, nowhere, to B, a solid publishing project. Fundamental manufacturer/investor relations, maybe, but not an ordinary concept for most little magazine editors.

Having said so much, and without disgressing altogether from the business of angels, it's not only interesting but under some circumstances crucial to create conditions in which it becomes possible to solicit work from various professional artists and writers for fees that are substantially lower than they are accustomed to. When Lawrence Levy and I first conceived the idea of a photo-narrative (*TriQuarterly 37*, "Going to Heaven"), we decided that we wanted to work directly against the avant-garde grain, that is, we wanted photographs of the highest professional and commercial quality, we wanted a set fit for display in the finest art and fashion magazines, and we wanted models who were both pretty and trained in the business of posing for pictures. Such photographers, models and sets do not come cheap, however, and we knew that in order to do what we'd set out to do we'd have to use the *TriQuarterly* format to its most natural advantage— we'd have to oppose art to business (an unnatural opposition in some circumstances), and we'd have to convince the people involved that out of this opposition would come their greatest good, exposure to an art audience that typically paid little attention to the art in the work that each typically performed, which attention would necessarily benefit each participant, including the owners of the set, a lawyer and his wife from Galena, Illinois. We were even able to retain the services of a professional horse-trainer from Montana for no fee at all.

The business here is fairly simple in concept but rather complicated in practice; or at least sticky. The strategy is obvious enough, only its execution is subject to the variables of personality and art benefits.

This holds true not only for specific magazine projects, but for the management of a magazine as well. When a staff, however professional, is obliged to work for less than the going rate over long hours to produce a magazine that ultimately reflects more credit on its editor than on those who have had the most to do with it, that staff will quite naturally begin to look for other rewards. *TriQuarterly* has had its ups and downs with staff in the past and often I have found myself in the position of having to ask for more work from people as a favor, knowing full well that I'd never be able to repay the favor, neither with money nor with any other currency.

Out of the context of the angels, *TriQuarterly* is one of a field of roughly three thousand little magazines and small presses in this country. Of that considerable number there are in my estimation maybe two dozen worth reading regularly, and of that two dozen no more than ten worth ongoing private or federal support. The fact of the matter, however, is that virtually anyone with the mind to turn a mimeo-crank and the staying-power to fill out an application blank can qualify for such support. When, as happened a couple of years ago, grants committees acting on behalf of the National Endowment for the Arts via the Coordinating Council of Literary Magazines, chose to make magazine awards by dividing available monies equally among all applicants without regard for quality or need—when editors with magazines costing anywhere from eight to ten thousand dollars per issue were lumped with those whose total annual budgets did not exceed a thousand dollars, good became bad and better worse.

The problem is compounded because of all the arts, at least at the non-commercial level, and especially at the level of the shortest-run mimeo publications, literature is the cheapest to produce in quantity. I suppose the same could be said for comic books or Xerox art, but I mean by comparison the opera companies, symphony orchestras, and theatrical groups that divide up most of the private foundation and federal arts pie. Once the opening night black-tie and bonhomie people have stepped down from the NEA table, there is something like three percent left over for literature— precious little for the handful of quality magazines and small presses, not to mention individual grants applicants and the Poetry in the Schools crowd. Now if the idea is to spread the money around and the rationale for distribution is an arts democracy, the shorter run, less expensive publications take on a certain luster. And if the idea is also to recognize quite rightly that groups of people in this country, among them blacks, chicanos, women and gays, have suffered unfairly and to presume therefore that each is entitled to its own piece of the action, ethnic and minority publications take on a luster with facets.

The impulses to democratize literature are many and stem in large part from the justified impression of a large number of little magazine editors and small press publishers that the noncommercial field was long dominated by representatives of some the larger and more established magazines, *TriQuarterly* among them. Public funds, such editors have cried, unfair, unfair. Well maybe so, but the alternative of one man, one editor, one public dollar, has only further fractured what is already a fractured audience, certifying in the process standards of mediocrity in the literary interests of no one.

In the end, I suppose, what we need is a Czar for Literature, a kind of ultimate angel, some one person with the political savvy to suggest that the solution to the problem— given the diminished range of literary services available from New York—has less to do with democratic versus elitist notions of magazine funding than with principles of literary organization and acceptable standards of quality. This should put the half-wits in a frenzy and set the stage for a new permanent Committee of Ten, each one an editor empowered to award himself a future.

THE STRUGGLE AGAINST CENSORSHIP A ROUND TABLE DISCUSSION
with Maurice Girodias, William Burroughs, Allen Ginsberg, Carl Solomon and James Grauerholz

Official censorship by the government and the resultant climate of self-censorship among publishers in this country during the late fifties and early sixties is the subject of this round table discussion. The participants are Maurice Girodias founder of Olympia Press, William Burroughs, Allen Ginsburg, Carl Solomon who published Burrough's first book, Junkie, *as a pulp paperback when he was an editor at A.A. Lynn Company, and James Grauerholz who is Burrough's agent. Maurice Girodias discusses the function of Olympia Press in Paris and how the Traveller's Companion Series included literary works by writers who would gain recognition at the end of the fifties and early sixties: Vladimir Nabokov, Lawrence Durell, J.P. Donleavy, Henry Miller, William Burroughs, and Terry Southern. These authors were published in the United States only after a long systematic campaign fought against censorship in the courts by Grove Press and other publishers. The restrictions which created the need for an Olympia Press in the first place cast Girodias into the limbo of running a clandestine press with his copyrights voided before the law both here and in France. Within this context, William Burroughs and Allen Ginsberg recount the events leading to the publication of Burroughs'* Naked Lunch *by Olympia Press in 1959, followed by* The Soft Machine *and* The Ticket That Exploded. *This account of the conditions in France which caused the demise of Olympia Press and the legal gains which made possible the publication of its major writers in this country reveals certain elements in the shifting of the creative center for the arts from Paris to New York during this period of time.*

The following remarks were adapted from a discussion taped by me in 1974 as part of a series of radio programs for New York's WBAI. The station manager at the time vehemently resisted broadcast of these programs because the station was in litigation about its

212

*license with the FCC over obscenities charges. When the programs
were finally scheduled for broadcast each was slotted so that the
portions of the program containing "questionable language" would
go on the air after ten p.m. Every word that might be considered
"obscene" and bring complaints by the listeners against the station
was listed on forms signed by the station manager, program
director and producer attesting that the language came from literary
texts of merit. This illustrates how the censorship to which publishing was subject in the fifties is currently to be found in other areas of
the communications field.*

Charles E. Ruas

M.G. - *It was Allen who first brought the manuscript [of*
Naked Lunch] *to me, in '58, in Paris. I was publishing
books in the English language at the time, books which
were unpublishable in America . . . the prose was
scintillating but the typing was pretty horrendous. I
don't know what happened to that manuscript before it
reached me.*

A.G. - *Kerouac had typed part of it in '57 in Tangier and
Alen Ansen had typed part of it and I typed part of it.
It was a composite of different typings.*

M.G. - *It was dazzling, but it was difficult to make out. So, I
must say that I reacted very badly. I remember saying,
'This is great but I can't even get a straight judgement
on this book. Can you do something about it?' That
was our first conversation. I also remember your
looking like a very elegant, dapper young American.
You looked extremely business-like, you were doing
your job as an agent, I suppose. 'Come back later', I
said, 'and bring me a better manuscript' . . .—A
month later, Allen came back with a retyped, rear-
ranged manuscript which was published in 1959.*

W.B. - *The point is that the manuscript which you saw in 1958
was not even approximately similar to the manuscript
published in 1959.*

M.G. - *A lot of work was done.*

W.B. - *Yes. As I remember the story, you became interested after publication of excerpts in* Chicago Review *and then in* Big Table. *One morning, Sinclair Beiles came to see me and said you did want to publish the manuscript and that you wanted it in two weeks. So, we all got busy and reorganized the material. The manuscript you got then was not at all the same as the manuscript you saw in 1958, which was really fragmentary and confused.*

A.G. - *I must have taken the initiative to see you at the time we were preparing the material for* Big Table.

M.G. - *I remember the meeting very clearly. When the* Big Table *piece came out and reminded me about the whole thing, we got into it and the book was published.*

W.B. - *The book was out on the stands one month after the morning Sinclair Beiles came to see me. I think that's a record. We had made the selections from about one thousand pages of material which overflowed into* The Soft Machine, *into* The Ticked That Exploded *and into* Nova Express *as well. You got it printed and out in two weeks. I was producing it in pieces, and as soon as you got it, it was sent to the printer. When it came back from the printer instead of rearranging the proofs, Brion Gysin, myself and Sinclair Beiles took one look and said, "this is the order, just leave it the way it is."*

A.G. - *It was all happening about one block from the Seine river within a few streets from each other from rue Git-le-Coeur to rue Saint Severin. We were living on rue Git-le-Coeur in Paris, so actually, it was a very short walk back and forth. It was in the neighborhood and everybody was seeing each other for coffee in the mornings anyway.*

214

M.G. - *Everything was happening within a radius of three hundred yards or so.*

A.G. - *That's one reason why it was possible to do it so fast.*

M.G. - *That's only one reason. I still can't understand what all the rush was at the time, can you remember?*

A.G. - *We wanted to take advantage of the publicity that was emanating from Chicago.*

W.B. - *Yes, that was part of it. But I remember Sinclair Beiles saying he wants to publish it and he wants to do it quickly, can you get it ready in two weeks? And I said yes, we can do it.*

A.G. - *Maurice, what other books were you publishing that year?*

M.G. - *Well, '58-59 was a bit slow. I had run through a number of pretty fantastic books in the mid-fifties. I started Olympia Press in 1953. My first list had a book by Samuel Beckett,* WATT, *and a book by De Sade, I think* The Bedroom Philosopher *or* Justine, *I don't remember which and a book by Henry Miller,* Plexus. *It was a great start for a completely new imprint and a new publishing firm with no money in the bank. We were very lucky. We really had a nice literary list to start with.*

A.G. - *And you also had a long series of books written by young Americans in Paris.*

M.G. - *Yes. Mason Hoffenberg was one of them, Iris Owen was another.*

W.B. - *Ed Bryant . . .*

M.G. - *Yes, and others, like Chester Himes, but his book was published under his own name. All the other ones were*

215

pseudonyms and we invented colorful names for everybody such as Akbar Del Piombo, that was Norman Rubington, and Ataullah Mardaan.

W.B. - *Yes, people still ask me if I'm Akbar Del Piombo.*

A.G. - *We may as well stop the myth that Burroughs is the author of that Piombo work once and for all.*

M.G. - *Yes. I never understood why so many people have thought that William Burroughs had written* Fuzz Against Junk. *Years later, I was asked for the first time, whether Burroughs had written* Fuzz Against Junk. *I discovered that there was once a mistake by which you were credited in the contract page. The copyright page had been misplaced by the printers, this was the reason for the mistake. I think it was all my fault and I apologize profusely. I never understood it until many years later . . .*

A.G. - *Norman Rubington was the author of* Fuzz Against Junk.

J.G. - *Didn't he write* Diary of a Beatnik?

A.G. - *Yes, but many years later.*

M.G. - *That was published in America when I was trying to reestablish Olympia Press in the late '60's.*

W.B. - *Maurice, didn't you publish* Zazie in the Metro *in '59?*

M.G. - *Yes. After the mid-fifties, when I published* Lolita, The Ginger Man, Candy *which came out in '58 and a number of books by Beckett. My list was fluid and bizarre in those days. The last important thing I did then was* Naked Lunch *in 1959. After that, it was a downhill evolution. I had been harassed by the French administration to the point where I was almost out of*

216

business. Also, censorship had started to receed in America and it became possible, partly thanks to Barney Rosset's Grove Press, to publish, in America, some of the books I had first published in France. Unfortunately, this happened years after their publication in French and because of the American copyright regulations, most of those books were out of copyright, and were pirated later by American publishers. But that was not the case with Naked Lunch. Naked Lunch *and* Lolita *were the only two that escaped being pirated. So, after '59, there were two other books that we published by William Burroughs. The first one was* The Soft Machine, *I think in '61 or '62 and after that,* The Ticket that Exploded. . . . *Well, after that, the next step was the publication, in America, of* Naked Lunch *by Grove Press in '64. There was a long interval and you must realize that in '59 there were still incredible problems that most American citizens have completely forgotten about. For example, the fact that in '59,* Lady Chatterley's Lover *was published for the first time by Grove Press. It was a breakthrough and a very daring thing to do.*

M.G. - *That was only a short time ago. It's a hard thing to believe.*

A.G. - *The point I'd like to make is that most of the American literary establishment, the publishers and the editors, adopted a party line which said that the reason "obscene" books were not published in America was that there were not very many of literary merit anyway. They were claiming that they were not leading any kind of fight, because there were no real manuscripts of great importance.*

M.B. - *That's a very devious cover.*

A.G. - *For present historical memory, I think the point should be made, that the cover story for not publishing this book was that there were no books.*

217

W.B. - *Allen, I remember the correspondence between Barney Rosset and Maurice Girodias. Barney was saying, very emphatically, "Do you really think* **Naked Lunch** *could be published? You're absolutely out of your mind. It is impossible. It must be done in a series of steps starting with* **Lady Chatterley's Lover** *and then, Miller. Perhaps, after that, depending on how the litigation goes. . . ."*

A.G. - *That's right. There was a world's delay on publishing* **Naked Lunch**.

M.G. - *Yes. That's what Rosset did, and I see that it was a rational approach. It worked very well. He slipped in Jean Genet and Frank Harris. It had to be that way. It's very interesting to see that, in fact, it's the publication of a number of books like that which really changed the rules of an entire generation and made things possible that were impossible before. What happened by way of books was extended to all our forms of expression.*

A.G. - *By the time* **Naked Lunch** *was published, that was precisely the time of the great battle in N.Y. over Lenny Bruce and of the battle of the movies over Jack Smith's* **Flaming Creatures** *with New York Filmakers, There had been a meeting of district attorneys in New York, somewhere in the early sixties, to take concerted action against one or another of Grove's items to see if they could break it.*

J.G. - *So in fact, there was a kind of conspiracy.*

A.G. - *I would say a concerted effort, not a conspiracy, because it was very public.*

M.G. - *It was quite open and funds were poured into attacking publishers. In fact, it was not expensive for the establishment side to do because, of course, they had the police and the courts at their disposal so they could do it easily.*

J.G. - *I mean conspiracy in a sense, like Barney Rosset's having to plan which books to publish.*

M.G. - *Oh, yes, it was on both sides.*

A.G. - *But I don't think of the word conspiracy there. I would say a concerted effort, because conspiracy involves secrecy, and this was done very openly.*

J.G. - *Yes, it was planned. The point is that he had planned a series of progressive, more liberal steps.*

W.B. - *Yes, definitely Barney did plan a series of steps.*

A.G. - *Brilliantly, I think.*

M.G. - *The first step, before Grove Press did anything, was the publication of* Lolita *in 1958 by Putnam's. I think it was the first event of this sort, an open challenge to censorship, which Putnam's did not follow up. The district attorneys had to let go of* Lolita *because of a completely stupid, irrelevant incident of a copy sent to a literary critic in N.Y. which had been stopped by the customs people and which had been released. I wrote a letter to this customs officer after hearing about this incident and asked him if indeed he had stopped a copy of* Lolita, *examined that book and released it after examining it. He answered in the affirmative. Therefore one copy of* Lolita *had been processed through customs. Since customs was one of the two bodies which were actively in charge of censorship, the other being the Post Office, this created a legal situation whereby an American publisher could then publish* Lolita *and have a precedent strong enough to defeat the effort to suppress the book in court. It's very weird but this is really what started the whole thing going.*

A.G. - *There were a couple of books of small explosions before that. One was with* Howl *in San Francisco. It was printed in England and then brought back to City Lights Bookstore in San Francisco. The customs stopped it. But we got it out of customs. Then a local vice squad officer picked it up in City Lights and it was prosecuted. We won a trial there. That was while I was in Tangier and in Paris, visiting Bill. Then there was a* Big Table *thing, which was a censorship battle in '58. The other thing I remember, was the battle about* Lady Chatterley, *which involved Arthur Summerfield who was the Postmaster General. He put a copy of* Lady Chatterley *on President Eisenhower's desk with the dirty words and passages underlined. Eisenhower was quoted, in* Time *or* Newsweek, *as saying "Terrible, we can't have that." He gave Summerfield the green light, "Go ahead and prosecute anywhere possible* 'Lady Chatterley!.'' *That involved a couple of hundred thousand dollars in legal fees expended by Grove Press to defend it.*

M.G. - Lady Chatterley's Lover *didn't get as much opposition as* Tropic of Cancer *which was the next one on the list and was published by Grove Press in 1960. That's where they really had trouble with local police and cases being started against them all around the country. They fought, and finally won all the cases when the whole thing was reviewed by the court.*

A.G. - *. . . The other thing that should be pointed out, is that when Grove went over the barbed wire and got* Lady Chatterley's Lover *legalized, immediately all the other publishing companies in New York jumped in, Putnam's among others and printed their own editions of* Lady Chatterley.

M.G. - *That's when the notion of public domain and copyright came out.*

A.G. - *Well, what I mean is that all the other publishers were*

220

too chicken, or too cowardly or conservative to actu-
ally fight for their own rights in regard to the earlier
classic texts. As soon as Grove established the classic
legal nature of Lady Chatterley, *they began pirating*
it . . .

A.G. - *The government's attitude in those years was in some*
way expressed by J. Edgar Hoover, who made a public
statement in the early '60's, saying that the three
greatest threats to America were the Communists, the
Beatniks and the Egg-heads.

M.G. - *There were editorials in the* New York Daily News,
attacking either the new culture, or literary publishing
or freedom of letters. So there was, to some extent, a
concerted government conspiracy which involved the
FBI who officially had started its counter-intelligence
program back in 1956. There may have been illegal
manipulations by the FBI to discredit the literary
community that far back to say nothing of the ac-
tivities of the CIA. An international literary atmos-
phere which was a big wet blanket was created to
discredit any literary breakthough of either the old or
the new classics that would have been considered
obscene.

W.B. - *Yes, it's true that* Encounter *magazine, which*
definitely turned out to be partially subsidized by the
CIA, was among the bitterest critics of my work and
also of Maurice Girodias. There was an article against
Maurice and Olympia Press written by George
Steiner.

A.G. - *Yes. We sent early chapters of* Naked Lunch *to*
Stephen Spender when he was working on Encounter.
That was in '58 when manuscripts were being solicited
by Grove Press for Evergreen *and* Big Table *in*
Chicago, Spender wrote back that the chapters that I
had sent might be of interest to a psychiatrist but that
they were not literary material.

M.G. - *Well, that's typical of Stephen Spender.*

W.B. - *You were the first to publish Genet in English, were you not?*

M.G. - *Well, there had been a privately printed edition of* Our Lady of the Flowers . . .

C.S. - *I bought it in the Gotham Book Mart under the counter.*

M.G. - *It was published by a Cocteau protege whose name was Maurian and who shortly after that started the Club Mediterranee and made a fortune, which he didn't do as a publisher. He was trying to run a very interesting bookstore and publishing firm and he was the first one to publish the book in English . . . But that was only a few hundred copies and it was never really put for sale in bookstores.*

A.G. - *Well, the copy that Carl had, I saw in Kerouac's room. It had a tremendous effect on us.*

C.S. - *I came into contact with Genet's work when I lived in Paris, in '47. I had jumped ship and I had a girlfriend there, a prostitute whom I took out. She took me to see a Genet play and so then I wanted to read Genet in French so I bought* Pompe Funebre *and was really carried away by it.*

M.G. - *He was a great discovery for French letters at the time. That was during the late forties.*

A.G. *It's funny, it made such an impression here, too, just at that time. At least, in our small circle of people.*

M.G. - *I suppose the first shocker the French had was Celine, before the war, but there was nothing else which was that provocative and that intense in French letters until Genet came out. Of course, he was another of my* *authors, I published two of his books in English,* Our Lady of the Flowers *and* The Thief's Journal. *I got into serious trouble with the French authorities because of Genet. At the same time, the French version of his books were published by Galimard who was a great importer and wealthy literary publisher.*

A.G. - *Didn't Gallimard publish edited versions of Genet?*

M.G. - *No. They were the complete texts. My English versions were banned and I was prosecuted for it by the French, which doesn't make much sense. But that was another illustration of what we were saying earlier: that it was really not just an American effort to stop the liberation of writing and thinking but it was really an international effort. My problems in Paris started with the British Government bringing pressure through Interpol and the French Government to stop me from publishing those horrible books in English.*

A.G. - *The Traveler's Companion which you were carrying across the Channel.*

M.G. - *Right, they were a mixed bag in which I had some amusing pornography written by very good writers who were doing this as a lark.*

A.G. - *And to make some money.*

M.G. - *Yes, these were interspersed with books like* Lolita, *which I could only sell because I was selling them as if they were dirty books. It was the only way to get the nice tourists to grab a copy and pay the nine francs that we were charging for them. Of course, we had to take the position that we were publishers of pornography, which we were to a very large extent—and very proud to be that at that time. But there was also a counter effort to stop us and to completely wipe me out of existence because I was the only publisher in the world who was able to publish books in English* *and who made an effort to select these books and to try to give an audience to good writers. So this is how, after weeks and weeks of litigation, I was completely run out of business by the French administration. They took my case seriously because they had been told it was important by their British colleagues and presumably, by their American colleagues.*

A.G. - *Well, if Summerfield was taking the matter up with President Eisenhower and they were having such a shocked reaction in the Oval Office, then obviously it was an international plot.*

W.B. - *Well, I think that Wilhelm Reich made this point as well in his* **The Sexual Revolution.** *From their point of view, it seems very rational that this would be a menace to their position and that the cultural revolution is the important revolution. Thus we know that in Russia, even in the Tzarist days, they were always oriented toward the control of thought. They regarded this as highly important.*

M.G. - *We also know that one of the aims of the revolution was, at first, sexual freedom.*

A.G. - *The Russian Revolution?*

M.G. - *Yes, and the Bolsheviks immediately wiped it out from the revolutionary program because it was a cause of social disorder.*

J.G. - *Well, in fact, the Bolsheviks in 1917, repealed all the laws against so called sexual perversion or homosexuality. It wasn't until the years of Stalin that the laws were reinstated. Now this is only what is on the books.*

M.G. - *In practice I think that one was actually forced to get married, one was forced by social, or professional pressures to lead a straight life. Morality among*

Communists is still the iron rule. You can't deviate, and if you do, you really get in trouble with the Party. No person of authority in the Party can have a mistress and things like that.

A.G. - *In the western world, what was the reason for such concerted action that would have stretched through Interpol, through Arthur Summerfield, the Postmaster, through President Eisenhower, through the British; what was their motive?*

M.G. - *I think that their motive was the suppression of any discussion, any free discussion of sex. Remember the problems that Freud himself had in those same years, and before those years. He was fighting the same fight. In fact, now, we have forgotten the political aspect of the fight that Freud and all his followers were having at the time. It was exactly the same thing. I think it springs from the beginnings of the industrial revolution, particularly in England which was the most conservative and repressive country in Europe, and the world at the time. There was a necessity to keep working classes well-disciplined and the notion that sexual freedom would destroy the social order completely. To force the people to follow moral rules in their sex life was the only way to impose the same old rules in terms of politics and social conduct. I think that a package was imposed, and the way to impose this was by sexual repression and by forbidding people to read certain books. So you had the British society in the Victorian era split in two; the working classes were not allowed to read anything and the upper classes were having a good time, quite deviously.*

A.G. - *Enjoying privately printed, deluxe editions of* Fanny Hill.

M.G. - *That's right. But this was not the French attitude at all. Before WWII France was probably the only free country in the entire world. Then it was knocked out of*

225

existence by Germany and was subjected to the rule of the German Army for the four years of Occupation, during which the French middle class got a taste of censorship and found out what it could do with censorship. After the war, when "Petain's disciple," de Gaulle, came into power, he just adopted the rules which Petain had followed during the war: he applied censorship, not just political censorship, or military censorship, but moral censorship as well. So this is really, in a very practical and historical sense, a fascist weapon to keep the masses under control.

A.G. - *Probably 'authoritarian' would be a better word there, because we are applying this to the condition in Russia as well as to the West . . .*

M.G. - *In my case, it was pretty atrocious because I was publishing books in English in France. The French Police are absolutely unable to understand the English language . . . I was being prosecuted and sentenced for books in English that the judges could not read. So, this gave life to very strange court scenes. But this was not just an accident. If the French authorities were trying so hard to suppress me and my production purely because I was a dangerous element in a well organized society then Interpol was playing this wonderful role of a liason between the various police forces in England, America, France and Italy.*

A.G. - *How do you know it was Interpol?*

M.G. - *Because I saw the files on me.*

A.G. - *Interpol files?*

M.G. - *Yes. I mean the French Police more or less willingly let me see some of the files denouncing me and in particular right before* Lolita *was banned which was my first big brush with the French authorities. I saw a big file and letters from the British police, addressed through Interpol to the French police, asking them to*

226

do something about stopping the crazy activities I was engaged in in Paris.

A.G. - *The point I was making before was that if Summerfield actually approached President Eisenhower in his White House office, to put pressure on, and Eisenhower gave the go ahead to prosecute* Lady Chatterley, *then it must have involved a very large police bureaucracy push from every direction.*

M.G. - *I'm sure that Hoover was playing a very positive role in all that. I mean, he was trying very hard. He was the great fighter against pornography, obscenity, and any kind of leniency.*

W.B. - *I think that the point that Maurice has made, I've always said the same, that all censorship is political.*

M.G. - *It's not moral censorship per se, I mean it has always meant to serve the purposes of the ruling class, or the party.*

W.B. - *But that attitude in England I've heard this directly from the upper English class, 'Well, it's alright for us to read books like this, but we don't want them to get into the hands of the working class', about my book for example.*

A.G. - *Well, what is their reasoning on that or didn't they ever propose reasons?*

W.B. - *They just don't want the working class to think. It's as crude as that. I've heard this also from the upper class English, 'We just don't want them to think, we want to keep them in ignorance.' In those very words.*

M.G. - *I mean, if reading is a secret pleasure, it's the first one to be supressed.*

A.G. - *Well, the conclusion that I would derive from all of our experiences, is that there is a great fluctuation back and forth in this question of liberty, and the old American saying 'eternal vigilance is the price of liberty.' It would be a good thing for later generations to bear in mind that you can't take it for granted that the ruling classes will allow questionable works to circulate freely. You always have to fight for them, and probably, we'll still have to continue battling for them for the next decade or so. Especially as there will be greater and greater repression.*

W.B. - *Certainly. Well, at some point, of course it becomes difficult for the ruling class to take back liberties which they've had. . .*

A.G. - *Well, they'd have to ban the books, bring out a bunch of police to arrest people for possession.*

W.B. - *No, they would not do that. They would have a war. That's what happened in France.*

M.G. - *Exactly. You have to have a military regime in charge. . .*

A.G. - *Well, one fantasy I had very early in the game in the mid and late fifties, was that once a few of these books were put through, like* **Lady Chatterley**, *or I'm thinking about in the case of* **Howl**, *or once* **Naked Lunch** *got out, once those books got out, and Henry Miller was out in hundreds of thousands of copies, in paperback and was secretly hidden on people's bookshelves and dining rooms and attics, they'd never be able to completely roll everything back because there would always be these secret artifacts, which younger generations would be able to pick up on secretly within the family.*

M.G. - *Oh yes, I mean in the healthy society, the desire to fight the rules is so strong that freedom is bound to win, but it can take several generations, it's a waste of time and a waste of life. Look at the two or three generations in Soviet Russia. . .*

I've been through the experience of the French Occupation, the war in France and the occupation by the Germans and I can assure you that it is absolutely devastating to see how a completely free country, educated and raised in the culture of freedom and in the respect of absolute freedom, individual freedom, can turn around and in a few months become a nation of slaves and idiots. I mean it's dazzling.

A.G. - *There is that point though, that they never will be able to completely suppress the new liberated mind because there are all these new copies around so that new little pubescent boys will be able to go up in the attic and find grandfather's books.*

M.G. - *Well, let's hope there are too many copies around. . . .*

TRUE CONFESSIONS
OF A FAILED READER
by Gordon Lish

Gordon Lish was co-editor of CHRYSALIS REVIEW, *editor of* GENESIS WEST, *fiction editor of* ESQUIRE, *and is now an editor at Knopf.*

I want you to hear this tale beginning to end, from start to finish.

This is because tricks of narrative give me a headache. It is also because I show up good when I started and got bad as I went along, and you won't know just *how* bad unless I cover the progress in its natural order. So I'm taking you back to Reggie Lish *kvelling* at the spectacle of her son as he lay staring at her through the ribs of the crib.

I think my first thought was that staring suited me. Forty-six years, hard drink, a cowardly intellect, and a couple of lapses into broken brain have united forces to beat my memory into retreat. But I am convinced I am reporting it right. I like to stare, is what I thought.

I think I would have been okay if I let it go at that. I mean, if I just went on staring at my mother, or the wall, and having a good time.

230

But what happened was—(this was maybe when I was six, five, in there)—what happened was, I started *thinking* about it. Well, the truth is, it was pressed on me—thinking about liking to stare.

My friend Andy and my friend Stevie wanted to shovel sand. But I said I wanted to sit on the curb and stare at the stuff in the gutter—which on a good day was twigs, gum wrappers, maybe something unknowable and all glinty with mystery. Anyhow, your usual dreck. I did not actually say this to Andy and Stevie—(even then I knew that too much truth is bad for everybody's complexion)—(everybody always knows that)—but I thought it, all right, and then I thought—(it was right in here that I started getting to be where I am today)—it was *then* I thought: better go to that sandbox and shovel sand.

And I did it.

I believe, indeed, that I acquitted myself that day of some exceptionally strenuous and distinguished shoveling. The stress was terrific, but the net effect was wonderful. The net effect on Andy and Stevie, that is.

Thereafter, when it came to shoveling sand, Andy and Stevie watched my moves. It was understood that Gordo would brook no shit, that I was up to serious business: a kind of competition, I suppose they thought: whereas, in fact, it was just work.

A kid does a little sitting on the curb and staring at the stuff in the gutter, and a generous fear gives him a vocation.

I have been working like crazy ever since.

Shoveling sand gave way to frontiers infinite in opportunity. I can remember catch-a-fly-is-up, kick-the-can, mumbly-peg, ring-a-levio. I was unbeatable. I can remember baseball, wrestling, soccer. There was no containing me. I can remember getting grades, getting girls, getting wild. There was nothing like me at any weight.

Andy and Stevie watched my moves.

I read *Finnegan's Wake,* they read it too. I read Huysmans, they read him too. So I read Jackson MacLow, and whipped their ass.

But I was a worker: cleaning a customer's plow was just a

lovely by-product. I mean, it wasn't *central,* in a manner of speaking.

I had looked into the delights of a dreamy gutter and seen what poet people call the void. Get busy, my chicken-heart told me—get busy, and *stay* busy, and dig like hell in that sand.

But I was pure in this, you understand. There was nothing in me but a large fear, and if the fear yielded work and the work was good, who's to fuss? On the contrary, Andy and Stevie applauded. The dumb bunnies even figured I was having fun.

Well, one thing led to another, and I came barreling after. I won't deny that certain people—by this time in my tale their names must be Doctor Andy and Doctor Stevie—I won't deny that certain persons took a look and said, who sees barreling? We see tumbling.

At all events, one thing was leading to another, and I say my progress was a pursuit.

Now here's the part where I start to look seriously worse than I did before. I was occupying space at San Francisco State College and I was working really strong. I met Billy. Billy's name was John Herrmann, and Billy liked a strong worker. Billy said you can staple the pages and I'll set your name in type right under mine. My name was Slade Molloy or Rake Blaze, but from now on, Billy said, I am calling you co-editor. Just get the staples in there.

This was very good. I liked my name in Bondoni Bold.

I did a lot of staring at it, in any type that Billy picked.

There was something glinty there, all right. And I don't think I saw what a poet person would call a void.

Let's see some more of this, I told Billy, as soon as he flashed a little Andy to me.

Enough is enough, said Billy, my name goes on top.

Well, friends and neighbors, this was very distressing. Your fellow who is a really great stapler does not like to hear enough is enough. So I went away from there—I would describe my mode in this as barreling, if you will honor my impression—I went away from there and got my own pages to staple. These I called *Genesis West*—because the Billy business was called *Chrysalis Review,* and it is wrong to think that

232

when a worker is brought forth from a starer, the imagination is not damaged in the doing.

Anyhow, my name went on top. It was editor, editor-in-chief, editorial director, editor-in-full-charge.

I picked the glintiest typeface vacation money could buy. And I did some colossal staring. I kept it private, of course. If I went into the garage at three in the morning to stare at all those stacked-up copies, the good it did me was no public sin.

And by now I knew there were plenty of Billys around doing the same thing.

Some of the fear was emptying out of me. Which is, I think, a bad thing.

But I did not think that then.

That's okay, I thought. Besides, there was another okay part of this: I was meeting customers with names like Spike, Dirk, Bruno, Alf, The Grip, Chuck, Fast Betty. Some of these were Jack Gilbert, Edward Loomis, George P. Elliott, Herbert Gold, Diane Wakoski, Hayden Carruth, Russell Edson, Curtis Zahn, Mort Elevitch, Vern Rutsala, Carol Berge, Tuli Kupferberg, Donald Barthelme, Grace Paley, Tillie Olsen, Leslie Fiedler, Leonard Gardner, Paul Bowles, Ivan Gold, Leroi Jones, Gil Orlovitz, John Hawkes, Dave Godfrey, Gina Berriault, Ben Maddow, and most stupendously of all, Ken Kesey and Neal Cassady.

These people had gorgeous names. But I picked the face and point-size.

I was editor-in-total-charge—and if a couple of these cuties couldn't keep a decent professional distance, if one or two of these intrepid starers sidled up to me and exhorted, "Come on in, the void is fine"—well, what was the harm? Isn't an editor-in-total-charge a fellow in halfway possession of himself? Such a fellow can go ahead and sit on a curb every once in a while—what's to really hurt?

I conceded some loss of purity in this. Whereas the fear had once filled me from top to bottom, now there were pockets where boldness intruded. And it's an old story from this point forward.

Nature took its nasty course.

The boldness spread and I went with it—still barreling, I

am absolutely convinced, though there have been opinions registered to the contrary. But I will further concede that boldness got entirely out of hand—arguing, nonetheless, that this was at my bidding. When you're an editor-in-total-charge, you can permit a thing like that, knowing all the while you have only to take up the leash by however many fistfuls.

So I just let the lead go out, and followed after, stepping smartly. All the astonishingly swift miles from the glory of my garage to the glorious immensity of *Esquire*. And, Jesus God, there I am, taking my bourbon with a shoveler call Rust! This is no mere Spike, no buster named Chuck! This is . . . a . . . Rust!

Well sir, I never saw one of those.

This is a name to conjure with. So that is, of course, what I did.

Not for nothing did I learn the lesson of the glinty, unknowable thing in the gutter.

Okay, I am quieting the tension now. This Rust, he tapped my shoulder and pointed to his chair. He needn't have bothered: I knew exactly where it was. I tapped his shoulder and wished him a tranquil life ever after.

We shook hands like armed men.

I never got to know if staring paid off for him and how much he paid off to it. He only pointed to the sandbox and took it for granted I had a shovel. I think I had a stick.

A bit after this, it began to look to me that what I had was a magic wand.

(You can see in here that here is where I am sharply going from bad to worse.)

In any case, the sandbox was chuggyjam. But now it was all boldness that was in me. A trifling gesture of my wrist, and—that—sand—flew!

Digging was not spoken here. For it turned out *everybody* had his wand, and it was a sad-assed kid who put his down to wipe his nose.

Anyway, I was working hard.

This is what you do: you make a little pass here and a little pass there: not entirely right for us, doesn't do a job for me, doesn't meet my immediate needs, not for the next four hundred years—and the sand moves something fierce.

234

This is really very good, you say—and *they* say, this kid is pretty quick with a wand. They say, what this kid maybe has is a new kind of wand, the which seems equipped with some heavy innovative shit. Let's watch his moves, they say.

Lenny and Tommy confer in the matter—over negronis and spritzers at the Italian Pavilion. Lenny and Tommy do a diagram on the tablecloth. They want to draw your wand, take the blueprint to the right shop, get the thing made, move more sand.

There is a new kid in the sandbox and he is stirring things up, and it is very clear to everybody he must be doing all this *tummeling* with a weird wand of Western design.

Meanwhile, back at the sandbox, the kid is getting plenty fed up with metaphor.

Well, he had to get fed up with something.

All this is happening—the story that I am telling you—all this is happening in a place where people just have to get fed up. Those that don't, they stay too long, and wind up with final notices before the show is out. I cite here the recent rotten examples of David Segal and Henry Robbins, wand-handlers of the rarest order.

Anyhow, the new kid is on page seven now: the story's getting long—he's in a terrible hurry to finish up and hear that crash of applause. A little litcrit can fix this. Metaphor is a goddamn dodge, so the new kid, in his bashing about, decides. Vladimir Nabokov, the new kid proclaims: there's nothing figurative in that!

The new kid likes this.

Well, boldness is making the new kid crazy.

Oh, this boldness is an dreamy language: it is like speaking in tongues. Only a crazy would make a habit of it.

Well, well, well—the new kid mounts a policy against metaphor. Give it to me literal, the new kid screams. Oh, he is shrieking now. He shrieks, Norman Mailer, Tom Wolfe, Philip Roth, John Cheever, Bernard Malamud! *This* is literal. These are nouns that don't fool around. Their considerable dimension, all their pretty amplitude, is right there in front of your snoot.

The kid is crazy in this coveting of the literal. Give me James Purdy, John Barth, Jorge Luis Borges, Saul Bellow,

Samuel Beckett! Because these are nouns that stand for what they are!

The new kid is making a terrible racket.

I want F. Scott Fitzgerald, I want Ernest Hemingway—and, by golly, he gets them.

Metaphors, the new kid declares to the balcony seats, are crap.

Hemingway? Hemingway is like counting to one hundred by tens.

Oh, listen to the new kid talk: here is what he says as he handles his bourbon: Oh, yeah, he says—well, last night I was shooting the shit with Gabo—you know, Gabriel Gárcía Márquez? And here is what the crazy kid means in this: he means *Gabriel Gárcía Márquez,* and that's it and that's it and that's it. He means, here is a noun too large to represent anything greater than itself because there is nothing that is bigger than *it* is.

But did I say this kid is crazy? Listen, this kid is around a very important bend. By the middle of page eight, this kid, God bless him, he wants Charles Dickens!

All right, there is organic conflict in this story. The literal vocabulary is finite: you use it all up and then what?

The kid finds this out.

But I am crazed now, now I am good and proper mad.

Which has its uses, as you all know, and as you also all know, invention is chief among these.

(Now here is where the fall hastens.)

I invent new metaphors. These are metaphors of a new design, and I think I really believe I made them all up. Here are some favorites. Listen: Raymond Carver, Barry Hannah, Mary Robison.

These are figures of speech whose powers work a treacherous business, angry tropes that advance belly-down and take you by the ankle with murderous teeth.

Just listen to the wondrous angling of their linguistics: David Huddle, James S. Reinbold, Sam Koperwas, John Deck, Jerry Bumpus, Gail Godwin, John Gardner, David Ohle, Thomas Bontly, Joy Williams, John Irving, Raymond Kennedy, Alan V. Hewat, Alma Stone, Leslie Epstein, Frederick Busch, David Kranes, Alexander Theroux, James

Thomas, William Kotzwinkle, Patricia Zelver, Robley Wilson, Jonathan Baumbach, Milan Kundera, William Harrison, Hilma Wolitzer, Reynolds Price, T. Boyle, John L'Houreux, Tom Cole, Stanley Crawford, and—get this, just listen to this—Cynthia Ozick and Harold Brodkey and Don DeLillo.

But make no mistake. The devising of a new metaphor will make a fellow crazy—and *this* fellow, the subject of my tale—well, he was nutsy from the very start.

But this is not news.

Not any of this has been news.

And a good story ought to convey some news—so here comes the news.

All of this is play for me. It is all just horsing around.

I don't think it used to be, but I guess that's what it is now. When I had my start, back there at the curb, I knew staring was what I did best. I could do it for hours, right through meals, with my mom threatening to break one of her blood vessels if I did not cut it the hell out. Of course, the glinty, unknowable thing got to be a book in time—and I just sat there and stared, happy as a clam. It was all mindless stuff, the way I stared. I never thought a thought. I just stayed fixed on that glinty thing and chewed Uneeda Biscuits. I'd be the first one to tell you I felt lots of feelings, and as bad as they got they shaped up good. But I never thought a thought, and I slept like a baby, deep adream.

Time passed fast.

My mother could break her blood vessel, but Stevie and Andy needed merely to exchange a sly, sidewise look.

I took to work and made it to meals. I was happy as a shrimp.

I came that way to New York, frantic to scavenge, scare up food—nutrition for the national literature, I thought—do a fine day's labor in the service of my stomach, the place where all my wanting resides.

Oh, did time pass now. The national literature could starve, but Lenny and Tommy need only slip me an invitation to the New York Literary Pavillon. I was beginning to see that bourbon was no profit to great artistic purpose. Masterpieces thrived on negronis and spritzers. Three for lunch at the New York Literary Establishment, and sometimes, if there were a lull in the chit-chat, I could even get in a few words in the general vicinity of my *kishkes*.

There was no real problem with any of this. Eccentrics are tolerated by truly mandarin folks. And if Tommy and Lenny had to go to the head to touch up their sneers, I could always check out the menu and try to learn some useful French.

I was happy as a minnow darting hither and yon.

I had thought the world was simpler—all mankind cleaved in twain. Here were your starers—and there were your workers. No one ever told me the thing was all complicated with types that in solemn purpose are just horsing around.

I just gave you a big illumination.

It concerns clutter.

If you want to be really childish about it, it concerns a kind of evil.

But as says the fellow the husband catches hiding beneath the wife's bed, *everybody has got to be someplace*.

It's like that, I suppose—mainly players, at the upper reaches, I striving hysterically to insert myself among them.

Not infrequently I play until four, five in the morning, weekends right into the bargain. The day's manuscripts and my felt-tip pens describe the playground on my bed. You wouldn't believe the sand it can hold.

I play until the wit is emptied out of me.

It runs out much faster than does boldness or fear.

I haven't done a good piece of staring in years. And the digging I have done will never fool Andy and Stevie.

It thus remains to see what Lenny and Tommy are up to. It is altogether likely that those good fellows will presently contrive yet a new delightful drink, something cool and vivacious for the very hot weather that is surely ahead.

THE STORY OF
MY PRINTING PRESS
By Anais Nin

Anais Nin arrived in the United States from Europe in the winter of 1939. Her early work was rejected by commercial publishers, so she published it herself—an experience that has been an inspiration to do-it-yourself publishers ever since.

In the 1940's, two of my books, *Winter of Artifice* and *Under a Glass Bell,* were rejected by American publishers. *Winter of Artifice* had been published in France, in English, and had been praised by Rebecca West, Henry Miller, Lawrence Durrell, Kay Boyle and Stuart Gilbert. Both books were considered uncommercial. I want writers to know where they stand in relation to such verdicts from commercial publishers, and to offer a solution which is still effective today. I am thinking of writers who are the equivalent of researchers in science, whose appeal does not elicit immediate gain.

I did not accept the verdict and decided to print my own books. For seventy-five dollars I bought a second-hand press. It was foot powered like the old sewing machines, and one had to press the treadle very hard to develop sufficient power to turn the wheel.

Frances Steloff, who owned the Gotham Book Mart in New York, loaned me one hundred dollars for the enterprise, and Thurema Sokol loaned me another hundred. I bought type for a hundred dollars, orange crates for shelves and paper remnants, which is like buying remnants of materials to make a dress. Some of this paper was quite beautiful, left over from deluxe editions. A friend, Gonzalo More, helped me. He had a gift for designing books. I learned to set type, and he ran the machine. We learned printing from library books which gave rise to comical accidents. For example, the book said: "oil the rollers," so we oiled the entire rollers including the rubber part, and wondered why we could not print for a week.

James Cooney, of *Phoenix* magazine, gave us helpful technical advice. Our lack of technical knowledge of printed English also led to such comic errors as my own (now famous) word separation in *Winter of Artifice:* "LO - VE." But more important than anything else, setting each letter by hand taught me economy of style. After living with a page for a whole day, I could detect the superfluous words. At the end of each line I thought: "Is this word, is this phrase absolutely necessary?"

It was hard work. Patient work, to typeset prose, to lock the tray, to carry the heavy lead tray to the machine, to run the machine itself, which had to be inked by hand. Setting the copper plates (for the illustration) on inch-thick wood supports in order to print them. Printing copper plates meant inking each plate separately, cleaning it after one printing, and starting the process over again. It took me months to typeset *Under a Glass Bell* and *Winter of Artifice.* Then there were the printed pages to be placed between blotters and later cut, put together for the binder and gathered into signatures. Then the type had to be redistributed in the boxes.

We had problems finding a bookbinder willing to take on such small editions and to accept the unconventional shape of the books.

Frances Steloff agreed to distribute them and gave me an autograph party at the Gotham Book Mart. The completed books were beautiful and have now become collector's items.

The first printing of *Winter of Artifice* was three hundred copies, and one publisher I met at a party exclaimed: "I don't know how you managed to become so well known with only three hundred books."

Under a Glass Bell was given to Edmund Wilson by Frances Steloff. He reviewed it favorably in *The New Yorker*, and immediately all the publishers were ready to reprint both books in commercial editions.

We did not use the word *underground* then, but this tiny press and word of mouth enabled my writing to be discovered. The only handicap was that newspapers and magazines took no notice of books by small presses, and it was almost impossible to obtain a review. Edmund Wilson's review was an exception. It launched me. I owe him that and am only sorry that his acceptance did not extend to the rest of my work.

I had to reprint both books with a loan from Samuel Goldberg, the lawyer.

Someone thought I should send the story of the press to the *Reader's Digest*. The *Digest*'s response was that if I had to print the books myself, they must be bad. Many people still believe that, and for many years there was a suspicion that my difficulties with publishers indicated a doubtful quality in my work. A year before the publication of the *Diary,* a Harvard student wrote in *The Harvard Advocate* that the silence of critics and the indifference of commercial publishers must necessarily mean the work was flawed.

A three-hundred-copy edition of *Winter of Artifice,* press, type and bookbinding cost four hundred dollars. The books sold for three dollars. I printed announcements and circularized friends and acquaintances. The entire edition of both books was sold out.

But the physical work was so overwhelming that it interfered with my writing. This is the only reason I accepted the offer of a commercial publisher and surrendered the press. Otherwise I would have liked to continue with my own press, controlling both the content and design of the books.

I regretted giving up the press, for with the commercial publishers my troubles began. Then, as today, they wanted quick and large returns. This gamble for quick returns has nothing whatever to do with the deeper needs of the public, nor can a publisher's selection of a book be considered as representative of the people's choice. The impetus starts with the belief of the publisher, who backs his choice with advertising disguised as literary judgement. Thus books are imposed on the public like any other commercial product. In my case the illogical attitude of publishers was clear. They took me on as a prestige writer, but a prestige writer does not rate publicity, and therefore sales were modest. Five thousand copies of commercially published *Ladders to Fire* was not enough.

The universal quality in good writing which publishers claim to recognize is impossible to define. My books, which were not supposed to have this universal quality, were nevertheless bought and read by all kinds of people.

Today, instead of feeling embittered by the opposition of publishers, I am happy they opposed me, for the press had given me independence and confidence. I felt in direct contact with my public, and it was enough to sustain me through the following years. My early dealings with commercial publishers ended in disaster. They were not satisfied with the immediate sales, and neither the publishers nor the bookstores were interested in long-range sales. But fortunately, I found Alan Swallow in Denver, Colorado, a self-made and independent publisher who had started with a press in his garage. He adopted what he called his "maverick writers." He kept all my books in print, was content with simply earning a living, and our common struggles created a strong bond. He had the same problems with distribution and reviewing I had known, and we helped each other. He lived long enough to see the beginning of my popularity, the success of the diaries, to see the books he kept alive taught in universities. I am writing his story in volume five of the diaries.

What this story implies is that commercial publishers, being large corporate establishments, should sustain explorative and experimental writers, just as business sustains researchers, and not expect huge immediate gains from them. They herald new attitudes, new consciousness, new evolutions in the taste and minds of people. They are the research-ers who sustain the industry. Today my work is in harmony with the new values, the new search and state of mind of the young. This synchronicity is one nobody could have foreseen, except by remaining open minded to innovation and pioneer-ing.

PUBLISHING THOMAS WOLFE
by Maxwell Perkins

Maxwell Perkins was a distinguished editor at Charles Scribner's Sons. He was preparing the following memoir when he died suddenly on June 17, 1947.

I think that there is not in any one place so nearly complete a collection of an author's writings and records as that of Thomas Wolfe's now in the Harvard Library. When he died on that sad day in September 1938, when war was impending, or soon after that, I learned that I was his executor and that he had actually left little—as he would have thought, and as it seemed then—besides his manuscripts. It was my obligation to dispose of them to the advantage of his beneficiaries and his memory, and though the times were bad, and Wolfe had not then been recognized as what he now is, I could have sold them commercially, piece-meal, through dealers, for more money than they ever brought. I was determined that this

The article is printed in the form received from Mr. Perkins's secretary two days after his death, with some slight modifications in punctuation and with the addition of a title.

literary estate should remain a unit, available to writers and students, and I tried to sell it as such; but at that time, with war clouds gathering and soon bursting, I could find no adequate buyer.

Then Aline Bernstein, to whom Wolfe had given the manuscript of *Look Homeward, Angel,* sold it by auction for the relief of her people in misfortune, on the understanding that it would be given to Harvard. Not long after that William B. Wisdom, who had recognized Wolfe as a writer of genius on the publication of the *Angel,* and whose faith in him had never wavered, offered to purchase all of his manuscripts and records. He had already accumulated a notable collection of Wolfiana. His correspondence showed me that he thought as I did—that the point of supreme importance was that these records and writings should not be scattered to the four winds, that they be kept intact. And so the whole great packing case of material—letters, bills, documents, notebooks and manuscripts—went to him on the stipulation, which I never need have asked for, that he would will it all to one institution. Since *Look Homeward, Angel* was already in Harvard, since Tom Wolfe had loved the reading room of the Library where, as he so often told me, he devoured his hundreds of books and spent most of his Harvard years, Mr. Wisdom made a gift of all this to Harvard. And there it now is.

Though I had worked as an editor with Thomas Wolfe on two huge manuscripts, *Look Homeward, Angel* and *Of Time and the River,* I was astonished on that Spring evening of 1935 when Tom, about to sail for England, brought to our house on East 49th Street, because Scribner's was closed, the huge packing case containing all his literary material. Tom and I and the taxi man carried it in and set it down. Then Tom said to the man, 'What is your name?' He said, 'Lucky.' 'Lucky!' said Tom—I think it was perhaps an Americanization of some Italian name—and grasped his hand. It seemed a good omen. We three had done something together. We were together for that moment. We all shook hands. But for days, that huge packing case blocked our hall, until I got it removed to Scribner's.

The first time I heard of Thomas Wolfe I had a sense of foreboding. I who love the man say this. Every good thing that comes is accompanied by trouble. It was in 1928 when Madeleine Boyd, a literary agent, came in. She talked of several manuscripts which did not much interest me, but frequently interrupted herself to tell of a wonderful novel about an American boy. I several times said to her, 'Why don't you bring it in here, Madeleine?' and she seemed to evade the question. But finally she said, 'I will bring it, if you promise to read every word of it.' I did promise, but she told me other things that made me realize that Wolfe was a turbulent spirit, and that we were in for turbulence. When the manuscript came, I was fascinated by the first scene where Eugene's father, Oliver W. Gant, with his brother, two little boys, stood by a roadside in Pennsylvania and saw a division of Lee's Army on the march to Gettysburg.

But then there came some ninety-odd pages about Oliver Gant's life in Newport News, and Baltimore, and elsewhere. All this was what Wolfe had heard, and had no actual association with which to reconcile it, and it was inferior to the first episode, and in fact to all the rest of the book. I was turned off to other work and gave the manuscript to Wallace Meyer, thinking, 'Here is another promising novel that probably will come to nothing.' Then Meyer showed me that wonderful night scene in the cafe where Ben was with the Doctors, and Horse Hines, the undertaker, came in . I dropped everything and began to read again, and all of us were reading the book simultaneously, you might say, including John Hall Wheelock, and there never was the slightest disagreement among us as to its importance.

After some correspondence between me and Wolfe, and between him and Madeleine Boyd, from which we learned how at the October Fair in Germany he had been almost beaten to death—when I realized again that we had a Moby Dick to deal with—Wolfe arrived in New York and stood in the doorway of my boxstall of an office leaning against the door jamb. When I looked up and saw his wild hair and bright countenance—although he was so altogether different physically—I thought of Shelley. *He* was fair, but his hair was wild, and his face was bright and his head disproportionately small.

We then began to work upon the book and the first thing

we did, to give it unity, was to cut out that wonderful scene it began with and the ninety-odd pages that followed, because it seemed to me, and he agreed, that the whole tale should be unfolded through the memories and senses of the boy, Eugene, who was born in Asheville. We both thought that the story was compassed by that child's realization; that it was life and the world as he came to realize them. When he had tried to go back into the life of his father before he arrived in Asheville, without the inherent memory of events, the reality and the poignance were diminished—but for years it was on my conscience that I had persuaded Tom to cut out that first scene of the two little boys on the roadside with Gettysburg impending.

And then what happened? In *Of Time and the River* he brought the scene back to greater effect when old Gant was dying on the gallery of the hospital in Baltimore and in memory recalled his olden days. After that occurred I felt much less anxiety in suggesting cuts: I began then to realize that nothing Wolfe wrote was ever lost, that omissions from one book were restored in a later one. An extreme example of this is the fact that the whole second half of *The Web and the Rock* was originally intended to be the concluding episode in *Of Time and the River*. But most, and perhaps almost all, of those early incidents of Gant's life were worked into *The Web and the Rock* and *You Can't Go Home Again*.

I had realized, for Tom had prefaced his manuscript with a statement to that effect, that *Look Homeward, Angel* was autobiographical, but I had come to think of it as being so in the sense that *David Copperfield* is, or *War and Peace,* or *Pendennis*. But when we were working together, I suddenly saw that it was often almost literally autobiographical—that these people in it were his people. I am sure my face took on a look of alarm, and Tom saw it and he said, 'But Mr. Perkins, you don't understand. I think these people are *great* people and that they should be told about.' He was right. He had written a great book, and it had to be taken substantially as it was. And in truth, the extent of cutting in that book has somehow come to be greatly exaggerated. Really, it was more a matter of reorganization. For instance, Tom had that wonderful episode when Gant came back from his far-wandering and rode in early morning on the trolley car through the town and heard about who had died and who had been born and saw all the scenes that were so familiar to Tom or Eugene, as the old trolley rumbled along. This was immediately followed by an episode of a similar kind where Eugene, with his friends, walked home from school through the town of Asheville. That was presented in a Joycean way, but it was the same sort of thing—some one going through the town and through his perceptions revealing it to the reader. By putting these episodes next to each other the effect of each was diminished, and I think we gave both much greater value by separating them. We did a great deal of detailed cutting, but it was such things as that I speak of that constituted perhaps the greater part of the work.

Of Time and the River was a much greater struggle for Tom. Eventually, I think it was on Thanksgiving Day 1933, he brought me in desperation about two feet of typescript. The first scene in this was the platform of the railroad station in Asheville when Eugene was about to set out for Harvard, and his family had come to see him off. It must have run to about 30,000 words and I cut it to perhaps 10,000 and showed it to Tom. He approved it. When you are waiting for a train to come in, there is suspense. Something is going to happen. You must, it seemed to me, maintain that sense of suspense and you can't to the extent of 30,000 words. There never was any cutting that Tom did not agree to. He knew that cutting was necessary. His whole impulse was to utter what he felt and he had no time to revise and compress.

So then we began a year of nights of work, including Sundays, and every cut, and change, and interpolation, was argued about and about. The principle that I was working on was that this book, too, got its unity and its form through the senses of Eugene, and I remember how, if I had had my way, we should, by sticking to that principle, have lost one of the most wonderful episodes Wolfe ever wrote—the death of Gant. One night we agreed that certain transitions should be written in, but instead of doing them Wolfe brought on the next night some five thousand words about Eugene's sister in Asheville when her father was ill, and a doctor there and a nurse. I said, 'Tom, this is all outside the story, and you know

248

it. Eugene was not there, he was in Cambridge; all of this was outside his perception and knowledge at the time.' Tom agreed with me, but the next night, he brought me another five thousand words or so which got up into the death of Gant. And then I realized I was wrong, even if right in theory. What he was doing was too good to let any rule of form impede him.

It is said that Tolstoy never willingly parted with the manuscript of *War and Peace*. One could imagine him working on it all through his life. Certainly Thomas Wolfe never willingly parted from the proofs of *Of Time and the River*. He sat brooding over them for weeks in the Scribner library and not reading. John Wheelock read them and we sent them to the printer and told Tom it had been done. I could believe that otherwise he might have clung to them to the end.

He dedicated that book to me in most extravagant terms. I never saw the dedication until the book was published and though I was most grateful for it, I had forebodings when I heard of his intention. I think it was that dedication that threw him off his stride and broke his magnificent scheme. It gave shallow people the impression that Wolfe could not function as a writer without collaboration, and one critic even used some such phrases as, 'Wolfe and Perkins—Perkins and Wolfe, what way is that to write a novel.' Nobody with the slightest comprehension of the nature of a writer could accept such an assumption. No writer could possibly tolerate the assumption, which perhaps Tom almost himself did, that he was dependent as a writer upon anyone else. He had to prove to himself and to the world that this was not so.

And that was the fundamental reason that he turned to another publisher. If he had not—but by the time he did it was plain that he had to tell, in the medium of fiction and through the transmutation of his amazing imagination, the story of his own life—he never would have broken his own great plan by distorting Eugene Gant into George Webber. That was a horrible mistake. I think Edward Aswell, of Harper & Brothers, agrees with me in this, but when the manuscript that came to form *The Web and the Rock* and *You Can't Go Home Again* got to him to work on, and in some degree to me, as Wolfe's executor, Tom was dead, and things had to be taken as they were.

The trouble began after the publication of *Of Time and the River,* which the reviewers enormously praised—but many of them asserted that Wolfe could only write about himself, that he could not see the world or anything objectively, with detachment—that he was always autobiographical. Wolfe was extremely sensitive to criticism for all his tremendous faith in his genius as an obligation put upon him to fulfill. One day when I lived on East 49th Street near Second Avenue, and he on First Avenue, just off the corner of 49th, I met him as I was going home. He said he wanted to talk to me, as we did talk every evening about that time, and we went into the Waldorf. He referred to the criticisms against him, and said that he wanted to write a completely objective, unautobiographical book, and that it would show how strangely different everything is from what a person expects it to be. One might say that he was thinking of the theme that has run through so many great books, such as *Pickwick Papers* and *Don Quixote,* where a man, young or old, goes hopefully out into the world slap into the face of outrageous reality. He was going to put on the title page what was said by Prince Andrei, in *War and Peace,* after his first battle, when the praise fell upon those who had done nothing and blame almost fell upon one who had done everything. Prince Andrei, who saved the battery commander who most of all had held back the French from the blame that Little Tushin would have accepted, walked out with him into the night. Then as Tushin left, Tolstoy said, 'Prince Andrei looked up at the stars and sighed; everything was so different from what he thought it was going to be.'

Tom was in a desperate state. It was not only what the critics said that made him wish to write objectively, but that he knew that what he had written had given great pain even to those he loved the most. The conclusion of our talk was that if he could write such an objective book on this theme within a year, say, to the extent of perhaps a hundred thousand words, it might be well to do it. It was this that turned him to George Webber, but once he began on that he really and irresistibly resumed the one story he was destined to write, which was that of himself, or Eugene Gant.

And so, the first half of *The Web and the Rock,* of which

there is only a typescript, is a re-telling in different terms of *Look Homeward, Angel*. Wolfe was diverted from his natural purpose—and even had he lived, what could have been done? Some of his finest writing is that first half of *The Web and the Rock*. Could anybody have just tossed it out?

But if Tom had held to his scheme and completed the whole story of his life as transmuted into fiction through his imagination, I think the accusation that he had no sense of form could not have stood. He wrote one long story, 'The Web of Earth,' which had perfect form, for all its intricacy. I remember saying to him, 'Not one word of this should be changed.' One might say that as his own physical dimensions were huge so was his conception of a book. He had one book to write about a vast, sprawling, turbulent land—America—as perceived by Eugene Gant. Even when he was in Europe, it was of America he thought. If he had not been diverted and had lived to complete it, I think it would have had the form that was suited to the subject.

His detractors say he could only write about himself, but all that he wrote of was transformed by his imagination. For instance, in *You Can't Go Home Again* he shows the character Foxhall Edwards at breakfast. Edwards's young daughter enters 'as swiftly and silently as a ray of light.' She is very shy and in a hurry to get to school. She tells of a theme she has written on Walt Whitman and what the teacher said of Whitman. When Edwards urges her not to hurry and makes various observations, she says, 'Oh, Daddy, you're so funny!' What Tom did was to make one unforgettable little character out of three daughters of Foxhall Edwards.

He got the ray of light many years ago when he was with me in my house in New Canaan, Connecticut, and one daughter, at the age of about eight or ten, came in and met this gigantic stranger. After she was introduced she fluttered all about the room in her embarrassment, but radiant, like a sunbeam. Then Tom was present when another daughter, in Radcliffe, consulted me about a paper she was writing on Whitman, but he put this back into her school days. The third, of which he composed a single character, was the youngest, who often did say, partly perhaps, because she was not at ease when Tom was there, 'Oh, Daddy, you're so silly.' That is how Tom worked. He created something new and something meaningful through a transmutation of what he saw, heard, and realized.

I think no one could understand Thomas Wolfe who had not seen nor properly imagined the place in which he was born and grew up. Asheville, North Carolina, is encircled by mountains. The trains wind in and out through labyrinths of passes. A boy of Wolfe's imagination imprisoned there could think that what was beyond was all wonderful—different from what it was where there was not for him enough of anything. Whatever happened, Wolfe would have been what he was. I remember on the day of his death saying to his sister Mabel that I thought it amazing in an American family that one of the sons who wanted to be a writer should have been given the support that was given Tom, and that they all deserved great credit for that. She said it didn't matter, that nothing could have prevented Tom from doing what he did.

That is true, but I think that those mountainous walls which his imagination valuted gave him the vision of an America with which his books are fundamentally concerned. He often spoke of the artist in America—how the whole color and character of the country was completely new—never interpreted; how in England, for instance, the writer inherited a long accretion of accepted expression from which he could start. But Tom would say—and he had seen the world—'who has ever made you know the color of an American box car?' Wolfe was in those mountains—he tells of the train whistles at night—the trains were winding their way out into the great world where it seemed to the boy there was everything desirable, and vast, and wonderful.

It was partly that which made him want to see everything, and read everything, and experience everything, and say everything. There was a night when he lived on First Avenue that Nancy Hale, who lived on East 49th Street near Third Avenue, heard a kind of chant, which grew louder. She got up and looked out of the window at two or three in the morning and there was the great figure of Thomas Wolfe, advancing in his long countryman's stride, with his swaying black raincoat, and what he was chanting was, 'I wrote ten thousand words today—I wrote ten thousand words today.'

252

Tom must have lived in eight or nine different parts of New York and Brooklyn for a year or more. He knew in the end every aspect of the City—he walked the streets endlessly—but he was not a city man. The city fascinated him but he did not really belong in it and was never satisfied to live in it. He was always thinking of America as a whole and planning trips to some part that he had not yet seen, and in the end taking them. His various quarters in town always looked as if he had just moved in, to camp for awhile. This was partly because he really had no interest in possessions of any kind, but it was also because he was in his very nature a Far Wanderer, bent upon seeing all places, and his rooms were just necessities into which he never settled. Even when he was there his mind was not. He needed a continent to range over, actually and in imagination. And his place was all America. It was with America he was most deeply concerned and I believe he opened it up as no other writer ever did for the people of his time and for the writers and artists and poets of tomorrow. Surely he had a thing to tell us.

ON SPAGHETTI AND
THE ALICE JAMES COOPERATIVE
by Marjorie Fletcher

Marjorie Fletcher is a poet and a founder of The Alice James Poetry Cooperative.

Now that so many formerly independent publishers have been absorbed by conglomerates, a conflict has developed between this country's best authors and a majority of our commercial houses. When a publisher's prime obligation is to amass profits, whether or not the titles issued have some literary merit, the basic interests of every writer whose first concern is to create literature are in opposition to that publisher's objectives. But, no responsible executive in any conglomerate would act against stockholders' interests and reject all books that are poorly written despite favorable sales projections. And thus, unfortunately, all U.S. writers now face a preponderance of publishing houses in which every commitment to the well-written book must bow to the pursuit of the buck.

254

Years ago all of us knew who was responsible for determining which titles appeared on bookstore shelves. Before subsidiary rights sales were measured in the millions, before Gulf and Western acquired Simon & Schuster and RCA controlled Random House, we knew whom to praise. We also knew who was the culprit. The men and women who made the decisions were identified with the books they issued. They were not mere entrepreneurs, but publishers and editors. The quality of the volumes with which they were associated reflected their judgements only. And many of them felt it was their obligation to issue work of merit. Charles Scribner, II, boasted, "I am proud of my imprint. I cannot publish fiction that is without literary value."

But now, "A lot of publishing houses are being run by accountants, businessmen and lawyers who have very little concern for the books. They could just as well be selling string or spaghetti," according to Roger Straus, Jr. Now established editors like William Targ are leaving the industry because they can no longer bear the atmosphere. Now the executives in most of our commercial houses must answer to the boards of conglomerates. Whom can we blame? Whom can we hold accountable for the quality of this country's literature? Gulf and Western's senior vice-presidents? RCA stockholders? The marketing director of The Music Corporation of America? Who in these huge corporations combines the power to effect financial decisions with an abiding commitment to the publication of literature?

The answer, I fear, is that no individual or group in the conglomerates combines these two attributes and, as a result, the conflict that now exists between most U.S. houses and all serious writers will not simply disappear: today, tomorrow, or even next year. The situation is untenable for authors. We must have alternatives.

For fiction writers this conflict of interest has only recently become a crisis. However, for a variety of different and complex reasons, both poets and feminist authors have long felt the aims of the commercial houses were unsympathetic to their basic interests. Both have found alternatives. The alternative that I find most interesting is cooperative publishing. In 1973, with two men and four women, all poets, I helped found

255

Alice James Poetry Cooperative. Certainly, the double burden of acting as both a writer and publisher is not desirable for an entire career; but, when a significant number of like-minded authors are faced with inhospitable publishers, one effective solution is to band together for the purpose of printing and distributing books that those writers judge meritorious. And now, when the businessmen who run our large houses display a frightening inability to distinguish literature from spaghetti, one way to insure that quality poetry and fiction will be issued in the future is to form publishing ventures that are owned and run by authors.

Publishing, however, is demanding. At Alice James all authors are required to attend regular meetings, to share office duties and work on production for approximately one year. Together we prepare mammoth mailings. We apply for grants. We fill orders. And mail books to distributors, debate current issues, trek to bookfairs, keep financial records, send out review copies, consult with the printer, dun bookstores for long overdue payments, draft press releases, pay bills. Somebody has to write the academics that, "no, we do not hand out free copies." Someone has to empty the wastebasket. Although Alice James now employs part-time help, for five years only the authors performed the tasks necessary for publishing.

Even though publishing demands time and energy, the member of a writers' cooperative gains several distinct benefits. An author who, in concert with other authors, operates the house which publishes his or her work effectively influences two crucial areas: the appearance of the volume and the marketing effort made after publication. Although the cooperative has final approval, at Alice James all authors select the art for their covers, design a format for their interiors, choose a typeface, consult with our printer. With the support and advice of experienced members, each assumes primary responsibility for the production of his or her volume. Then, once the books are printed, the author becomes involved in promotion. He or she draws up a list of reviewers who will receive copies, including those who might be sympathetic—e.g., gay reviewers, traditionalists, feminists. Each author also compiles a list of individuals to whom ordering information is mailed. And every author in the cooperative has the opportunity to effect the tenor of publicity by soliciting pre-publication comments, by writing blurbs and press releases. To an extent unknown in commercial houses, Alice James' authors can control both the physical aspects of their books and the sales efforts. Also, because all decisions are made by writers, the basic interests of an Alice James author seldom conflict with the publisher. For instance, not only will the cooperative never shred books, but it is our intent to keep every book issued in print; and, because we are thoroughly committed to each manuscript accepted, the cooperative promotes each book equally and does not favor one title over another.

And it works. Alice James has published thirty collections of poetry. More are currently scheduled. Six of our books contain the work of two or more poets. The remainder are by one author only. Although our first four books were issued in runs of one thousand, that number was doubled for all subsequent volumes. Six titles have been reprinted. And Alice James has gained a national reputation even though all members must live in the New England area because every author is required to devote time to the cooperative. Our books have been reviewed in periodicals as diverse and far afield as *Aspect Magazine, Publishers Weekly, Madamoiselle, The New York Times Book Review, The Beloit Poetry Journal, 13th Moon, The Chicago Daily News, Aspen Leaves, the Pacific Sun Literary Quarterly.* Articles describing the venture have appeared in *The Christian Science Monitor, New Times, Coda* and many other periodicals. Nearly every book issued by the cooperative has been attended to in one of the major review vehicles for libraries, which guarantees an immediate spate of orders. One Alice James title received honorable mention for The Elliston Book Award. Two have been selected by the Small Press Book Club. Several of our members have received NEA Fellowships for work that Alice James issued. Several have been recognized by state arts councils. Many individual poems published by the cooperative have been awarded prestigious prizes. Many have been anthologized. And poetry printed by Alice James has received accolades from Adrienne Rich, Jean Valentine, Mark Strand, May Sarton, Rosellen Brown, Michael Benedikt, George Plimpton, Marge Piercy, Louis

Simpson, Helen Vendler, Robert Pinsky, Maxine Kumin and dozens of other critics and authors.

But writers involved in cooperative publishing must eventually resolve some unique issues. When a manuscript is being discussed, should the author's desirability as a group member also be considered? Although I have on occasion regretted my conviction, I continue to feel strongly that the personality of a candidate must be irrelevent. Should the corporation become non-profit and, thereby, sacrifice members' royalties in order to receive lower postage rates and certain tax benefits? Alice James may pay any author for mopping the floor or setting type, but he or she is paid with copies of books for writing poetry because the IRS considers that royalties are profits and, therefore, prohibits such payments. Once a writer's book is published, how can he or she be enticed to remain with the cooperative? The problem of how to convince authors to stay on as members once their vested interests have diminished is, I feel, a central dilemma for this sort of venture since, unless experienced members remain, the cooperative is always beginning again. Contracts have to be written that favor neither the writer nor the publisher. By-laws that define the various relationships must also be drafted. But while these and the other special problems created by forming a publishing venture are being discussed by a cooperative's authors, the perfect poem or the great American novel must lie in the drawer unfinished.

Someday in paradise all poetry and fiction writers will live in secluded towers and publishers will have to fall on their knees to beg us three times, "Pretty please." But just now the number of independent commercial publishers in this country is diminishing so rapidly that everyone of us who cherishes literature had better act on behalf of that interest. We must urge that existing anti-trust laws be brought to bear on houses owned by conglomerates. We must encourage the efforts of independents to remain autonomous. We must support small houses. And, I think, we ought to form more publishing ventures of our own. Although we will surely disagree about what constitutes literature, when we read books that are tangled and sloppy we, at least, know they are spaghetti.

258

DEALING
WITH MAMBRINO'S HELMET
by David Ray

David Ray is a poet and editor of NEW LETTERS.

To confess is to ask for pardon; and the whole confusing process brings out too much self-pity and too many small emotions in general. For people like myself to look back is a task. It is like re-entering a trap, or a labyrinth, from which one has only too lately, and too narrowly, escaped.

Louise Bogan

Concerning their statement that this is a basin and not a helmet, I have already answered; but as to declaring whether that is a pack-saddle or a harness, I am not so bold as to give a definitive decision, but leave the matter to your worship's better judgement. Perhaps, since none of you are knights, as I am, the spells in this place will have no effect on you, your understanding will be free, and you will be able to judge of the affairs of this castle as they really and truly are, and not as they appear to me.

Don Quixote

259

A. H. Maslow, in *The Farther Reaches of Human Nature,* states "Who is interested in creativity?"And my answer is that practically everybody is. This interest is no longer confined to psychologists and psychiatrists. Now it has become a question of national and international policy as well . . ." He doesn't say 'editors' (perhaps he was thinking first and foremost of those 'creative' scientists who might figure out how to live under the deep ice of the coming glaciers, or the 'creative' encounter leaders who offer procedural tips for better orgasms), but surely editors are among those particularly interested in creativity, specialists of a sort, their own creativity either displaced or sublimated or involved in endlessly sifting through the 'creative' efforts of others. Since editing itself is sometimes said to be creative it should, as a job, attract such types as poets and painters. Sylvia Plath went to Manhattan as a *Mademoiselle* guest editor while still in college. But did she discover the hitch? I notice she did not remain an editor. If she had, the daily masochism associated with the role might have drained off the intensity needed for suicide. A bizarre speculation, but there *is* a hitch (or two) to what at first appears a delightful task. Maslow touches on one in defining the *ambiente* of creativity itself: "*Acceptance: the Positive Attitude.* In moments of here-now immersion and self-forgetfulness we are apt to become more 'positive' and less negative in still another way, namely, in giving up criticism (editing, picking and choosing, correcting, skepticism, improving, doubting, rejecting, judging, evaluating). This is like saying that we accept. We don't reject or disapprove or selectively pick and choose. No blocks against the matter-in-hand means that we let it flow in upon us. We let it wreak its will upon us. We let it have its way. We let it be itself. Perhaps we can even approve of its being itself. This makes it easier to be Taoistic in the sense of humility, non-interference, receptivity."

"Acceptance" and "Rejection," the crucial polarities: writers and editors speak of them incessantly, and they are also emotional states, the bliss of acceptance, the writer's happiness. "My poem's coming out in *The New Yorker*"—

Love, recognition, smiles, self-respect. "My daily rejection slip!"—self-hatred, thoughts of self-slaughter, feelings of worthlessness. Like the writer, the editor who sent the rejection slip is led into his work by his own creativity, and his respect for that of others. But is he permitted to give up "editing, picking and choosing, correcting, skepticism, improving, doubting, rejecting, judging, evaluating?" A fine editor he would be! "Either it's a pack-saddle or, as your worships say, it isn't." (*Don Quixote*) And thus the editor, who wants to affirm, to love, to give—who does so when he can respect and accept a work—becomes a Nay-sayer, a Rejector, a person who makes other people feel like self-slaughter. If his magazine is good enough to attract writers, at least ninety-nine percent, probably more, of all the material he reads, reacts to, wants to bless with his acceptance, must be returned. His labor will never show, though he may feel it as a great cumulative weight of negation, may share the rejection and defeat others feel through his non-cooperation with their ambitions. Yet, like Sancho, if he is an honest man, he must cry, "What I see and perceive is nothing but a man on a grey ass like mine with something glittering on his head." No gold helmet at all—just a barber's basin. When work that does not deserve publication appears in print we might say the editor has shared in the writer's self-delusions, agreeing with Don Quixote rather than Sancho: "Why, that is Mambrino's helmet. Stand aside . . ." Every editor needs a Sancho to caution: "I could probably give you some reasons that would make your worship see that you are mistaken."

Not only is the editor's habitual, unavoidable negation the polar opposite of what he intended to express, but insofar as he identifies with the writer (which he certainly does if he is also a writer or if he has himself suffered from rejection during his lifetime), the editor has drifted into a near insoluble dilemma. How can he accept his function as the hated Nay-sayer for so many, the person who dishes out to others what he himself most dreads? It is a sadomasochistic situation. He works harder to find the highs of the job more satisfying, to distance the lows, not to feel them, not to identify with the rejected writers, though this is more difficult to do when he reads his not infrequent hate mail.

We have a rather profound problem here, and I want to emphasize its importance. I am sure a variation of it is involved in many professions. It is touched upon by recent research on right brain-left brain activity (so different are the roles demanded by the job). For example, in a recent book about television, Jerry Mander writes: "The right half of the brain, which deals with more subjective cognitive processes—dream images, fantasy, intuition—continues to receive the television images. But, because the bridge between the right and left brains has been effectively shattered [by the hypnotic effect of watching], all cross-processing—the making conscious of the unconscious data, so that the information is useable—is eliminated. The information goes in, but it cannot be easily recalled or thought about." He cites A. R. Luria: "No organized thought is possible in these phasic states, and selective associations are replaced by nonselective association, deprived of their purposive character." Mander concludes that "television information enters unfiltered and whole, directly into the memory banks but it is not available for conscious analysis, understanding or learning." He concludes also that intellectuals are fooling themselves if they think television can serve any rational purpose (e.g., solving particular social problems). Television has blottoed the rational left brain, after a few hypnotizing moments. One cannot think in "the conscious level of somnambulism" which is television-watching. And yet many contemporary poets have been writing about the pre-digested experiences offered them by television, seemingly unaware that they are not directly experiencing anything but a dream state. Yet, reading such books and television-derived poems in manuscript I am left with the feeling that almost all material derived from television shares the effects described in research; and I agree with McLuhan that the television-reared individual is a new and different creature altogether. The T.V. child may not know the difference between a gunshot and a dirty look, a beheading and a playful swat; the poet does not seem to know the difference between a Magda Goebbels and a housewife with dishpan hands. Where is the rage, the indignation one should feel? How can Americans sit, sip their beer and watch the affluent war criminal rehash the statistics of his crimes? And of course, in vivid documentary, watch the crimes, interview the survivors, stare at their scars? Of course poetry is *possible* from this: but surely a poetry that knows the difference between victim and aggressor, a crime and a pastime. Surely a numbed morality never qualified an artist. "Such a cruel pastime could only result in developing a coarse and brutal people," it was said of the Romans, voyeurs of violence.

In dealing daily with manuscript material like this, as well as a garden variety of other aesthetic devotions, the editor's entire being is on the line each time he makes a judgement. One editor awards the T.V. poems a prize; another, like myself, sees merely another example of decline and fall. Either, if serious, feels that his gesture is important to his culture.

The editor too switches on the T.V., sits down to experience the hypnotic, non-judging, all trusting state of blissful complete acceptance of whatever the author is doing. But like a teacher spotting misspellings, his trusting and loving and approving and indeed his own creativity are abruptly blocked: he reaches for the rejection slip. The editor is expected to respond with the most loving of I-Thou encounters to each offering (no one wants less of him), and yet the most 'rational' performance is also expected of him—he must demonstrate his delight with the offered manuscript, correct those spellings, proof-read, coordinate the work with other offerings, and then set about getting the material reviewed if possible. (Note: the little magazine editor is not simply an 'editor;' he is lucky if he is spared the work of typesetting.) The editor is, in short, the great lover. He is expected (by those who offer it) to praise warmly each gift of new material. The relationship of author and editor has vestiges of the mother-child relationship, the infant's offerings to the all-loving mother, the earlier nursing experience itself. The editor is modern midwife, also footstool: "an attendant lord . . . Advise the prince; no doubt, an easy tool,/Deferential, glad to be of use,/politic, cautious, and meticulous; . . . but a bit obtuse;/At times, indeed, almost ridiculous—" (An editor wrote that poem.) When a writer complains that he didn't get a proper reading he means he didn't get unconditional acceptance, love, assent to his dreams. Who wants merely the rubber stamp of logic? And he is right. Thus the ideal editor-writer relationship is rare. That's why you see the same names crop up as "regular contributors"—winners of true love. But what a bagful of hate, resentment, disappointment, spins on from anything less! The editor crops up as hated figure in more shoptalk than the devil himself.

II

"Freeing the enchained, releasing prisoners, succouring the unfortunate, raising the fallen, relieving the needy? You infamous brood whose low and vile intelligence deserves no revelation from heaven of that virtue which lies in knight errantry, nor any knowledge of your sin and ignorance in not reverencing the shadow—how much more the actual presence—of a knight errant! Come here, you pack of thieves, for you are no troopers, but highwaymen licensed by the Holy Brotherhood! Tell me, who was the dolt who signed a warrant of arrest against such a knight as I am?"

Don Quixote

Come in with high ideals! Tilt the windmills! It is possible to play both F. Scott Fitzgerald and Maxwell Perkins! I asked a young associate what he thought of editing now, after six months of it. "A different thing altogether," he said. "I didn't know writers were such . . ." He could not find the word for it, like the outraged wife in *To Have and Have Not,* reaching for the vilest word imaginable and coming up only with "Writer." The thanklessness. The sibling rivalry. ("She's no good, send that stuff back and I'll give you enough for the full issue, give me a month.") The associate still has ideals because he has not yet been destroyed by the grind. One comes to understand the cynicism, the defeat, in some of those Max Perkins letters. I prefer, to the Perkins' pained grimace, the picture on my wall, torn from an old *Life,* of Hemingway kicking a can on a lonesome road.

Hired in 1971 by the University of Missouri-Kansas City to teach half-time and edit *The University Review* (once *the University of Kansas City Review*), I was not only provided with the inherited wealth of an already established magazine, but also with the opportunity to do—within limits—what I wanted with it. Though my wife Judy, who helped greatly

264

from the outset, shared my admiration for what retiring Professor Alexander Cappon had done with the *Review,* we felt it was a bit too scholarly for our tastes: Alex had published the important essays that launched the Chicago school of criticism, and his early issues abound in Grant Wood and Thomas Hart Benton woodcuts; he had published an unknown writer named J.D. Salinger in 1940, and a terrific, as yet unpublished, anthology has been created by choosing the William Carlos Williams, Weldon Kees, e.e. cummings, Winfield Townley Scott, John Ciardi items scattered through the forty years of back issues. Nevertheless, the magazine had become better known for scholarship; we therefore changed the focus, format, title and emphasis, and if we'd known how hard it would be to build a subscription list we might have changed it more radically—perhaps to *Nude Lovers* rather than *New Letters.* Our kickoff issue had a new Thomas Hart Benton story, "Ali," his first venture at fiction so far as I know.

I renewed acquaintance with those I had published earlier, either in *Chicago Review* or *Epoch;* some of them were still creating work that was literally too good for the Establishment. (Though others had slipped away from the Littles into their deserved recognition—people like Philip Roth, Joyce Carol Oates, Don DeLillo). Many too had been told, on New York or Boston letterhead, "Get Thee Hence!" their manuscripts returned unread. Those writers go on resisting the tendency of everything in our day to turn into vinyl; they make up what some of us mean by a viable counter-culture. They operate despite those critics who fear dealing with living literature, and they ignore snubs like rain; they go on functioning. At *New Letters* they could at least get a reading based on response to the work, not projected sales figures. I also scouted, and urged others to scout for us, in archives, widows' cupboards, old beerboxes. We soon found we were specializing in work that had been ignored, Melvin B. Tolson's fiction, e.g., written in the Thirties, when no Black Lit enthusiasts were around to thump for him. Both our Richard Wright issue (reprinted as a book) and our Paul Goodman book issue were rescue operations. Yet these efforts received not a single review! Would that have been the case if they had come out of New York? Countee Cullen's essay about his love affair with Isadora Duncan was a hot find. We reprinted J.D. Salinger's story from 1940, though he had taken what he wanted from the little magazines and didn't care to look back long enough to grant us permission. Ironically that single act got *New Letters* more attention, and more new subscriptions, than all the really original work we had found. Victims of the system, reviewers who called complained that the Salinger story was not as good as most work found in *New Letters,* even though they continued to maintain they could not review work on the basis of its quality alone. In our culture, only the name matters, and everyone wants the same people, whether for jobs, profile articles, reviews, or whatever. To us there is also magic in the name Richard Wright or Paul Goodman, but we are not really in touch. We even find magic in names that others have not yet discovered at all. For some, we have perhaps helped keep their heads above the water line; we have provided an outlet when the Establishment offered nothing. And our real highs still come from work with Becoming, not Being. We still try to spot the real thing before it's quite the real thing. Frank London Brown and Cyrus Colter remain two of my favorite writers because I was privileged to work with them at a point in their careers when my interest could mean more than a bystander's approval.

Someone has to offer alternatives to slick magazines, T.V., slick fiction, formulas. The little magazines offer a counter-culture; I believe that as I did in college—though clearly the value of this counter-culture erodes if the littles lose their sense of role, if, as is occasionally the case, an editor merely imitates more popular fashions. Our literary life would be incredibly diminished without the little magazines. Yet, when two Bucknell professors asked me for advice about starting their own little magazine I tried to talk them out of it, tried to give them some sense of the pain associated with the job—and of the costs to one's own work (both were also writers). "It'll make it twice (or six times) as hard for your own work to get a fair hearing," I said. "You'll be typecast as an editor. Don't wear three hats—you're already wearing two." Will they turn from editing at the point when they begin to say, like my young associate, "Why do writers have to be such . . . ?" Have they yet read Melanie Klein's *Envy and*

Gratitude, which offers insight into a syndrome common to artists, be they Frost or Hemingway or lesser fry? Klein relates the repayment of generosity with malice to regressive tendencies common to artists—back to early nursing experience, the stage in which the hungry child ('the hunger artist') bites, hates, and smears the breast which has served so well. For many in the helping professions (which includes editing), such behavior has often proved painful, bewildering, and sometimes tragic. Is this one of the reasons psychiatrists as a group lead the suicide list? Did such mistreatment by fellow artists of Ezra Pound help produce his later sickness, a terrible projection of mistreatment and victimization? I believe it was Hemingway who said that Pound fed and clothed writers, gave them handouts, did his best to get them published and reviewed, got them jobs, etc., and he was unseasonably lucky if they didn't stab him in the back within six months. With few exceptions I'd consider that an accurate description of the experience of others who have made helping others in their careers primary.

A dangerous role, rescuing anyone. The Karpman triangle: the Victim becomes the Persecutor; the Rescuer becomes the Victim, scorned and hated, discarded. We rescue a writer everytime we say "We are happy to accept . . ." Hemingway pilloried Sherwood Anderson in a vicious satire. Anderson's crime? Doing everything he could for Hemingway. Anyone who has read biographies of artists and writers knows the syndrome. Henry James wrote delightful stories about such pain, comedic when one manages a distance.

III

Though editorial talent is as rare as any other kind, editors don't audition or play the violin to obtain their positions, some of which give them immense power—not only to print but to keep out of print. One must, if assessing an editor honestly, wonder what talents he has crushed, not simply take his word for his enumerated glories as midwife. I am amused when reading memoirs of editors who Homerically rollcall the artists they have personally created by their generosity (wasn't I tempted to do it myself a page or two back!). You'd never know from one of the 'best' that he also rejected folks like John Steinbeck. Let's see the account book, Sir! As an editor I can only pray that I myself have not been too rejecting, too deadly an influence, in any artist's life.

Though little magazines are not at the "red hot center" of our culture, we don't have to excuse our own preference for trivia by citing "readership studies"! We don't have to dance to the trios of our advertisers. We seldom make the excuse that "we were only following orders." Once one has decided, as commercial editors feel they must, to follow capitalism with its dead-end rule that whatever and only what is profitable is of any value, one's soul is surely lost. I have files full of letters from powerful editors telling me they have no power. If it's not readership studies they cite for their helplessness it's sales surveys. "I can't publish it just because it's good," an Establishment editor told me. Such men can say, "Your work is too good for this world," and mean it. "We aren't permitted to publish anything that won't sell fifty thousand paperbacks," another states. "How did you get that Richard Wright material?" one asked me, saying that he had futilely offered Ellen Wright a dollar a word for such rights. "By not offering her a dollar a word," I replied to his deaf and uncomprehending ears. He couldn't understand that sort of thing, a relationship based on appreciation but then again, he probably hadn't read *Don Quixote*, who goes on tilting in a fog of scorn.

THE CURSE OF THE EDITORIAL CLASS
by Gerald Howard

Gerald Howard is an editor at W. W. Norton. He previously was an editor at Viking Penguin and New American Library.

Before Cork Smith became my friend he was my hero. Not that I knew who he was, but I knew *somebody* at Viking had to be Thomas Pynchon's editor, and since I was a two-time reader of *Gravity's Rainbow* and a Xeroxer of uncollected Pynchon stories in back issues of *Epoch* and *The Saturday Evening Post* (sic!), that person naturally assumed heroic stature in my mind. So when I came to Viking Penguin in 1980 as a young editor through the paperback portal, I made it my business to chat up this Cork Smith, who had been Pynchon's editor since 1960 when he bought the story "Lowlands" for *New World Writing.* He was everything you could hope for in a literary editor: dry, witty, kind, with a roster of authors past and current that included Jimmy Breslin, Robertson Davies, Leonard Cohen, Muriel Spark, Harper Lee, and Roger Angell, and a rich and deeply instructive fund of publishing anecdotes. In about a year and a half, first at Viking and then at Ticknor and Fields, Cork published the first novels of Harriet Doerr, Gloria Naylor, Madison Smartt Bell, and Carolyn Chute, and the fourth novel of a down-on-his-luck Albany scribe named Willian Kennedy—*Ironweed*. His eye for literary talent was, and is, phenomenal, almost spooky. In January Cork Smith became the casualty of the decimation of the Harcourt Brace adult trade department, of which he was editor-in-chief.

Also dismissed from Harcourt was another editor friend of mine, Patricia Strachan. Pat worked for a decade and a half at Farrar, Straus and Giroux, where she helped Tom Wolfe transform *The Bonfire of the Vanities* from its unsatisfactory *Rolling Stone* version into the signature novel of the 1980s. Her feel for the pure American literary voice is wonderful: she has edited Padgett Powell's *Edisto,* Larry Heinemann's *Paco's Story,* and Ian Frazier's *Great Plains,* that wildly original piece of Americana.

The casualty list stretches on. Houghton Mifflin closes its Ticknor and Fields imprint and out the door go John Herman (Robert Stone, William Gass, Frederick Barthelme) and Cynthia Spiegel (Kathleen Norris). Paramount Publishing purchases the Macmillan Company and shuts down the Atheneum imprint, canning Lee Goerner (Michael Herr, Charles Johnson, Reynolds Price, Isabel Allende). Earlier Paramount had dissolved the Poseidon Press imprint run by Ann Patty (Harry Crews, Patrick McGrath, Steve Erickson). HarperCollins folds the imprints of veteran editors Aaron Asher (Milan Kundera, Arthur Miller, Saul Bellow, Philip Roth) and Ed Burlingame (Ron Hansen, Jonathan Raban). Everybody waits to see just how many Macmillan jobs will disappear in the ongoing merger (a lot, it appears, as of this writing), and for over a year William Morrow, a commercial house that nonetheless published the likes of Richard Powers and Sven Birkerts, twisted slowly in the breeze while their owner, the Hearst Corporation, cruelly fished for a purchase offer that never came.

In short, the great fear is upon New York publishing, as houses and imprints gutter out and the careers of dozens of the most respected professionals in the business appear at dire risk. The merger mania and fiscal shenanigans of the eighties seem to

270

be replaying themselves, but this time with a chilling endgame flavor.

And what of it, a former employee of a steel mill or an auto assembly plant or a defense contractor or a semi-conductor manufacturer might ask? Wrenching change and economic dislocation are the lot of all industries, and why should an elite communications industry like trade publishing be immune to the bruising body blows of postindustrial capitalists? No reason at all. It should be said, though, that in my small corner of the media world, the Quality Lit and High End nonfiction district, the mentality is beginning to feel distinctly Southern Californian: i.e., is this the Big One? Print culture in general and book culture in particular seem suspended in an uneasy hiatus as the digital revolution bears down upon us and will absolutely certainly without a doubt change everything unless it doesn't. Are we, the purveyors of quality printed and bound goods since 1455, to be in the end nothing more than road kill along the information highway?

It's a hard situation to get your mind around. The things you can grasp are tiresomely obvious and everything else is unnervingly imponderable. In the first category is the fact that the dynamics of large corporations have nothing whatsoever to do with literary and intellectual values. Please note carefully: I am *not* saying the big corporate publishers do not put out superb, challenging books on a regular basis, or that they do not serve broad constituencies well above the lowest-common-denominator audience. A visit to your local bookstore will give the lie to that notion. In fact, the joint (and complementary) concentrations of power in publishing and bookselling, have, a bit paradoxically, generated an explosion in the availability of books.

I will say, though, that there is an increasingly autonomic and savorless quality to all this publishing activity, as the remaining big publishing combines compete for the same books and seek to serve all the markets. Unlike the great names in American publishing in the earlier part of this century, Alfred Knopf and Harold Guinzburg of Viking and Bennett Cerf of Random House and Alfred Harcourt and, yes, Roger Straus (still very much alive and publishing, of course, but certainly a great name) and Warder Norton, the men and women at the very top of the corporate houses do not have very strongly defined tastes in books—they cannot afford them. Instead they seek to achieve their goals of rationalizing their business and maximizing their profits through value-free and taste-neutral managerial and financial techniques. (In their positions I'd do the same thing.) Billings are billings, whether generated by *Private Parts* or *To the Lighthouse.* Doubtless as private citizens they would prefer Virginia Woolf dollars to Howard Stern dollars . . . but in the end it doesn't matter. To the corporation, that is. To the culture at large it matters very much.

Prominent in the unnervingly imponderable category is the question of the audience for serious books. Is it shrinking? Nothing in American culture—its dismal education system, its increasingly ideological and instrumental university atmosphere, the time pressures on its best educated citizens, the inexorable claims of electronic media, its indifference to and contempt for the life of the mind and the free play of the imagination—would lead you to guess otherwise. And yet, the most surprising books from Michael Ondaatje's *The English Patient* to John Berendt's *Midnight in the Garden of Good and Evil* to Patrick O'Brian's erudite and Austenesque novels of the sea to the astounding Edith Wharton revival, find substantial audiences. Again, there are those cultural treasures shelved at bookstores across the country. My own feeling is that the readers are out there and are hungry for good books, but that serious publishers are broadcasting on a band width that takes in no more than one-twentieth of the population, absent a *Schindler's List* or *The Age of Innocence* media boom. But cutting through the noise of the American media to deliver a quieter message to those twelve million souls—that is a daunting challenge indeed.

In late January *The New York Times Book Review* ran a superb two-part story by Michael Norman on the marketing efforts applied to a first novel by Mark Richard, *Fishboy,* on the part of his publisher Doubleday, his editor Nan Talese, and the author himself. Every writer and publisher I know read the article, and it seems to have elicited the sorts of ambiguous anxiety-laden responses that the surrealists sought to provoke with their sculptures and objects. Writers seemed to feel that the publicity marathon that Richard engaged in was at the same time not quite respectable and certainly beneath them, yet something they devoutly wish *their* publishers would make them do.

I had my own conflicted thoughts, of course. I marveled at

272

the shrewd strategizing of Nan Talese and the tireless spinning and plugging of the publicist, Marly Rusoff, a lot of it in the face of not very encouraging early auspices. Surely this disproves the perception that corporate houses have no commitment to literary fiction? (Doubleday is owned by Bertelsmann, one of the largest media companies in the world.) Surely it must be heartening for writers to know that such efforts and resources can be marshalled on behalf of a book whose prose and narrative are challenging and unconventional?

Well, yes twice. But attend: After all this striving, so man- and woman-hour intensive, Doubleday achieved a net sale of 12,000 copies, from which must be deducted the author's advance and royalties, the costs of producing the book, the advertising, the bound galleys, the review copies and author tour, as well as the overhead costs of keeping a big New York publishing house operating: salaries, employee benefits, warehousing, utilities (imagine Marly Rusoff's phone bill in an average month), postage, Federal Express, office rent, and so on. Doubleday probably made a modest profit on *Fishboy,* and if Mark Richard goes on to bigger things then the paperback will be a long-term generator of backlist income. But if you strip your perceptions free of any literary sentiment and look at the economics of *Fishboy* in the coolest possible way, my sense is that it has to look marginal, given the tremendous investment of time required to sell those 12,000 copies—maybe less after the returns are all in. And remember, in my world that is considered a *success.* To a media executive with no feeling for books and for the vagaries of literary fortune, it has to raise the question of whether there are not more remunerative activities for your employees to be engaged in and your money invested in. Indeed there are—and they almost certainly don't involve literary fiction written by someone outside the small handful of prestige authors.

Something like this seems to have been the point of view of Harcourt General as they effectively ceased publishing trade adult hardcover books in any meaningful way. Trade—i.e., book-store—publishing accounts for only three percent of that corporation's income and adult hardcover only a third of that. The rest is made by the large school and college textbook operations, professional publishing, and a large string of movie theaters. Apparently that department was losing some money—I image a Spec-4

Financial Technician back in San Diego headquarters yelling, "We're showing a loss of fiscal pressure in Sector G-12!"—so they just shut it down. The kind of publishing that Alfred Harcourt started his firm in 1919 to do, and which it did so brilliantly, bringing out the works of T.S. Eliot, Virginia Woolf, Sinclair Lewis, George Orwell, Mary McCarthy, E.M. Forster, Italo Calvino, Alice Walker, and Umberto Eco (to name a few)— kaput. I have to view this as a small, but real tragedy, a death in the cultural family. But then, I would.

The financial realists will say that no corporation is under any obligation to carry an imprint or subsidiary indefinitely if it is losing money, and that is certainly true. But I would also point out that a fair number of these publishing causalities constitute posthumous notches in the large belt of Robert Maxwell, whose grasp of financial reality was lethally nonexistent. Remember, Harcourt Brace Jovanovich (as the corporation was then called) was forced to take on a billion dollars of debt to defend its shares against Maxwell's takeover attempt in the eighties, a burden that, not surprisingly, led to its eventual bankruptcy and purchase by General Cinema. Maxwell, undeterred, bought the Macmillan publishing group, which in reasonably short order was swallowed up in the huge and scandalous disasters of his global empire that emerged after Captain Bob's fatal dip off his yacht. That is why Macmillan is now owned by Paramount (which is now owned by Viacom . . .), not through any fault of its own; Macmillan was making money.

So while the consolidation and conglomerization of publishing is certainly the single most salient and consequential fact of the past couple of decades, it is useful to remember that not every step in that process was inevitable, or even rational—that greed and heedlessness and loss of nerve and overreaching and incompetence played their part as well. The result of all these developments has been to create a publishing culture in which everybody—authors and agents and publishing employees alike—feels scared and miserable and compromised, with the exceptions of certain lickspittles, opportunists, beetlebrows, and white collar thugs.

People with a taste for quality suffer from these melancholy developments throughout all areas of publishing, but it is editors of the old school, actual and aspiring, who take the most direct hits. An editorial culture that nurtured and fought for and insisted upon literary excellence has become marginalized and demoralized. Every message editors get from the corporate publishing culture—"Don't care so much," "Okay is probably good enough," "Who reads this stuff, anyway?" "Is this going to pay off, and when?" "If they'll buy it, we'll publish it"—contradicts their training, their temperaments, their deepest instincts. You become cynical, you become slick, you become calculating and political and at some level you might not even acknowledge, you despair.

Well, we *are* in a fin de siècle mood, aren't we? I would like to believe that new imprints—smaller, more focused, lighter on their feet, deeply committed—will arise from this wreckage to carry on the literary mission that some of the corporate houses are abdicating. The problem is, literary culture itself may not be robust enough to bring forth a Barney Rossett and a Grove Press or a James Laughlin and a New Directions. The Balkanization of culture may mean that niche publishing must be the route to survival for the smaller houses, not the addressing of a broad cultural agenda. And while it is true that real book people are resilient and resourceful, and that excellent books will be emerging from houses big and small, likely and unlikely, for some time to come, they will increasingly be set to swim against the current.

See you downstream.

* * *

The above article appeared in the summer of 1994. The following comments were added in the summer of 1995.

Well, what a difference a year and change makes. After a sustained burst of economic prosperity the trade publishing business is in a bouyant and literally expansive mood. New or resurrected imprints are either in the works or already launched at Putnams (Riverhead) and Bantam Doubleday Dell (Dial and an as yet unnamed publishing division headed by Willian Shinker). William Morrow is once again a going concern, and even the Harcourt trade department has risen a certain distance from its ashes. Some of the editorial casualties cited are employed by these new imprints and elsewhere; some, disturbingly, are still unemployed; and one, ironically, sold a novel for $150,000 to Nan Talese—proving something, I'm sure.

What's the point? Besides indicating that I was a bit hysterical from seeing some of my best friends get it in the neck? I stand by most of my analysis of the ailments besetting serious trade publishing, since an economic downturn could cause them to flare up again, like a bout of malaria, in very short order. But one important lesson here is the resilience of book people—and you'd better be resilient in this line of work, in this culture. I still think that the current is carrying us downstream, but that is no excuse for ceasing to swim against it.